MISSIONVILLE

GREED   DESPERATION   HUMANITY

ALEX BROWN

Author of *Greatness and Goodness: Barbaro And His Legacy*

Missionville
Copyright @2017 by Alex Brown

Published by
Glen View Media

ISBN: 978-1-9997963-0-3
eISBN: 978-1-9997963-1-0

Cover Art: Lynden Godsoe

Cover and Interior Design: GKS Creative

Praise for *Missionville*

"There are two versions of horse racing in the American narrative: the sunny version where everyone loves their horses like children and a stakes win is just a dream away, and the dark clouds version where every horse is marked for death from the day it is foaled, handled by so-called horsemen who couldn't care less as long as there's a paycheck. Naturally the truth lays well in-between. In *Missionville*, racing insider Alex Brown tells it like it is: a deeply flawed industry where even passionate horsemen and women can be dragged down by a tough lifestyle, hopeless options, and sheer hard luck. Unflinching and yet not overwrought, this book lays bare a fractured world of horses, the people who love them, and the people who exploit them, which somehow isn't yet beyond redemption."

—Natalie Keller Reinert, author of *Turning for Home*

"Alex Brown, a lifelong horseman, takes you on a journey few are capable of providing, to life on the backside of a hardscrabble Pennsylvania racetrack, showing the pressures that bear on both the horses and the humans, and the possibilities for it all going off the track. He takes you to the real underbelly of the sport. He gives you characters you can root for as they face moral dilemmas. He tells a good tale while he's giving you the tour. A terrific read."

—Mike Jensen, journalist, *Philadelphia Inquirer*, winner of an Eclipse Award

"Behind the grandeur and pageantry of American horse racing there is a dark secret playing out. Author Alex Brown transports his readers to rural Pennsylvania, where heart-pounding action and heartbreak intertwine at the Missionville Racetrack. A captivating read, *Missionville* excels in its narrative of love, life—and death—on the racetrack's backside."

—Jordan Schatz, Sports Editor, *Cecil Whig*

"Set at the Missionville Racetrack, this novel is a close-up look at the backside culture at a racetrack that lets us in on the worries, triumphs, and concerns for the horses that are at the mercies of their owners. This is a fast-paced read that is educational as well as entertaining."

—Shelley Mickle, author of *Barbaro* and *American Pharoah*

"An intriguing horse mystery written by someone who obviously knows the industry. A great mix of horse knowledge, racing highlights, romance and an inside scoop on the controversial slaughtering of retired racehorses."

—Christine Meunier, author of the Thoroughbred Breeders series

"While bringing such rich life to the largely hidden world of Missionville Racetrack, Alex Brown turns an unflinching eye on the modern horse racing industry, its flaws along with its many virtues. A must read for anyone with even a passing interest in the sport."

—Dan Ross, journalist with bylines in *Newsweek* and the *Guardian*

"*Missionville* is a fast-paced read that grips the reader from the start and provides a ride that is both eye-opening and entertaining. It's not easy to make the seedy underground network that drives horse racing and horse slaughter entertaining, but Brown manages to pull it off with vivid characters and a gripping storyline. In the end, he presents no easy answers for the complexities of the issue, but leaves the reader with hope for the future of the nation's horses. Highly recommend; a great piece of work."

—Sharon Boeckle, filmmaker, director and producer, *From the Kill Pen*

"Alex Brown is a prominent opponent of horse slaughter whose blog posts about Barbaro held the Kentucky Derby winner's fans in thrall as the colt struggled, and ultimately failed, to recover from a broken leg. Brown's fans will be glad to see his byline again, this time on a novel that reports from one of Thoroughbred racing's low rungs: the fictional Missionville Racetrack in Pennsylvania, where denizens of the track confront, and sometimes challenge, their own moral decay in a world where horses are used, discarded, and 'disappear' into the slaughter pipeline, even as others try to adhere to their love for the animals and protect them from such a fate. Brown's first effort as a novelist provides a rare insight into the little-covered nuts and bolts of how horses once considered valuable can end up in a dreadful situation, as well as the thought processes of the people who put them there, the people who come to question those decisions, and those who work to change a world where desperation can lead to serious moral peril. It is a bleak tale, but not without a few happy endings, some human redemption, and an education for the reader."

—Glenye Cain Oakford, author of *The Home Run Horse*

"*Missionville* is fiction based on fact, but don't think Alex Brown's book in any way exaggerates or distorts the truth to make it more sensationalist, far from it. Brown has worked in the industry and knows at first-hand what goes on. Brown tells it like it is, and tells it very well."

—Will Jones, author of *The Black Horse Inside Coolmore*

"I could not put it down. It is a riveting read, a thrilling equine literary ride. Alex Brown illustrates a realistic narrative of the racing world culture and paints a wonderful landscape of the backside dynamics. Brown's book also provides a clear lens into the equine slaughter pipeline."

—Kristen Halverson, author of *A Horse's Magical Neigh*

"Alex Brown provides an authentic insight into what lies beneath the glamour of horse racing. Brown holds a mirror up to a disturbing side of the horse industry, exposing deep flaws and depraved deeds."

—Caitlin Taylor, OTTB Designs

This book is dedicated to all backstretch
workers and their racehorses.

This is a work of fiction.
The truth would be unbelievable.

CHAPTER 1

PETE, THURSDAY

THE SIREN BLASTS ACROSS THE RACETRACK. Either a horse got loose or broke down; whatever it is, it's not a good start to training after the mid-morning break. But it happens, especially during these cold winter months. I walk out of my barn to take a look and see the horse ambulance moving slowly onto the racetrack. The track will be closed for another fifteen to twenty minutes.

My phone vibrates in my pocket. Pulling it out, I stare at the screen to see Ray, the guy who owns the horses I train, calling me.

"Thunder Clouds's in tonight," Ray says.

"Yeah, saw that, in the $10k claimer, dropping down from $15k last time."

"I think we should take him."

"Sure, if you want me to. He hasn't won for a while. If he doesn't win tonight, he'll be eligible for some decent conditions."

"Good. Have a look at him in the paddock. If he looks OK, take him. Let's hope he runs decent, without winning."

"Sounds good. I'll call you after the race."

As I put my phone in my pocket, my vet strolls into my shedrow.

"All OK, Pete?" James asks.

"Good, thanks. Will need a pre-race over the weekend for my filly if she gets in for Monday?"

"Sure." James nods and walks on down the shedrow. He stops by one of Mike's stalls; the stall of a horse that is racing tonight. I can see he has a syringe in his hand as he enters the stall. Moments later James leaves the barn.

I have one horse left to train today. I head to my tack room to get some equipment. Hairy is fast asleep in the corner. It is getting late in the morning, but the nice thing about training only a few horses and doing most of the work myself is that I can also keep my own schedule. Alfie is my only help. He's worked for me since I started training at Missionville more than ten years ago. He's a hotwalker who has pretty much held every job on the racetrack. He was a leading jockey here in the 1970s. He lives on the backside and, frankly, I don't think he's left the racetrack over the last twenty years.

I typically train four horses at Missionville. I have four stalls in the same barn as the leading trainer at the track, Mike Franks. While currently only three of my stalls are filled, I should be back up to four if we claim Thunder Clouds tonight.

I train for one guy, Ray. I claim horses for him. We try to win one or two races with the horses we claim, and then try to lose the horses back through the claim box. The math is simple: claim a horse for $10k, win one or two purses of about $20k total, and then drop the horse to $5k and lose it. It's a winning formula when it works. Of course it doesn't always work. Sometimes the horse we claim is a dud, and we cannot win anything with it. Sometimes the horse we claim keeps running well and we keep it longer. The key then is to drop it down to a low claiming race before it runs poorly, which will almost always happen.

I eke out a living this way; I earn training fees from Ray that barely cover my expenses. I also get an additional bonus when we win a race. And if I have to sell one of Ray's horses to Jake, I keep the two hundred dollars Jake gives me.

My training career wasn't supposed to last forever, but I got sucked into it. The feeling I get from winning a race keeps me going; it's like a drug-infused adrenaline rush. But weeks can go by between wins. Sometimes it gets financially grim, but I hang on; I wait for that next big hit.

Alfie pulls out my last horse and gives him a turn around the barn.

"Ready, boss?"

"Thanks, Alfie." I jump aboard as Alfie holds my horse's head.

We walk out to the racetrack. I'm wrapped up well; it's another bitterly cold February morning, and the wind has picked up as it always seems to do after the training break. Because it's late in the morning, the racetrack is pretty empty. I nod to a couple of riders who are leaving the track as I enter. I stand my horse in.

"Last horse, Pete?"

"Yes, Jess. Time to get finished and warmed back up again."

"No kidding, standing here all morning is no picnic." Jess is part of the clockers' team. She radios up to the track clockers when a horse enters the track for an official work.

"Wouldn't be my choice of work, Jess." I head off and jog my horse back to the wire. We turn around and I let him stand for a little while, and then we gallop an easy mile and a half. I pull up, turn around and begin to return to the gap. I walk back with one of the two outriders, who is getting ready to close the track.

"Did the horse break down?" I ask, referring to the commotion just after the track break.

"Yes. One of Johnson's was working. Looks like he blew an ankle coming down the lane."

"Damn. Taken back to the barn?"

"Yeah, looks 50-50. Depends if they want to spend the money I suppose. The jock had him pulled up pretty quick."

Alfie takes my horse when I return to the barn, so I start grooming my other two horses and bandaging their legs. With the wear and tear of dirt track racing, each horse in my care needs some kind of work on its legs to try to keep it in racing condition. We can't afford to give our horses any time off, not with the claim–race–race–drop program that we follow. I am a pretty good leg guy and when I can't fix something up with the remedies I have, I work with James to see if we can use some additional medication to fix things for the short term. Three to four races, that's all we need from each of our horses.

Once all the horses are back in their stalls after training, and are groomed and bandaged, it's feeding time, and time to leave the horses in peace for a while. I head over to the track kitchen with my dog, Hairy. It's time for a quick sandwich, and to catch up on any gossip.

"Usual, Pete?"

"Thanks, Alice." This is an almost everyday exchange. Alice runs the track kitchen, which she has done since well before my time.

The draw for Monday's races is about to take place. After my sandwich, I go over to the racing secretary's office to see if my filly got in. I'm pretty excited about her prospects after her last race – her first for me, and a decent third place finish.

They used her race, race seven, where she drew post three, with Emma Sparks aboard. I scan the names of the other runners in the eight-horse field. The horse that had finished second in my filly's last race is back in, and there are also one or two names I don't recognize.

Time to head home for a few hours before returning to the races this evening.

Racing at Missionville is an odd experience. We rarely have much of a crowd to watch the live program, even though the parking lot fills up. Most customers at the racetrack are here to gamble at the casino rather than watch horses.

The casino became part of the racetrack about eight years ago. The way I understood it, the only legal venue for gambling in the state was at the racetracks, so that's where they put the casinos. The hope was that those interested in gambling at casinos would become interested in horse racing. Unfortunately that hasn't happened; not at Missionville, nor at the other racetracks across the country which have developed into racinos.

Thankfully the casino has brought extra money into the purses of the race-track, which is great for us. Prior to the introduction of the casinos, a $5,000 claiming race – a race where any licensed owner can buy any horse running in the race before the race for $5,000 – would have a purse of around $5,000. Now the purse is about $10,000 for that same race. If a horse is claimed, the new owner pays the claiming price, and the old owner keeps the purse money. There are inflated purses for the higher level claimers too. This makes things very interesting for us horsemen, who like to gamble and trade horses.

Thunder Clouds, the horse I am hoping to claim tonight, is in the fourth race, the $10,000 claimer, going six furlongs. I head to Pokers, a bar adjacent to the paddock. Pokers is frequented by the horsemen who have horses in the races, their hangers on, and a few seriously loyal racegoers. No matter which day of racing, I will know people at the bar. It is a good way to kill time, while also keeping on top of the goings on at the racetrack. Even trainers who don't have horses to race that night will go. Like me, they might be seeking a horse to claim. Claiming activity at our racetrack is pretty common; two or three horses change hands most race nights.

Mike Franks is in his usual spot, at one of the tables, amongst a group that includes a couple of his grooms and exercise riders, and an owner who has one horse with him. Mike's main owner is Harry Mitchell, who owns this racetrack. Harry probably has twenty horses with Mike and is very active in the claiming game, though you seldom see him at the races. Their horse is in the third race tonight, a $15,000 claimer. That horse hasn't raced for Mike before because they claimed it from its last start, for $10,000. Mike also has another runner in a later race. I assume the owner who is with them at the table is the owner of that second horse.

I take a seat at the bar.

"Budweiser, Pete?"

"Thanks, Mary." Mary is part of the furniture here at Pokers. She works every race night, and knows her customers well.

"Shopping tonight, or just browsing?" Having already studied tonight's program, Mary knows that I don't have a horse in.

"Just enjoying another night of racing." I like to keep my cards close to my chest. I like Mary, but I don't really know her. I take a gulp of my Budweiser and open my copy of the *Daily Racing Form* to take a more serious look at who's running tonight. Part of my job as a trainer isn't just to worry about my own horses, but to keep an eye on everyone else's. Their horses may soon be mine, and I need to seek out horses that I think I could make money with, without completely using them up.

The first race is a maiden claiming race, for horses that have not won a race. For this type of race, I just watch. I won't claim a maiden horse for Ray, it's too risky. Young and unproven, these horses need more time to show me what they are made of.

I go out to the paddock to see these young horses as they are saddled and readied for the race. It's brutally cold, which is typical for a February evening. The wind is whipping around, making the conditions uncomfortable for both man and beast. Besides myself and two other horsemen, there are only three spectators willing to brave the elements to view the horses in the paddock – a young woman and her two small children.

When the jockeys come out to meet with the trainers and get ready to mount, they are in full winter gear, including a balaclava to protect their faces from the frozen weather and the rock-hard kick back of the dirt track – working on this circuit isn't a jockey's dream.

Marcus Longman, the leading jockey at Missionville, has a mount in the first race. Longman had shown a lot of potential when he was a bug rider in his youth, but he has his demons. Longman was suspended, not long after he finished riding out his bug, after he was found with a battery in his car. A battery is a small device meant to shock a horse into running faster. When Longman returned to the races a year later, his reputation as a plug-in jockey haunted him all the way to Missionville. Rumor has it he still uses a battery once in a while. He's clever though and hasn't been caught again – either that or no one is really that bothered around here. It's a shame, as he does have the talent to outride this jockey colony when his head is right.

Emma Sparks also has a ride in the race. She's the jockey I like to use. A local girl, she has plied her trade on the Pennsylvania and Ohio circuits for most of her career. Any time I have a horse to breeze in the mornings, I try to get Emma to do it. She can really tell me things about a horse that I might miss. A good honest horsewoman, that's what Emma is, and a pleasure to work with. I always root for her in her races. After she was legged up on her horse, she comes by and smiles down at me.

"Good luck, Emma. Can you swing by the barn in the morning?"

"Thanks. Yes, I'll be there sometime after the break."

The race itself is pretty uneventful. Seven horses break from the gate, one goes very fast early and stretches the field out. That horse then slows down as it runs out of energy and one of the horses that is near the back manages to scramble past the field to win its first race. Emma's horse is fourth, Longman's mount never factors and only beats the early leader.

The second race is a $20,000 claimer, for non-winners of two races. This contest has some interesting horses that might have a bright future. After studying the form for the race at the bar, I walk out to the paddock to assess how the horses look. This is my usual routine, for every race, throughout race night.

I have my eye on one of the horses, a beautiful and big grey gelding called Jacob's Will. He won his first race, a maiden race, three starts back, and then ran a couple of decent races in this condition, without winning. Longman is on him for the first time, which I thought was an interesting switch. His trainer, June Buttersmith, isn't usually able to get Longman to ride. He is the third favorite at 5-1. I place a ten dollar bet.

When the gates open, Jacob's Will goes straight to the lead. In his previous starts, he had been held back early. Longman is riding a 'catch-me-if-you-can' race, and he's probably the best rider on the grounds at doing this because he's a great judge of pace. Jacob's Will is five lengths in front turning for home, and wins the race easily. I collect my winnings, which will pay for my night's entertainment.

Mike and Harry's horse is running in the third race. He was a recent claim for $10,000, when he was second, and is now running for a $15,000 claiming price. On paper it seemed like an odd claim, but the horse was quite useful in his earlier racing days.

I go to the paddock to see how he looks. His groom, Jennifer, is leading him around. She's wrapped in a large coat and a thick woolly hat. She smiles as she leads her horse past me, I nod. Small bits of communication between two people that have known each other for a long time, without truly knowing each other at all.

Longman, who rides most of Harry's horses, is in the irons. The horse should have been an outsider in the field, but people are more wary when the leading owner-trainer combination has a runner. The bettors make the horse the third favorite.

The race is a short five-furlong sprint. Longman repeats his performance from the last race and guns the horse to the lead early, and he's able to hang on to his advantage down the stretch.

Nice, that's tomorrow's breakfast. There will be plenty of doughnuts in the barn, as is tradition after a win.

I return to the bar, order another Budweiser and study the form of Thunder Clouds, who is up next. An eight-year-old, he had won a number of stakes races at top racetracks in his early years. He had real class and talent; he might be the most accomplished racehorse at Missionville right now. Unfortunately for him, it looks like he must have had an injury; he had a year off from the races from 2012-2013. When he came back, his form dropped to the claiming ranks. Three years later he is here, plying his trade near the bottom of the system. The question for us, Ray and me, is – does he have three or four races left in him, and can we make money from him? It's a gamble, but if I can fix him up, I figure he has the talent to win at this level with ease.

I go to the paddock to take a look at Thunder Clouds. He's a big brown horse, probably close to 17 hands tall. He has a nice loping walk. His only marking is a white star in the middle of his forehead. His front legs are heavily bandaged, which could be a sign of trouble, but could also be a bluff by his current trainer, Randy Marsh. The bandages are removed as he's being saddled. I watch him walk around the paddock again, and he seems to move quite freely.

I put in our claim. Win or lose, finish or fall, Thunder Clouds will be ours after the race, unless someone else has also put in a claim. If that's the case, we would have our names placed in a hat, and the winner would be drawn. It's all part of the drama of a claiming track.

Having multiple connections trying to claim a horse is not unusual, especially at racinos where the purse money for a claiming race is higher than the claim price. I think the record at Missionville is six people in for a claim; sadly that horse was vanned off in a horse ambulance after the race and never ran again. The new connections that 'won' the shake had to eat that claim.

Thunder Clouds breaks alertly, and races well for the first part of the contest in second and third position. Turning for home he holds his place as the front runner starts to slow down, and a couple of horses behind him start to gather their momentum. Running down the lane, Thunder Clouds makes a mild bid for the lead, but gives way easily and ultimately finishes fourth. It is good for us that he didn't win, since it gives us more racing options, but I would have liked to have seen him finish stronger. No one else had put a claim in for him. Thunder Clouds is now Ray's horse, with me as trainer.

I leave a message on Ray's phone, "Ray, we have the horse. He's on his way back to the barn. I'll call you in the morning and let you know how he is."

Alfie leads Thunder Clouds back to our barn to take care of him. I remain on the frontside and continue my routine of studying the form, viewing horses in the paddock, and watching the races. The rest of the evening is fairly uneventful. A horse named Harbor Lights was vanned off after the sixth race, after he stopped very quickly as they were running down the backside; it didn't look good. Three other horses were claimed – two horses out of the very competitive seventh race, which was a 'never won three races' $15,000 claimer.

I catch up with Mike later in the evening and ask him about Harry's horse in New York. While Harry owns this racetrack and has a large string here with Mike, he also has a small string on the New York circuit. One of his horses, Dancer's Foil, is being pointed for the Triple Crown series. This is a big deal for Harry, who is new to the top end of horse racing. Mike mentions that the horse is running in the Gotham Stakes on Saturday, which is a prep race for the Wood Memorial in early April. If he wins on Saturday, they will go to the Wood Memorial, which is a step closer to the Kentucky Derby.

CHAPTER 2

PETE, FRIDAY

SIX O'CLOCK IN THE MORNING THE NEXT DAY, I'm back in the frigid barn. My first job is to feed my four horses. My second job, in the winter, is to swill out their icy water buckets and refill them with fresh water. During this time of year, you have to be careful of water buckets freezing. Without reliable access to water, horses can colic – a digestive ailment that can be catastrophic. Most winter nights Alfie will swing by the barn late in the evening and reset the horses' waters for me.

Hairy follows me around in the barn in the early mornings, before he retreats to his spot in the tack room when I start training. I enjoy this time of day, even in the cold winter months. The first fifteen minutes are peaceful, before the barn begins to buzz as Mike's grooms arrive to start mucking their horses' stalls. The track doesn't open for training until seven, but his grooms will generally arrive at around six fifteen to get a head start on their stalls before getting their first horses ready to train. Mike's exercise riders arrive at six thirty and get their tack for their first two horses, based on the set list that Mike has put together. Mike's help includes his assistant trainer, David Arts, who basically runs the barn and is there from the early morning to the end of training, and again in the evening until their last horse races. Mike also has nine grooms, four exercise riders, and eight hotwalkers.

In the early morning my routine is different from most. I like to watch my horses eat; you can learn a lot about their health from how they attack their food. After they finish their breakfast, I will strip off the bandages on each of my horses and spend some time assessing their legs. This morning I save Thunder Clouds for last, I am curious to see what sort of injuries he might have. I also want to wait until Alfie is here. He usually gets in around seven. Alfie doesn't muck stalls or groom the horses; he helps me out walking the horses after their exercise or instead of their exercise, and when we have a runner at night he will take it over to the races and bring it back for me after its race.

I had finished up with the other three horses' inspections, and was about to start mucking out a stall, when Alfie appears.

"Hey, boss, you want me to pull out the new guy?"

"Yes, please. He's ready. Ate everything up too, which is cool."

Alfie goes into Thunder Clouds's stall and pulls him out. The horse looks pretty impressive standing under the shedrow lights. Alfie moves away with the horse and they start jogging up the shedrow, away from me. He looks a little gimpy on the right front leg. Alfie turns him around and jogs him back towards me. Yes, definitely something up with the right front. No doubt there's a reason why this horse has lost some of his past form. Let's hope I can figure it out and fix the problem, even just temporarily.

As I run my hands down his right front leg, I see that his ankle is clearly swollen and there is some heat in there too. It's hard for me to tell if this is a new injury, or more likely an on-going issue that the horse has had to deal with. I'll get James to look at it.

"Thanks, Alfie. You can put him in. If James stops by when I'm out on the track, can you ask him to come back when I'm around? I need to chat to him about this guy."

"Sure. You want me to walk him for thirty minutes?"

"Yes please, then cold-water hose that right front ankle for twenty minutes before you put him in."

"OK, boss."

I have to muck some stalls and train the rest of the horses, but not before grabbing a coffee from Mike's tack room – a doughnut would go down well right around now. I meander down the shedrow, saying hi to a few of Mike's help along the way. Jennifer is busying herself around her latest winner.

"Congratulations! Didn't really expect to see you in the winner's circle yesterday, but it's always good when it happens."

"Thanks, Pete. I was hopeful; first time we've run him. Grab a doughnut."

"I'm on my way."

Jorge, another of Mike's grooms, is in the tack room pouring himself a coffee.

"Que pasa, Jorge?"

"Bien. You good? How's your new horse?"

"All good. New horse seems cool. Will know more in a day or two."

"Good luck! Doughnut?" Jorge passes me the box of doughnuts.

"Of course. Gracias."

I return to my small part of the shedrow, and start mucking a stall. I want to get two horses out to train before the training break, so I need to start hustling along a little bit. After finishing the first stall I get some tack. Hairy is now fast asleep in his usual spot in the tack room.

I tack up the filly that's racing on Monday. She's a small filly which we claimed a little over a month ago for $10,000. I've run her back once in a $15,000 claimer and she ran a decent third place. I really need to win with her on Monday. She's back in for the $15,000 tag and looks to be competitive. Emma worked her on Tuesday over a half-mile. She breezed very well, and Emma was pretty excited about her when she returned.

We go up to the track. It's bitterly cold. It is always a challenge to wear enough clothes to keep warm, but not so many you can't move freely when you're galloping. This is especially true with your extremities. I wear a decent pair of gloves and a facemask to ensure that none of my skin is exposed. If you're not careful, it's not unusual to suffer from a bit of frostbite in these conditions. Horses seem to handle this weather better than humans, although they can get a little frisky.

At this time of morning the track is pretty busy, and this morning is no exception. I enter the track behind a group of horses from another barn. I turn my filly in and let her watch the training for a few moments. I find this useful, especially for fillies, to help them relax. I then jog her 'the wrong way,' which is clockwise, to just past the wire. I turn her in and let her stand for a few minutes. We watch a few horses working down the lane, horses getting ready for their races in the next week or so, no doubt. More horses gallop by us, some in groups of two and three, and a few on their own. One exercise rider, Hector, is clearly struggling to keep his horse under control; sadly for the horse, Hector's hands are a little 'heavy,' probably not helped by this brutal weather. They probably gallop farther and faster than their trainer would have liked.

Hector is one of those riders who seems to have been around the racetrack forever. He was freelancing here when I arrived fifteen years ago, and is doing the same now. Sometimes he also takes a job during the races, on the starting gate. He's a pleasant enough guy, but also hard to get to know. I don't know if he likes horses. Some of the riders here just seem to be doing it to earn a dollar, lacking the compassion that is key to a true horseman. Others, though, are really good with horses, and it shows with everything they do. I would put Emma in that category.

I set off to gallop my filly and she takes a strong hold of the bit in the early part of the exercise, then eases herself comfortably into the bridle. My hands are buried into her neck, my left hand holding both reins – called a half-bridge – and the neck strap and a good chunk of mane.

The filly gallops a nice mile and a half. Once I eased her up and brought her back to the entrance of the track we stand again and just watch. All this is to help keep her a little calm. When I first claimed her, she was a bit of a tear-away. I knew that before making the claim, as I had seen her train for another barn. You hope that by changing them just a little, you can improve them a lot at the races.

"Your filly's looking good, Pete, nice and relaxed when she galloped around." Jess doesn't miss much, but always has a pleasant word.

"Thanks," I say to Jess through my facemask. "Been working on trying to keep her settled. I was worried the work earlier this week might have fired her back up, but she seems good."

"I think you might have a decent one there. Good luck on Monday." Everyone knows everyone's business around here.

Once I return to the barn I walk the filly into her stall and strip her tack. Alfie is there to collect her and cool her out.

"All good?" Alfie asks as he gets ready to walk the horse.

"Yep, fingers crossed she seems to have come out of her work on Tuesday in good shape." I rub her on her left ear and leave her stall.

I repeat the routine with my next horse. Tack him up, pull him out of his stall, and give him a turn around the shedrow. I then climb aboard and head to the track. I'm just in time to get him exercised before the training break.

He's an older claiming horse. I've had him for two months now, and I'm hoping for one more win before we drop him down a level to try to get him claimed. When I gallop him, he generally wants to ease to the outside of the racetrack; we call it 'lugging out.' I've tried a few things to fix it, but nothing has really worked. I've learned to ride him with his idiosyncrasies.

I trot back the wrong way to the wire, and we perform the same routine as I just did with the filly. This is pretty standard training for all my horses, unless I need to work one. Usually six days before I have a race picked out for a horse, I will work the horse at racing speed, to make sure everything is going well with it. I usually have one of the jockeys aboard for the work, most of the time Emma Sparks. She tells me how she thinks the horse is doing, and then hopefully she will ride it in the race. Of course each trainer has his (or her) own training routine with their horses. I know this well from my days as a freelance exercise rider working for many different barns. You pick up what works for different horsemen, then apply what you like to your own routine.

By the break time I only have one horse left to train and two stalls to muck. Alfie is busy walking circles around the barn. The vet strolls into my shedrow, at the perfect time.

"James, can you look at the new horse we claimed?"

"Sure, do you want to bring him out?"

"Will do. Alfie, can you put that guy back in his stall, and get Thunder Clouds out?"

"Sure, boss."

In no time, Alfie has Thunder Clouds standing in the shedrow.

"The right front ankle has some filling. We cold-water hosed it for twenty minutes. He's a little short on it at the jog. Hard for me to tell if this is just an old injury he's been carrying, or whether it's getting worse."

"OK, could you trot him up for me?" James asks.

Alfie leads Thunder Clouds away at the jog. He looks a little less stiff, but that's likely a result of the hosing taking some of the filling away. Alfie turns Thunder Clouds and jogs him back toward us. Still a little short, but not as bad. James runs his hands down his right front leg.

"Definitely an old injury there. I imagine that the race last night didn't help it, but we should wait a couple of days, see how it responds to a little of your therapy, and then decide if we need to take more action. OK with you?"

"Sounds good, James. I'll call Ray and give him an update."

"Good. Will pre-race the filly tomorrow for Banamine, Bute Sunday."

"Thanks."

I take out my phone and leave Ray a message, "Ray, James just took a look at Thunder Clouds. There's an issue with his right front ankle. He wants us to wait a few days before we make any decisions regarding additional vet work. Right now the horse is a little short on that leg, but maybe I can fix him up. I'll let you know more as I know. The filly is in on Monday, seventh race, in case you didn't know. She's come out of her work nicely."

I have my last horse to gallop, a young gelding we claimed four months ago. We have won a race with this guy since the claim, and I'm hoping for one more win before letting him go to someone else. The trouble with younger horses is they typically have won only a few races. Each time they win an additional race, their competition, at the same claiming price, gets tougher. We claimed this horse for $10,000 in a race for horses that had not won three races. Now that he's won his third race, he has to face open company, including horses like Thunder Clouds, who has won twelve races in his career. Despite that, I'm hopeful this guy can win one more race for us before we drop him down a claiming level.

I get him ready to train and head out to the track for the final time this morning. Things are now quieter on the racetrack. We stand still after we enter the track and just take it all in. For a younger horse, he has an old head on his shoulders. Nothing much bothers him. We watch a horse and rider gallop by and then begin jogging back to the wire. Once into our gallop my horse stretches out into his large, loping stride. It's a shame we don't have a turf track here, as he feels like the sort of horse who would handle the firm turf well. Maybe one day he'll get a chance at a different racetrack, but that would be without me. We finish our gallop and I walk him toward the gap, the reins in a loop, as he stretches his neck and relaxes. I turn him in at the exit, nod to Jess, and leave the track.

Emma Sparks is waiting for me when I return to the barn. I put my horse in his stall, strip the tack, and let Alfie deal with him.

"Emma, good to see you."

"You too. How's the filly after her work?"

"She's doing really well. Pretty excited for Monday. Have you looked at the race yet?"

"Not yet. I did see the filly that finished in front of us is in there, but maybe we can get by her this time."

"Yes, I think she's improving. The move the other day was nice, right?"

"She felt terrific underneath me. I didn't need to urge her at all. Fingers crossed then."

"Great. You have any live mounts tonight?"

"Three rides, but I don't think I'll get my picture taken this time."

"Well, safe rides, and look forward to Monday."

"Thanks, Pete. Have a great weekend."

Jake, a pony rider who ponies a lot of Mike's horses in the mornings and evenings, is in the barn now that training has finished. Some horses aren't ridden by exercise riders because they have sore backs, or are barely rideable for other reasons. In these cases a trainer gets someone to pony the horse without an exercise rider. Sometimes a horse is ridden, but needs another horse and rider to keep it settled down. Again, a pony would be used. This is Jake's job, all morning, for a variety of trainers. Jake also ponies at the races in the evenings, taking horses down to the starting gate. He ponies Mike's horses, and ponies mine too if Mike doesn't have one in my race.

Jake is also a bit of a hustler. One of his sidelines is he buys horses from you for two hundred dollars, once they're finished racing. He rehabs some horses and sells them to people he knows off the track. Some go elsewhere. If I get stuck with a horse which isn't running well, that I can't get claimed, Jake will buy it, regardless of the type of horse or its injuries. He's bought three or four of my horses over the years.

Chatting with Jorge, Jake looks like he's taking one of Jorge's horses. His truck and trailer are outside the barn, with another horse in the trailer, waiting. I guess that horse might be Harbor Lights, the horse that was vanned off last night.

I finish up my morning barn work. I groom my four horses and attend to each of their legs with treatments that I've conjured up to help provide the necessary therapies. Thunder Clouds is obviously my newest project. I'm convinced that I can work some magic to improve the state of his right ankle, to get him back to his winning ways. For now, I just poultice the leg, to try to cool it out. I will probably do that for the next couple of days, then switch to sweating the ankle, rubbing in a bit of Furacin and DMSO, and then wrapping the inner layer with a film of plastic; I do this to draw out any additional filling. Of course, I think I'm pretty smart about all this stuff. The reality is that for a horse like this, most therapies have already been tried by his various keepers. But success would mean a big pay off at the races.

All finished for the morning, I head to the track kitchen for a sandwich and to buy the *Daily Racing Form* for tonight's races. When I arrive, I see one of the exercise riders from Jim Johnson's barn eating a sandwich on his own. I wander over.

"Jose, how's that horse that got hurt yesterday morning?"

"No bueno, senor. He could not make it."

"Sorry to hear that, man. Sad."

"Thanks. He was a nice runner."

This is a tough business. You have to wonder sometimes if we push these animals a little too much. But it's the business that I know, a business that has sucked me in.

I turn away and order my sandwich at the counter. Hairy's looking at me in the hope I would get him something too.

"Usual, Pete?" Alice knows what everyone likes on the backside. For me, it's a breakfast sandwich, eggs, bacon and tomato and brown toast.

Alice, looking down at Hairy with a smile, adds, "I have a couple of extra sausages for you. Here you go." She hands me the meat, and Hairy snatches the sausages from my hand in two swift chomps. His tail wags his appreciation.

I head home before returning to the races tonight.

Another race night: it's the last night of racing for the week. Wednesdays, Saturdays, and Sundays are 'dark days' for us. Racing resumes on Mondays. It might seem odd not to race on the weekends, but our racing doesn't attract too many fans. We rely more on money from our simulcast, where other tracks and off-track betting shops take our signal. I am told we do better when our signal doesn't compete with the big racetracks on the weekends. I also know John, the racing secretary, would prefer that we only raced three days a week; he struggles to fill races as the horse population here at Missionville continues to dwindle.

Tonight's program includes a $50,000 stakes race, the fifth race on the card. Half of the field for that race are from here, but half have shipped in from other tracks and training centers; which isn't unusual for our bigger races. Longman has the mount on the favorite, a ship-in from Aqueduct, New York. Other than the stakes race, the rest of the card is made up of our typical claiming events, starting with a maiden race for horses who have not won a race. The claiming price is $15,000.

I go out for the first race and take a look at the horses in the paddock. Like last night, and forever it seems now, it is brutally cold. It means that paddock time and the pre-race parade is shortened for the horses. There are only six fillies in the race, aged three and older. A couple of the runners have made lots of starts and are clearly not cut out for racing; one is a first-time starter, and three look like they might have a shot. I study those three in the paddock. One is from Jim Johnson's barn – she finished third last time. I like her. She has a really nice loping walk. The other two are from smaller barns, one of which is a ship-in from a local farm. They had both placed fourth in their last starts, but for maiden $20,000, this race is supposed to be a little easier.

I stick with the Jim Johnson filly, and decide to place a $10 bet. I was interested in potentially claiming her, but not tonight. She needs to win a race or two first to prove she's got what it takes to make me some money.

The race is pretty straightforward. The six fillies break together from the three-quarters of a mile starting gate. The filly I bet sits second for most of the race, then looms up to challenge the leader as they turn for home. She passes the leader willingly and strides away by three lengths. At 3-1, she earns me an extra thirty dollars. Not bad.

The second race is a claiming event for older horses that haven't won a race for six months. That is the condition, sometimes you will get horses in a race like this that have won a lot of races, but just not recently. We call these types of horses 'war horses.' They are battle-hardened, and have earned their connections quite a lot of money over the years. I look at the *Daily Racing Form* to see who is here for this type of race tonight, and of the seven runners, four have already earned over $300,000, and one has made over half a million! The claiming price for the race is $10,000. That's what these horses are now on offer for. I'm guessing one or two of these horses will get claimed. Once I get Thunder Clouds back to the races, this is the type of race he will be running in.

I look at the horses in the paddock. They just plod around the ring, they've done this so many times. One runner has actually raced over 50 times, which is very impressive for a Thoroughbred; he's done it over a span of seven years of racing, he is now nine.

The race itself is quite a good event, with three horses going head and head as they turn for home. The three jockeys are at full drive to push their mounts into the lead, but it isn't until inside the last sixteenth of a mile that the winner, on the outside of the three, draws away by half a length.

The horses are led away after the race, except for the winner, which is led into the winner's circle – all very routine at the track. The track announcer then announces a claim in the race – number four, Spicy Lemon, claimed by Harry Mitchell and trainer Mike Franks. The horse had finished fourth. I take a quick look at my *Daily Racing Form*: Spicy Lemon had been trained by Sarah Lester, who is a local ship-in trainer. The horse will now be in our barn, under Mike's care, for the racetrack owner, Harry. I am guessing Jorge will be his new groom, as he has an empty stall.

The following two races are uneventful. Emma Sparks had a third place finish in the third race; the horse actually ran quite well while appearing to be overmatched. In the fourth race there was another claim, this time by Jim Johnson's barn. Johnson is the second big trainer on the backside here at Missionville. He and Mike are not too friendly.

I go to the paddock to look at the horses for the stakes race. Alfie is leading the New York runner around the paddock. On race nights when we have no activity, Alfie sometimes tries to hustle some extra cash by freelancing for the shippers-in who need help. The horse looks pretty good. His form in New York would make it difficult for him to win a stakes race on that circuit, but at Missionville he appears to be a standout. His trainer is known for being able to place horses well in races.

Longman is legged up on the horse, after having a quick chat with a person who I assume is an assistant trainer. The runners are now ready to parade in front of the stands, before heading over to the three-quarters start.

The race itself is dull. The New York horse is hard ridden early from the gate by Longman, and goes on to win by a wide margin. No one is ever close enough to challenge. It is an easy 'smash and grab' win by an out-of-towner. This sort of stuff doesn't sit well with the local horsemen who like to keep the purse money amongst themselves. The one silver lining is that Longman is a generous guy after winning a feature race. Those who go down to our local bar, Jessup's, tonight, will benefit from his generosity.

While there are three races left on the card, I'm not interested in them. None of the horses in those races are horses that I've been watching for potential claims. I can watch the races online at some point over the weekend. I decide to head out of the racetrack and make a detour to Jessup's before going home.

Jessup's is about a mile from the racetrack, just inside the town of Mission-ville. There's nothing special about the place, but it's the bar that the horse-men like to frequent when off the track. Later tonight it will be hopping. It has an all-you-can-eat buffet, which some of the jockeys will gorge on.

They don't have to make weight now for two days, so this is their one night to let go. They will eat loads – some will then 'flip' – drink too much, and consume whatever else they need to unwind. It makes Saturday mornings on the racetrack rather quiet.

Longman will be in later with his posse of friends and miscreants. Two or three of the other jockeys will also be here. A few trainers will be out, and groups of grooms and exercise riders will also be here. It's actually quite fun, but I'm not up for it tonight. I'm planning to have just one or two drinks, and then get home before the partying really starts.

"Budweiser?" Charlie, the bar guy, asks.

"Thanks."

"Any luck at the track this week?"

"No runners, but claimed one yesterday, so fingers crossed. I have a filly in on Monday."

"Nice. Does she have a shot?"

"I think so. I haven't really looked at the race too much, but she's training well."

"Great. I'll look out for her. Good luck man."

"Thanks."

I recognize a couple of exercise riders in the corner of the bar, and walk over.

"Hey guys, long week." A casual opening remark to start a pointless conversation.

"Yeah. This weather is getting old. Next year I'm heading south for the winter," Tim says, who is always complaining about something.

"Come on Tim, you told me that last year."

"Maybe, but things didn't work out. Next year I'll find something. I can't handle another cold winter, I swear." He won't leave.

"You should just buy a better jacket." The other guy, Brian, prods him.

"Sure, but I just want to get out of here." He'll still be here next year.

This kind of conversation is repeated over and over again, throughout the winter, amongst the horsemen at Missionville. We all seem to want out of here, to move to a more hospitable environment for both man and horse; the reality is, very few of us escape. And those who do don't come back.

I order a second beer and watch a little shuffleboard. I enjoy playing the game. I'm actually pretty handy at it, but for now I just want to watch and relax. It's been a long week.

CHAPTER 3

AMANDA, SATURDAY

MY ALARM BLASTS, REMINDING ME THAT IT'S Saturday morning.

Each day during the week, I rise at seven thirty to get to the bank by eight thirty. But on Saturdays I go to the racetrack; it's six in the morning. I'm not sure if you could call this a hobby or an obsession, but I spend time on the backside of the racetrack and talk to the horsemen and look at horses. I go there to try to help a few horses retire. I know there are worse fates ahead for them otherwise.

I turn off the alarm on my phone; I see a voicemail message waiting for me.

"Amanda, it's Sarah. I'm freaking out. Mike Franks just claimed Spicy for Harry Mitchell. I don't get it. There were better horses in the race. You know I don't place my horses to lose them. You know those guys are bad. They'll win with Spicy and make me look bad, not that I care about that, but then he'll disappear. I know you can't do anything, but I needed to unload. Call me tomorrow?"

Sarah Lester trains a few horses she bred herself at a farm about thirty minutes from Missionville. We've been friends for a few years now. She helped me learn how the backside works at the track. Spicy, Spicy Lemon, is a favorite horse of hers. He is seven, he's won a few races, and she just loves him. When he's finished racing, she was looking forward to seeing if he would make a good equestrian horse. I remember going out to her barn one day and Sarah was up on Spicy. They looked like they adored each other.

I want to swing by to see Pete Wright when I'm at the track. He is in the same barn as Mike Franks. Pete just claimed Thunder Clouds. That horse really does deserve to retire – he hasn't won for a while now and is sliding down the claiming ranks. He used to be a very good horse. Something has to be wrong with him.

I arrive at the stable gate and pull out my track license. The guard nods and smiles at me. I was given a track vendor license a couple of years ago, when I started helping Shawn, the racetrack chaplain, with a new banking program I designed for the backstretch workers. I still run the program.

I drive through and turn to the left, parking outside the track kitchen. It's seven o'clock in the morning and still dark. And very cold. I go to the kitchen to get a hot steaming coffee to go. The kitchen has only just opened, so there really isn't anyone around yet.

My usual routine is to watch a little training for an hour, and chat with whomever comes up to the track to watch their horses train. This way I'm able to meet a good cross-section of the backside. After doing this for two years now, I'm known as the lady who would try to help place horses into good homes. Some horsemen choose to ignore me, a few tolerate me, and a few really want me to help them. After watching a little training, and hanging out with whomever I come upon, I visit a few barns, especially the barns that have the horses that I am advertising for second careers. I want to make sure that they are still around. But today I'll visit Pete Wright first.

I run a website where I advertise retired racehorses that are available for free. A trainer lets me know about a horse during my Saturday visits. I then visit the barn and get pictures of the horse, as well as a video of it jogging up and down. I then put together a general description of the horse and post everything to my site.

Typically I have between ten and fifteen Thoroughbreds posted on the site at any given time. Once a horse is adopted from the site, I follow up with the new owner every six months, and then get back to the trainer to let them know how their ex-racer is doing. The system isn't perfect. I know a couple of horses have ended up getting lost, but I've managed to help place more than a hundred over the last two years.

The hour I spend on the rail of the racetrack passes by without much action. Saturdays are generally quiet training days at Missionville. Because Friday is the last day of racing for the week, most trainers try to slow things down on Saturday before ramping back up for the next week. Quite a few of the jockeys take Saturday morning off; those who are here mostly just visit trainers to chat and catch up, rather than work horses.

Pete Wright enters the track on one of his horses. He acknowledges my presence, "Hey Amanda, it must be Saturday. Good to see you as usual." I like Pete, although I also find him to be very frustrating.

"Good to see you. I was planning on swinging by your barn. Could I take a look at Thunder Clouds?"

"Sure, I wondered if you'd be calling. It's one of the reasons I claimed him." He always has a sharp response. "He looks like a really nice horse. I hope I can do right by him." I really wish he would do right by him, but I wonder if Pete is still capable of such action. I think he's genuinely a decent guy, but he's been around here too long and has fallen into some of the bad habits of the racetrack.

"Great, what's a good time for you?" I ask.

"Well, I'm only training this filly today, she's in on Monday. So basically I'll be around my barn for the rest of the morning until about ten."

"Perfect, I'll stop by within the hour." Pete nods and trots away from me.

Of all the people I've met on the racetrack, Pete was the toughest nut to crack, or to understand. He seems like a great horseman; he is a terrific rider, just great to watch as he gallops by. He could take a rogue horse and if it's fixable, he'll fix it. Patience is his keyword, he has so much patience with his horses. But there's another side to him, in part driven by his need to make a living I guess, and in part, because of his owner, Ray. Pete has complained to me about him from time to time, Ray's constant pressure to get his horses racing, or lose them when they're no longer able to compete at a good level.

Pete's also very attractive in a roguish way. He has a thick mop of dark hair, with deep blue piercing eyes. His smile can make you melt.

"Hey, Amanda." John Swank interrupts my thoughts. A horse of his is currently being advertised on my site.

"John, good to see you. How's Rocket Road?"

"He's good, have you had any interest?" It has been three weeks since I placed his horse on the site.

"Not yet. I know it's tough, but if you can hang in there, I'll see if I can push his entry out to a few more online forums this weekend."

"That'll be great. I need to get another horse in to fill his stall. You know how it goes."

"I understand. Thanks for holding out a little. He seems like a sweet horse."

"He is. I really want the best for him, he's been good to me."

"I'll call you as soon as I hear something. Otherwise I'll stop by your barn next Saturday."

"Thanks," John says as he turns his attention to the horse he had come out to watch.

One of the issues I've run into with the site is advertising horses that, in the meantime, are sold or moved on via another means. It is frustrating, but these guys cannot afford to keep horses in their stalls that are not racing. The racing secretary is always looking for runners to fill the races, so he puts pressure on the trainers since the track is giving them free stalls. A horse that is not racing is taking up space that could be used by a horse that is racing; that's the bargain trainers make with the racetrack – race your horses, or lose your stalls. It's one of the reasons why I visit the auction in Owenscreek each Tuesday, in case advertised horses end up there; sadly, some have.

Jake, the pony guy, comes onto the racetrack with another horse in tow. He acknowledges me, and I offer a short, "Morning, Jake." Jake is the horse trader at this racetrack. He takes a horse for two hundred dollars, no questions asked. He tries to rehab a few on his small farm, which is fifteen minutes from here. But he takes a few up to the auction at Owenscreek. I see him there every Tuesday. He buys horses directly for Tom, who is one of the two kill buyers at the auction. Some horses he'll run through the sale. Jake and I have had our run-ins over the last couple of years. But we've also learned how to tolerate each other. Sometimes he shows me a horse that he thinks shouldn't go to kill that he can't place, so there is some good there. Anyway, it's better to work with your enemy than to be completely shut out.

The hour at the track passes by quickly. I head over to Pete's shedrow.

"Hello, Pete."

"Amanda, you're looking well, even under all your winter gear," Pete flirtatiously says.

"Thanks! Can I take a look at Thunder Clouds?"

"Sure, here he is." Thunder Clouds is looking at us over his stall webbing. He has lovely kind eyes and a white star on his forehead. He's also big with a deep brown coat.

"What do you think of him? Is he a good claim for you guys?"

"I hope so. He's got an old ankle injury I'll need to try to fix up. I'll know more in a week or so. I haven't ridden him yet; I'll put a saddle on him on Monday."

"You know I want this horse don't you? He deserves a place to retire." Thunder Clouds has been at Missionville now for more than two years. I want to get him off the racetrack and into another career if that's possible. My friend, Sarah, has told me she would have a space for him for a few months if needed.

"I'll look after him, don't worry. If we can't do anything with him, you will be the first to know." I hope Pete is being honest. I know he's given a couple of horses to Jake over the years. He knew the last one really upset me after I saw the horse at Owenscreek. I'd called him, a little hysterical at the time.

"You know the claim Mike made last night?" I ask.

"Spicy Lemon?"

"Yes, Spicy. Any chance you can keep an eye on him for me, just let me know if you hear anything? Sarah Lester left me a message on my phone last night. She's very upset."

"Sure, I'll see what I can find out next week, swing by next Saturday if you like. I'm guessing Jorge will be looking after him. He's a good groom. He'll let me know what he thinks."

"Thanks."

"No problem. Hey, what are you doing for the rest of the day?" It is an odd question and catches me by surprise.

"No plans yet. Once I get out of here, I need to update my website and make a couple of calls. Then relax. It's been a tough week at the bank."

"Harry has that runner in the Gotham Stakes in New York later today. Do you want to come and watch the race?"

Christ, is Pete asking me out on a date? It's weird, maybe I want to hang out with him a little more. It would also be a good way to learn more about what really goes on on the backside.

"I might do that. Where do you want to watch it?"

"Say we meet at Jessup's at four? Race goes off about six." I've never been to Jessup's but what the hell, I might as well do something.

"Sounds good. See you then."

As I leave Pete's shedrow, an odd feeling runs right through me. I haven't felt like this for a very long time.

I walk through a few more barns and check in on a couple of horses.

They're still here. I have a few brief conversations with their respective horsemen. It's now time for me to head home and relax for a few hours. But I need to call Sarah back first.

"Sarah?"

"Amanda, shit, I'm freaking out."

"Yes, I understand. I spoke to Pete Wright, who shares a barn with Franks. He said he'd do a little snooping."

"I'm sick about it. That horse doesn't deserve what might be coming to him. Those guys are doing something bad with their horses, I swear. Anyway, if you can find anything out, please let me know." Sarah knows the risks of racing at Missionville, but there really are no other options for her horses.

"I will. Unfortunately you know he won't be available for retirement from these guys."

"I know. I guess I could try to claim him back, but I just don't have the money right now."

"I'll call you back if I hear anything. We should plan to get dinner sometime soon and really catch up."

"I would love that. Can you come over here one day next week?"

"That should work. Let's plan something early in the week. I'll be heading to Owenscreek on Tuesday, as usual. Maybe I could stop by on my way back?"

"Plan on it, I'll fix some dinner."

Around three o'clock I start to get ready to meet Pete. It feels a bit strange; was this a date, or what casual friends do, just hang out and watch a horse race? Do I like Pete? The guy has done some bad things over the years, but is that behind him now, or is he broken? Can he help me?

I really need to get out a little more, but I've let my life slip into a routine where I don't want to risk any more personal disappointment.

What should I wear? Dress down and set no expectations, but I want to impress in a subtle way. Pete is a mystery to me, but a mystery that might be worth solving.

After lots of outfit changes, I go with a casual but smart look. Skinny jeans and a soft cream colored angora sweater, with a hint of make-up, but not too much. This is the first time Pete has suggested we get together. I didn't think he was interested. I didn't think I was interested.

I drive over to Jessup's, a short ten minutes from my house. I arrive a few minutes early so I drive on and circle the block for a while. I want to make sure Pete is there first; this is his bar, not mine.

I walk through the door, casually, at 4:05 p.m. precisely. I try to look relaxed, despite the anxiety churning away inside me. Pete is here, sitting at the bar, chatting to the bartender.

"Amanda, I was worried you might have changed your mind."

"Sorry, a little late."

"No worries. Charlie, this is a friend of mine, Amanda. What do you want to drink?"

"I'll take a glass of sauvignon blanc if they have it, thanks."

"Sure, welcome to Jessup's," Charlie responds, and goes to get the wine.

"It's good to see you outside of the track. Go and grab a table, I'll bring the drinks."

I find a booth and sit down. Pete looks pretty good, it's nice that he shaved. When I see him most Saturdays, he has a day or two's growth around his chin.

Pete comes over to the table with the drinks. He has a beer, and gives me my wine.

"Thanks for inviting me out. It's a little crazy, but I've never been in this bar, or hung out with racetrack guys."

"Well, don't label us all the same. I'm very glad you agreed to come; honestly I was a little nervous to ask you." Really, Pete appeared to be pretty cool and casual when he asked.

"I'm glad you did. I need to get out more, and I feel I half know some of you guys that work at the racetrack, without really knowing you at all."

"I know, odd really. We live these lives, we think we know people, but we rarely get to know them." Pete is sounding pretty philosophical. I know he is very good around horses, a very good horseman, but maybe there's more to him.

"So what do you do when you're not at the racetrack?" I ask.

"The track sucks up a lot of my time. Seven days a week in the mornings. Four days a week in the evenings. I'll admit to spending a little time here at Jessup's, but mostly I spend time with Hairy, my dog. He comes with me to the track in the mornings, you've seen him."

"Yes, mostly I've seen him asleep in your tack room."

"Yeah, that's Hairy. In the afternoons we head off to find somewhere to walk. We have a few favorite spots. He's a cool dude, and we hang out."

"Nice."

Our conversations are interrupted by awkward pauses as each of us tries to learn more about the other. I have to admit, I like a guy who sees his dog as a principle non-work occupation. It helps me explain my horse obsession, away from the bank.

"Have you always trained horses and worked on the backside?"

"Since I graduated college. I came to Missionville for the summer, while I was looking for a position with an accounting firm. I have a degree in business, good GPA too. Of course I got so sucked into the lifestyle of the racetrack that I've stayed ever since. Fifteen years now, five galloping horses, ten training them. I had a pretty good horse when I started out training, claimed him for $5,000 and won six straight races. I've been looking for another good horse ever since I guess. The last five years I've pretty much exclusively trained for Ray, my owner. I'm guessing my accounting career is on hold."

"I didn't know you went to college, not that it should matter. Where did you go?"

"Penn State. I had a good time and still keep in touch with a couple of buddies from there. One's a lawyer with a big firm in DC, the other went to Wall Street and works for a hedge fund. Both are on their second wives." Pete smiles.

"And you, never married?" Perhaps I shouldn't have asked.

"No. I've had a couple of serious relationships, but unfortunately the racetrack lifestyle makes things hard." Interesting, and something I can understand given my own lack of success.

"So how did you get involved in the racetrack?"

"I've ridden horses since I was a kid. Pony club, hunting, you name it. As a college student, it was an easy way to make extra money, freelance at the racetrack during school breaks. What about you? I'm doing all the talking."

"I also rode horses as a kid. I went to college and studied chemistry at a small liberal arts college in Connecticut. After I graduated I was supposed to go to grad school. I decided to get out of the sciences and applied for a job at our local bank in Connecticut. I did that for a while, moved up, and now I'm a manager for the Susquehanna Bank system. We have eight branches. I've kept horses as a passion of course."

"Impressive. I thought you were just a full-time tree hugger, or whatever we should call bleeding hearts. Ready for another?" I realize I've swallowed down my wine pretty quickly, but Pete seems pretty relaxed in his manner, so things must be going OK, I guess.

"Sure, but can you mix it, wine spritzer please?"

I need to start switching the conversation. I want to see what Pete knows about Harry and Mike. Clearly Sarah thinks that they do bad things to their horses. While I haven't seen their horses run through the auction, they dump them somehow. Sarah's concerns might be valid. But what are they doing at the track?

Pete returns with the drinks.

"I ordered a plate of nachos. I hope that's OK, or I can get you something else too?"

"No, that's great. Will help with the wine! Pete, can we talk about Harry and Mike for a minute?"

"Sure, what do you want to know?"

"Well, you know they just claimed Sarah's horse, and she's very stressed about it."

"Yes, no worries, I'll follow up with Jorge, see how he is."

"I appreciate that, but I wonder, Sarah seemed to imply that she thinks those guys cheat in some way. Make the horse better than it is for a race or two, then get rid of it when it can no longer run." Pete looks a little puzzled; perhaps he's preparing his words carefully, but it seems like something is troubling him.

"I don't know. All I can tell you is this: Harry is the track owner, so what he says goes. Security is not allowed anywhere near our barn, so if they're doing something dodgy, perhaps they can. Other than that, you know the rest. You go to the auction at Owenscreek. You know Jake." I know Jake is always at the auction, but I haven't identified any of Harry's horses, which is odd.

"How is it for you, the track I mean?" I try to keep things moving.

"It's my livelihood now. My accounting days were over before they even started. I wish things were better around the racetrack, but they aren't. I don't like Harry, but he helped me out after my accident, and that's where I'm at."

"I didn't know you had an accident. Sorry to hear that. What happened?"

"I was galloping one of Harry's horses in the morning. Its leg broke right underneath me. This was before I started training. I got hurt real bad. Harry paid all my medical bills, and when I started training, he gave me four stalls without any questions. That's why I'm in Mike's barn. I think it pisses Mike off a little, and it really annoys the racing secretary. I might be the only trainer on the grounds who isn't hassled to fill races, except for Mike of course. Anyway, Harry's an ass, but I don't make waves."

I'm worried I might have annoyed Pete a little. Time to chill out and relax for the rest of the afternoon. I'm enjoying being here.

Charlie drops off the plate of nachos.

"Thanks, Charlie," Pete says.

"So will Harry's horse win this afternoon?" I ask Pete.

"He's got a good shot. His last workout was good, and his trainer seems pretty bullish on him, top trainer too. He's only raced four times, but he has three wins, including two stakes races."

"Will they be pointing him for the Kentucky Derby?"

"If he wins today, he'll go to the Wood Memorial in April. That's the key Derby prep in New York. If he places in that race, he'll go to the Kentucky Derby."

"Harry must be excited?"

"We don't see him often at the track, but Mike says he's going nuts about this. I guess it's his way of trying to gain acceptance amongst racing's elite."

"I guess that's as good a reason as any for wanting to win," I say sarcastically, though Harry does seem like a bit of an ass.

All the TV screens in the bar are showing the races from Aqueduct; the horses are now in the paddock for the Gotham Stakes. While I have only seen Harry once or twice in the years I've been visiting the track, I recognize him in a close huddle with what I assume are his trainer and jockey.

"Have you ever raced at Aqueduct?" I ask Pete.

"No, sadly. I've only raced my horses at Missionville, and once or twice at other Pennsylvania tracks if Missionville didn't have a race for one of my horses. When I first started training, I thought I would start here, and then venture off to another circuit after a year or two. This place could teach me, but unfortunately I never really had the opportunity to move on. Now I don't see it happening. I'm stuck at Missionville, and Missionville is stuck with me."

The horses come out of the paddock at Aqueduct. Harry's horse, Dancer's Foil, is the 2-1 betting favorite. Jose Figuaro is in the saddle, the current leading rider in New York. Todd Brown, his trainer, is also the leading trainer on the circuit, so things look pretty good for Harry's horse.

"Do you see yourself here forever?"

"I stopped worrying about that a while ago. Losing your ambition can be a little soul-destroying. Now I just focus on my day-to-day existence, try to make the best of my situation. It's not all bad. There are some good people at Missionville and Hairy keeps me busy in the afternoons."

The way Pete says it, it doesn't sound good no matter how he coats it. While I'm not overly ambitious, I always want to make a difference, and I think my work retiring horses is starting to do that. It's funny, my bank job, managing a number of branches, is my career; people admire me for it, but it is my horse work that is my passion, and where I derive most of my satisfaction. There must be more to Pete now than simply surviving the day-to-day life on the backside at Missionville.

"OK, horses are loading, fingers crossed for Dancer's Foil, I guess." I'm not sure if I want Harry to win the race or not. But I don't know anyone else in the race. Watching racing is not something I usually do on a Saturday afternoon, or any time really.

Dancer's Foil leaves the gate and lets four horses move by him easily. His jockey has him settled about five lengths off the pace as they start to head down the backside.

"They're going too fast up front. I think Dancer's Foil's in the perfect spot. Should gallop by them coming off the turn." Pete vocalizes his thoughts. "Come on, Figuaro, let him run."

Dancer's Foil eases up to the leaders at the quarter pole, and Figuaro pulls him wide as they enter the homestretch. Dancer's Foil draws off to an easy victory. The TV camera focuses on Harry as his horse gallops out. He goes completely crazy, jumping up and down, high-fiving whoever he can. He's not the classiest of guys.

"There you go, Harry wins the big race. It'll be on to the Wood Memorial, which will be a sterner test." I'm not sure if Pete is happy for Harry, or just accepting of the whole situation. Nor am I sure if I could really like Pete, but I do want to know more about the goings on in that barn.

CHAPTER 4

PETE, MONDAY

WITH TWO HORSES TRAINED, IT'S TIME FOR A COFFEE while it's break time on the track.

"Hey, Pete, need anything?" James asks me.

"I'm good today. I haven't trained the new horse yet, but I'll catch up with you, maybe tomorrow, to discuss how he's doing. Hopefully we can make a plan for him?"

"Sounds good. Good luck tonight."

It's bugged me a little, what Amanda said on Saturday about Harry and Mike's operation. James is a little slick for sure, a very good vet, but I wonder if he would do anything beyond the rules. I'm sure he injected that horse last week on race day. I guess that's beyond the rules. While I didn't think anything of it at the time, perhaps I should have. The horse won, he shouldn't really have beaten a couple of horses in that race. Maybe I'll just keep a closer eye on James's comings and goings. Talk to him more, learn a little more about him. I don't think there's much point in sharing anything with Amanda right now. She'd probably go a little crazy with it. I remember her being upset with me on the phone when she found one of my horses at Owenscreek. That was bad all around. Jake had told me he would try to rehab the horse when I sold it to him. I should have pushed him a little more, but I didn't. Three weeks later the horse was at the auction.

Amanda is very cute. She has lovely green eyes and long reddish blonde hair. She is definitely not ordinary looking, and has a wonderful figure. I really didn't think she would come out to watch the race on Saturday, but she did, and seemed to enjoy it. I'll try to get her out again, hopefully sooner rather than later. I finish my coffee.

Hairy is snoring in the corner of my tack room as I get the tack for my final horse to train for the morning, Thunder Clouds.

I groom the old horse and tack him up. He seems very gentle and easy to be around when you're on the ground. He's a pleasure to have in the barn really. Alfie pulls him out of his stall to give him a turn around the shedrow.

"Ready, boss?"

"Thanks, Alfie," I mumble through my facemask, as he gives me a leg up.

At the entrance of the track we just stand and wait. The first time I ride a new horse that I don't really know, I'm always cautious. But I've seen this guy train a few times, so I figure he is going to be fine. He is. We start our jog over to the wire. Like most older horses, he has a little stiffness in his movement; he is definitely a little short on the right front leg. It's hard to notice, but over many years of riding at the track, you learn to feel even the most subtle imperfections. I start jogging on the left diagonal as usual, but when I switch to the right diagonal I can feel the shortness a little more. This is something a lot of exercise riders don't do, unless they went through pony club like me. Anyway, I'm not too worried, a bit of stiffness is to be expected.

I turn him in at the wire, and we wait for three to four minutes, watching other horses train. While it's another very cold morning, there is also bright sunshine and no wind. Mondays are typically busy days at the track, and we watch three workers come by, as well as a few horses gallop by. One pair of workers breeze down the lane head-to-head and spook a horse that's galloping in the middle of the track. That horse's exercise rider struggles for an eighth of a mile to get it back under control. Typical goings on for a Monday morning.

Thunder Clouds gallops his mile and a half in a leisurely fashion. When I gallop him tomorrow, I'll drop my irons a little. He sits on the bridle nicely, and is very easy going in his manner. The shortness in his stride that I detected at the jog is not there at the gallop. He switches his leads at the right places, in and out of the turns, but perhaps just falls back onto his left lead a little too easily. These are all signals to a horse's soundness. It's a decent gallop, probably as good as I could have expected. Time to head back to the barn. We stand in at the gap.

"Your new horse, Pete?" Jess asks.

"Yes. Classy old guy."

"How'd he go?"

"Great, thanks."

"Good luck with him. I've followed him for a couple of years now, a real war horse."

"He is. We'll do our best."

"See you tomorrow, Pete."

Marcus Longman is in my shedrow when we return.

"Long time since you've been in my shedrow," I note with a little sarcasm.

"Yes, too long. How's things?"

"It's Monday, all's well. The old horse trained well."

"He looks good. Just wanted to see if you had a plan for him yet?"

"Not yet. I see you rode him a while back."

"I won on him. I've not ridden him since, and he's not won since."

"I noticed that." It's true. A little over a year ago, Thunder Clouds won his last race with Longman aboard. The comment in the *Daily Racing Form* noted that he spurted away quickly at the quarter pole with an impressive change of pace. He hasn't done that since.

"I'd like to get back on him, if you need me. Just want to work him first."

"Thanks, Marcus, I'll let you know."

Longman heads to Mike's shedrow.

"Boss, he's no good," Alfie whispers to me as he passes me in the shedrow with Thunder Clouds.

"What do you mean 'no good'? Is the horse OK?"

"Sure. He's good. But Marcus is no good. Not worth it." Alfie knows the backside as well as anybody. At first appearance he seems to be someone of little consequence, but I have learned that if he tells me something, it is something I need to know. Longman should not ride Thunder Clouds.

I wander over to see Jorge, and how their new claim is settling in for him. Jorge is busying himself with his new horse.

"Hey, Jorge, this your new horse?"

"Si, Spicy Lemon, claimed last week."

"I figured it was him. Do you like him?"

"Nice old horse, easy to work around."

"Any problems with him?" There's a golden rule at the track, you don't claim horses from trainers in your own barn, nor discuss their horses with other trainers at the track. These are not written rules, but it's an understanding. Because of this, outfits in the same barn are generally more open about their horses.

"I think he's a little weak in his hind end, some back issues maybe. I'm working on some stuff. We shall see. Has not been to the track yet."

"Good luck with him."

"Gracias. Good luck tonight, I might bet on your filly."

"Thanks. Yes, me too!"

Jake is hanging out in Mike's shedrow as I'm chatting to Jorge. He is scheduled to pony my filly at the races tonight.

"All good for tonight, Pete?" Jake asks.

"Yes, thanks. I'll see you at the races."

"She looks good in the race. I'll take care of her."

"Thanks." For all his faults, Jake is a very good pony guy. You know your horse will be well taken care of before a race.

Ten minutes later I'm grooming one of my horses when Larry, the state vet, swings by my shedrow.

"Pete, can you pull your filly out for me?" Before a horse competes, it has to be approved, soundness-wise, by the state vet. Larry has worked at Missionville for many years, and I'm not sure how many horses he's scratched due to unsoundness, but it's only a few. Certainly there are quite a few times he should have scratched a horse, but Larry doesn't seem to be too bothered.

"Sure," I respond, I bring the filly into the shedrow. Larry quickly moves his hands down her front legs.

"OK, jog her away, and then jog back." It is a routine I know well. I trot her away for about five strides, ease her, turn her, and jog her back.

"Looks good. Lasix as usual, four hours out."

"Thanks, Larry. Alfie will be here when you guys come back."

"Good luck tonight."

"Thanks." With the state vet inspection over, time to head to the track kitchen and then home before tonight's races.

Alfie leads Pink Slippers into the paddock for the seventh race. She looks good; her bay coat shines under the lights. She has a big white stripe down her face which always makes her stand out from the other fillies.

"All good?" I check in with Alfie.

"No problems." Alfie waits with all my runners during the afternoon before the races. He needed to be there when the filly received her Lasix shot, he would then wait until it was time to bring her over for the race.

They circle the paddock with the seven other fillies who had been led over from the backside. I wait in the saddling box until the valet comes out with the jockey's saddle and number cloth. When he does, I nod to Alfie, who brings the filly in.

We tack her up and Alfie leads her back out for a few more turns around the paddock. Emma Sparks files out of the jocks' room with the other seven jockeys and comes over.

"What do you think?" I always like to ask jockeys first for their thoughts. There's a well-known saying on the backside, good jockeys will know how to ride the race and don't need instructions, bad jockeys can't follow instructions.

"There seems to be plenty of speed in the race, so I thought I'd just sit off it a little, and then bring her with a run once we straighten up for home."

"Sounds good to me." Alfie brings Pink Slippers back to the saddling stall.

"Riders up!" is the call from the paddock judge. Emma props up her left leg and I lift her up.

"Good luck, Emma. Have a safe trip."

"Thanks, Pete. She looks great." Emma gives Slippers a pat as they depart with Alfie.

I will admit it, I'm pretty much a nervous wreck when I run my own horses. There's plenty at stake. I want to know that I've done right by the horse by putting it in a race that it's ready to win. There's some vanity there, I want to prove to whomever that I am a good horseman, but I am also concerned for the horse. I want the horse to do well, while I have it in my care. Aside from all that, I kind of need this win. Money is getting very tight.

Alfie comes over to me, after leading Emma and the filly out to the track and handing them off to Jake.

"All good, boss."

"Thanks. Are you betting?" I ask Alfie.

"No, I just hope she wins for you."

"Thanks. I'll put ten dollars on for you." Alfie smiles. I walk away. I want to place a bet, and I need a Budweiser to settle my nerves.

"Mary, Budweiser please?"

"Here you go, it's ready for you. Good luck!"

"Thanks."

I head over to the betting windows. My filly, Pink Slippers, is the 3-1 second choice. I place a hundred dollars on her to win. Stupid really, because I need that cash, but I decide to go all in on this filly. If she wins tonight, we are in great shape for the next month or so. She's been training well, so I want to try to take an edge.

I watch the TV screen nervously as the horses are being loaded. My filly walks right into the starting gate with no problem. She looks calm and quiet, Emma appears to be relaxed. Exactly how you want it in the gates.

"They're in the gate," the commentator announces over the p.a. system. "And they're off!"

I watch the race unfold on the screen. She breaks well, maybe a little too well. Emma has Pink Slippers head and head on the lead. This could be good, this might not be good. The early fraction is fast, 22 and change. Christ, I hope Emma has plenty of horse underneath her.

They move around the turn. The horse on the inside of Emma begins to retreat, leaving my filly in front on her own. Emma has only one choice, to really go for it. She pulls out her stick and gives the filly a couple of quick cracks and then starts to hand ride. Coming off the turn they shoot three lengths clear.

"Come on, Slippers! Come on!" I start yelling, wrapped up in the moment. At the eighth pole she is still in front, but her lead is shrinking, she's tiring.

"Hold on! Hold on girl!" I yell. Her lead shrinks more and as they cross the wire two other horses flash by heads apart and a neck in front of her.

Damn. She'd run a great race, despite how the race set up, but the result is costly. I finish my Budweiser.

I wander down to where the horses are being unsaddled. Alfie is already with the filly. Emma and her valet are busy taking off her saddle.

"Sorry, Pete. She should have won that race."

"She ran a gutsy race. Tough loss in the end."

"Yes, she broke so well, I really didn't have much choice but to sit on the lead. This was unknown to her, but the other speed in the race never set up like I thought it would."

"No worries. I get it. You've got to make quick decisions, and then go for it. I thought it was going to work out at the eighth pole."

"Thanks, Pete. I know you really wanted this. I'll stop by tomorrow and catch up."

"Cool. Catch you later."

Now the hard part, I had to call Ray. He was probably expecting a win; I have been pretty enthusiastic about her training. When Ray's expecting a win, he bets big, not here at Missionville, but in Vegas, so as not to impact the odds.

I pull out my phone and call up Ray. I get his voicemail, which is a relief. "Ray, the filly ran third, only just got beat. The race didn't set up well, but she ran very game. I'll call you in the morning." Hopefully by tomorrow morning, if Ray's upset, he might have settled down a little. I put my phone back in my pocket. Thirty seconds later it vibrates.

"Hello, Ray."

"Pete, I saw the race."

"She was very game, things just didn't work out."

"Why was she on the lead? What was Emma thinking?"

"She broke so well she didn't have much choice."

"C'mon. This filly needs covering up. She has a late kick. We know that. She's not a speed horse."

"I really think Emma was taken by surprise by how well she broke. She made a decision, perhaps not the best decision, but she tried."

"She screwed up. I know you like Emma, but there's a reason she's not a leading rider at the track." I didn't like the direction of the conversation.

"I get what you're saying. But Emma's loyal, works our horses and for the most part does a decent and honest job. She only got beat less than half a length."

"That less than half a length just cost me thousands of dollars." It cost me a few hundred too, a few hundred I really need right now.

"I understand."

"I want to see Longman, or one of the other leading riders, on one or two of my horses more often."

"OK, Ray."

CHAPTER 5

AMANDA, TUESDAY

IT'S 11 A.M., TIME TO LEAVE THE BANK and head to Owenscreek. Because I've been with the bank now for a while and done well, I've been able to negotiate a half-day on Tuesdays so I can attend the horse auction. It's about an hour's drive from Missionville, and the horse sale usually starts at about one o'clock. There's always a tack sale first. I like to get there a little early so I can take a look at the horses in the corrals, before the sale. I change between leaving the bank and getting to the auction: shaggy sweater, woolly hat, jeans, and a thick coat.

Visiting kill auctions would not be everyone's choice for a hobby. But for me it's become a part of my weekly routine now for a couple of years. Every Tuesday, almost without fail. I watch out particularly for Thoroughbreds that are being run through the sale, and keep an eye on the two kill buyers who attend every week. Tom buys horses for the slaughterhouse in Massueville, Fred buys horses for the plant in St. Andre-Avellin. Both slaughterhouses are in Quebec, Canada. I've pulled a few Thoroughbreds out of the sale. Sarah Lester has helped me with quarantine arrangements, and finding other farms that will hold the horses temporarily. Sarah's basically been my mentor for all this. I'm looking forward to our dinner tonight.

I arrive at Owenscreek at about 12:15 p.m. The tack sale is underway as I enter. Rather than go into the gallery and watch, I head straight to the back of the sales barn where all the horses are waiting. There is a boardwalk over the top of the corrals where I wander along to look at the scope of the offering.

A few horses are in pens on their own, many are shoved into pens with others. There are horses of all shapes and sizes: working horses, kids' ponies, trotting horses, pleasure horses and a few Thoroughbreds. All discarded by their current owners. Thankfully at this time of year the sale typically comprises of only fifty horses a week. In September and October there will be upwards of one hundred and fifty horses run through.

I spy a group of horses that look like Thoroughbreds in the back of the barn. I head to the ground level and walk over to the two corrals that these horses are in. My goal is to try to identify who they are, while being discreet about it. I don't have any homes for them to go to at the moment, but I still think it's worthwhile to note the names and follow up with the previous owners, if at all possible. To do this I need to identify the lip tattoo that's under the top lip of any Thoroughbred that has raced.

I have a notepad, pencil, iPhone and mints – the tools of my trade. The first corral contains two of the Thoroughbreds. I walk in quietly, with a very calm voice.

One of the Thoroughbreds, a chestnut gelding, snorts at me as I approach, but he doesn't seem to mind me too much. He lets me get close. "Hey buddy, here's a mint." I pull up his top lip, he backs away and snorts again.

"Hey, hey, it's OK buddy, I'm just trying to figure out who you are." I move closer, he drops his head, looking for another mint.

"Here you go, pal." I give him another mint and stroke his neck. He starts to relax a little. I move to lift his top lip up with one hand, as I balance my phone in the other to take a few pictures. This is very tricky, but after doing it for a while now I've gotten pretty adept. I then slide my phone into my pocket and examine the lip tattoo again. I write down the numbers in my notepad. I also note the sales number that has been pasted to the horse's rump.

I repeat this routine for the three other horses. One of the Thoroughbred's tattoos is unreadable, I can't identify him. But three out of four is decent work.

Both of the kill buyers have their own pens, which will fill with horses as the sale progresses. Sometimes there are already horses in those pens, prior to the start of the sale; horses that are not offered for sale, but going directly to kill. There's one in Tom's pen. He's a Thoroughbred, they usually are. He's standing on his own with his head down. It's too risky for me to go over to identify him, that's part of the unwritten bargain I make with the auction. If I get too carried away with my work, I will be asked to leave. I used to get a little too emotional, but I have learned that emotion doesn't get me very far. I've seen other rescue folks over the years get overly zealous with their work, and then they don't return.

My pre-sale work is done, so I retreat to the gallery to wait for the horse sale to begin.

I sit down with my notepad and pencil in hand. My routine here is to note the number of horses each kill buyer purchases, and the prices paid. I also make particular note of the Thoroughbreds, what they go for, and to whom. My best estimate for a typical sale here at Owenscreek is that half the horses at the sale are bought by the two kill buyers, the remainder are bought by private buyers, rescues and other horse traders.

Sometimes I will do this type of observation work for an animal welfare group. They like to keep an eye on how the kill auctions work around the country. They want to know who the kill buyers are and for which slaughterhouses they have contracts. I find their work fascinating and have been happy to help.

The kill buyers here know who I am, and what I do. As long as I don't cause any disruption, they tolerate me. It's the same with Abel, the auctioneer, who owns the auction. They will even answer general questions I might pose to them, to help me understand the system more clearly.

I look around the gallery. A few familiar faces are in attendance, aside from the ever presence of the two kill buyers and Abel. There are a couple of horse traders I have come to know, and Jake, the pony guy from the track. Jake is pretty much always here, and I know why. He is the connection between the racetrack and the kill auction. Jake gives two hundred dollars a horse at the track and turns that into four hundred or so pretty quickly. Some of the horses he brings go through the sale. I have no doubt that one or two I checked this morning were brought here by Jake. I also wonder if the horse in Tom's kill pen is from Jake. There are also a couple of drivers here, the guys who ship the horses up to the slaughterhouses. Mark is one of them, he drives for Fred.

The odd thing about this place is that it's also a community gathering. Every Tuesday, the horse auction brings out the locals, many of whom are Amish; they come here not to trade horses, but to trade gossip and socialize. This is part of their way of life.

The horse sale gets underway as the first horse is herded into the ring.

The auctioneer provides brief detail, "Number 103, older mare, no foal. Signed paper." Signed paper means that the seller is willing to sign a form that says the horse is available for slaughter – it is basically drug-free. It's a relatively new hoop the slaughter system has to deal with, but it's bogus. I've seen the form they sign; the questions aren't well thought out, and anyone seems willing to sign. The four Thoroughbreds will sell with 'signed paper.' They always do.

Tom, the kill buyer, picks this old mare up for $250. I make a note of the sale.

Fifty horses doesn't take long to get through, and the sale is over in less than an hour. Each of the kill buyers bought two of the Thoroughbreds I had tried to identify. All told, they bought 22 of the horses on offer. The rest of the horses went to an assortment of new owners and local rescues, with various horse traders picking up about a dozen of them. I finish up all my notes, snap a couple more pictures with my iPhone and then leave.

Sarah's farm is always a pleasure to visit. There are paddocks on either side as you drive in, and horses are out grazing, looking very content. This is how to train horses, I think to myself. Give them plenty of outside time. The contrast to the backside of the racetrack at Missionville is stark. Those horses seem to spend more than 23 hours a day in their stall; I often think it's like comparing a 5-star resort to a prison camp.

I get out of my car and head over to the house. Because it's the middle of the afternoon, I assume Sarah has finished all her barn chores for the day other than bringing the horses in and feeding them, which happens a little later.

"Hey, Amanda," Sarah greets me as I open her kitchen door. "I heard your car coming up the driveway."

"Sarah, good to see you. It's been too long."

"No kidding. Coffee?"

"Sure."

"How was Owenscreek?"

"Another quiet sale today, with all the usual suspects in attendance. Four Thoroughbreds went through the sale, one was already in Tom's pen."

"Ugh. I'm proud of you for heading over there and witnessing all this. I'm not sure I could do it anymore."

"Well, you got me into it, so I blame it on you. I don't particularly like it, but it's becoming a bit of an obsession. I've not missed a sale for months now."

"Do you want to see if we can identify any of those Thoroughbreds?" Sarah hands me a coffee.

"Yes, that would be great. We might as well see who's getting rid of their horses."

Sarah pulls out her iPad and goes to the Jockey Club website. I hand her my notepad with the list of tattoos, while pulling up my iPhone so she can browse the pictures.

Sarah types in the numbers, one set after the other, and writes down a couple of names.

"I think we can identify two of them, both are five-year-olds, the first letter of the tattoo is an O. One is a filly, Dream Sweeper, the other a gelding named Harbor Lights. The third tattoo isn't matching a horse in the database. We'll have to take a closer look at those numbers on the photo and see if we can come up with a different combination."

"Thanks. It's always sad to uncover who these guys are, like it has to be a secret."

"That's how the game works. No one wants to admit to dumping their horses, would be bad publicity. But that track wouldn't survive if there wasn't an easy outlet for their waste." Sarah is clearly bitter about the goings on at Missionville. I didn't really want to bring up the subject of Spicy Lemon just yet. "That horse, Harbor Lights, his name is familiar. Not sure why, but I think I know him?" Sarah's thinking out loud.

"Sad stuff. All four horses were bought for kill, two each by the two kill buyers. I also wonder which horse was already in Tom's pen."

"You know whose horse I think it is. Harry's. That ass doesn't even let his horses run through the ring, in case they're rescued." Sarah is probably right about that. In all the times I've been to the sale I've never identified a horse of Harry's. But there are these horses, from time to time, in Tom's pen before the sale, always Tom's. Maybe one or two over the course of a month. They are always Thoroughbreds and they always look fit, just off the track.

We head out to the barn and start to get the horses in and readied for their feed time. Sarah has eight horses in training. She also has an assortment of horses that are either retired from racing, not yet ready to race, or breeding stock. It is a very nice operation. It's always good for the soul to come out here and help out a little. I don't stop by to see Sarah often enough.

Once we finish the barn chores and the horses are munching away on their dinners, I notice one stall remains empty – Spicy Lemon's no doubt.

Back in the house, Sarah pulls out a bottle of wine.

"Amanda, you have to stay tonight. This has been a week from hell for me." I thought about it for less than ten seconds. It's easy for me to stay the night, I have no one waiting for me to return home. I would just need to get up a little earlier than usual for a week day, head home and then get ready for the bank.

"I'd love to stay over. I need to unwind a little, and I know things are tough for you."

"Good, then it's settled." Sarah pours me a glass of wine. She gets two more bottles from a cupboard and places them in the fridge.

"Ugh. I feel so guilty about Spicy Lemon. Like I've betrayed him. He's been at the farm all his life, except of course when he raced for me. He was a great runner for me, very consistent. I owe him so much. Now look what's happened. Shit, if he ends up in that pen of Tom's at Owenscreek that'll be the end of it." I couldn't imagine how I would feel in the same situation. Sarah really does love her horses. She treats them so well, and they're so easy to handle, which I assume is because of the love and care she gives them. She's had one or two claimed off her over the years and she knows the reality of the claiming system far better than me, but this has rocked her.

"I don't understand why he was claimed. In that spot, he should have been safe. I was just hoping to pick up a small check with him. If I wanted him claimed, I would have run him in a cheaper race and tried to win with him too. Damn. I need to do something, but for the life of me I can't figure out what." I keep listening, as we both take swigs of our wine.

"He's got a weak hock, on his left hind leg. I was working with it, and he was managing fine with it. God knows what will happen now." The guilt in Sarah's voice is palpable.

I really want to change the conversation, so we could chat about some good stuff. I ask Sarah to tell me more about Spicy's younger days.

Sarah starts to recount how, in his first race, Spicy finished dead last. His jockey came back and was polite, but she could tell he didn't want to ride him again. She recalls each of his two-year-old races, it took Sarah six races to get Spicy to place in his first race. This wasn't unusual for her horses which sometimes take a little time to mature. After Spicy won his first race, Sarah goes on to tell about his second win as if she's in possession of a stakes horse. I could almost see her smile as she reminisces story after story. Perhaps this is good therapy for Sarah, for now. The wine is also sliding down very nicely, and Sarah has already opened a second bottle as she prepares our meal.

Dinner is delicious. Sarah is a great cook, and she seems glad to be able to cook for company. She has been divorced now for nearly three years. Her husband was having an affair with someone at his office; he's a lawyer, who ironically focuses on family affairs. She hasn't dated much since. We've become closer over the last few years as Sarah taught me more and more about how the racing system works. I've grown very fond of her.

"What do you know of Pete Wright?" I ask Sarah quizzically.

"He's an odd guy. Sometimes I think he's OK, there's no doubt he's a good horseman. But I don't like the owner he trains for, Ray. We know a couple of his horses have ended up at Owenscreek."

"Yes, I know. He asked me out the other day."

"What? Really? Did you go?"

"I did. We went to that bar in Missionville the horsemen over there go to, Jessup's, and watched Harry's horse in the Gotham."

"Wow, Amanda, you at that dive bar, you with Pete, and watching a horse of Harry's. Seems like the world has tilted the wrong way." Sarah is only half-joking.

"I know. It's odd. But Pete was actually pretty easy to hang out with outside of the track."

"Easy on the eye too, I should imagine." Sarah grins.

"Yes, that too. Anyway, since he's in Harry's barn, I figure I might try to hang out with him a little more. See if he can help any with Spicy."

Sarah seemed to sober up a little. I shouldn't have mentioned the horse.

After an awkward pause, she says, "Well, if anyone can do that, it's you. He'll enjoy your company no doubt, and want a little bit more. I can't imagine Pete's gay."

We crack open a third bottle of wine.

CHAPTER 6

PETE, FRIDAY

WITH THE TOUGH LOSS ON MONDAY, the week had started on a bad note and I'm ready for the weekend. I have no plans, but I am hoping I can get Amanda to come out again. She'll be stopping by tomorrow for sure. I had wanted to text her, but decided I should just wait. It's part of the game we play, I guess.

Ray called a couple of times in the last few days. He is serious about wanting to switch riders. I know I'll have to do it for a couple of mounts, but I'm hoping I can get Emma back in his good graces. Emma understands. I told her what Ray had said and she is good with it. She just told me to do what's best for the barn. That's what I want to do, keep riding Emma, that's what's best for the barn.

The filly has actually come out of the race well, so I'm hoping we can run her back in the same spot again pretty soon, and get the win she deserves. Unfortunately we know in racing, a win is tough to get. I'm not going to be overly confident. I'll just try to nurse her nicely to her next race.

"All good, Pete?" It's James, the vet.

"All good. Can we chat about Thunder Clouds when you have a few minutes?"

"Sure. Now's good."

"Alfie, can you bring Thunder Clouds out please?"

Alfie puts the gelding he was walking in its stall, then leads Thunder Clouds into the shedrow.

"He's been training well, James. It's hard to notice much when you're riding him, but he's slightly short on that right front, and he seems to almost fall onto the left lead when he's galloping. He's not bad for an older horse though." James takes a long look at the right front ankle, moving his hands up and down. He then lifts the leg up and flexes the joint a little.

"Alfie, jog him up there please, then back." Alfie does and after the flex, Thunder Clouds looks a little shorter on that right front.

"Hmmm. A tough one. That's an old ankle. I would guess it's been tapped a few times, but if you want it pain free on race day, that's what we should do, a week out, after a workout so you can walk him for a couple of days. You know the drill. We'll obviously know more about the joint when we tap it." James is referring to whether we see blood or a clear fluid. You can only tap a joint so many times; things could go wrong. It's a dangerous game we play with these horses.

"Thanks. I'll let you know when I've found a race for him, then work back from there. I'm guessing it'll be a couple more weeks."

"Sounds good."

"Things busy for you?" I inquire. I want to get to know more about James's business.

"Yes, Mike keeps me busy, you know that, you see me here all the time. Plus, with you and one or two other trainers on the backside, I have a full schedule."

"Cool, I guess if Mike uses you, I should," I say half-joking, and acknowledging that Mike is the leading trainer here at Missionville.

"Mike does do well here, and I'm grateful he's a client. You're a great horseman, so if there's anything I can do to help you, you've got it."

"I know, thanks, James. It's been tough here lately for me, especially with the filly's loss on Monday, but I've bounced back before."

"You will." James leaves, and heads down the shedrow to tend to more of Mike's needs for the day.

I'm grooming my last horse when Jake stops by.

"Any chance you have that twenty from Monday night?" Jake is referring to the twenty dollars I owe him for ponying the filly to the starting gate.

"Jake, things are really tight. Ray's getting a little late on the bills, you know how it is. Any chance I can give you the money next week?" I hate being behind with money.

"No worries, I know you're good for it." I am good for it. I never shirk my debts like a few others on the backside. But I admit things are getting worse than usual.

"Thanks, Jake. Appreciate it."

"No problem. That was a tough loss on Monday for you guys."

"Yes, it was. I was pretty bummed, even though she ran decent."

"She ran a winning race, just think the tactics were screwy."

"Yep, you're not the only one, I'm getting grief from Ray too."

"Well, you'll get her back to the races in good shape here soon, and she should be able to beat those fillies with a good ride."

"Thanks, Jake."

"See you."

CHAPTER 7

AMANDA, SATURDAY

I PULL UP OUTSIDE THE TRACK KITCHEN ready for my Saturday morning on the backside at Missionville. I'm a little nervous, which is an odd feeling. I will be seeing Pete at some stage this morning, and I really don't know how he or I will react. Part of me really wants to get to know him more, another part of me, the rational side, thinks not.

It had taken me a day to recover from hanging out with Sarah on Tuesday. We have done that before, sat up most of the night drinking wine and sharing our thoughts. Sarah is easy for me to do that with, and wine is a weakness of mine. I paid for it the next day. My job at the bank isn't a walk in the park. I oversee eight branches, and being a smallish community banking system, we are under pressure from the bigger banks and internet banking – just to survive. At the best of times it's a tough enough job to keep everything going. So on Wednesday it was tricky, but worth it. I plan to stop by and see Sarah more often, especially while Spicy Lemon is in Mike's barn. Hopefully Pete will have some news for me about the horse.

I grab a coffee from the track kitchen and head to the racetrack to watch and hang out. It's another brutally cold morning. I'm wrapped up in a thick coat, my woolly hat, gloves, scarf, and anything else I could think of putting on. I don't envy the exercise riders at all. Watching is different.

There is something magical about seeing horses in their training, early in the morning, when it's still dark and the track is under floodlights. The scene is almost mystical. The sound of the hooves crunching the ground, the horses' heavy breathing, which you can see as they exhale into the frozen air, all add to the majesty of the moment; it takes me far away from my banking world. I stand on the rail for ten minutes, just taking it all in before I'm interrupted.

"Amanda, I was hoping to see you here."

"Hi, John, good morning," I greet John Swank, who has Rocket Road listed on my site.

"Any luck with my horse?"

"Yes, actually. There's a person in Ohio who emailed me on Thursday night. She's looking for a project horse, maybe to do a little trail riding and showing. She likes the pictures and video."

"That's great. Any chance you can connect us? I need to get him out of that stall by the end of next week. I have a new horse coming in."

"Sure, let me get her number." I reach into my pocket for my notepad. I had written her number down to give to John this morning.

"216-555-1247. Her name is Jane Kinley. Call me if there's a problem and you can't get the horse moved?"

"Will do. If this works out, I will owe you big time."

"I really hope it does, but don't just let him go if it doesn't. Call me, right?"

"Sure. Thanks again."

John seems like one of the good guys. He cares about his horses, but I know how hard it can be for these guys. If it comes down to it, I will ask Sarah if she has a spare stall for a month. Rocket Road seems nice and should be easy enough to place.

I return my attention to watching the training. It is light enough now that the track lights have been turned off. I chat with one or two other trainers, and promise to stop by one of their barns to take a look at a horse. In the meantime, Pete enters the track on one of his horses, and stands him in for a little while, as he seems to always do.

"Hey, Amanda, good to see you. Here's your horse."

"Thunder Clouds? Great. It'll be nice to watch him train."

"He's been doing well. Are you stopping by later?" He asked, that's good.

"Yes, it'll be good to catch up." I try not to sound too eager.

Pete rides off. It is a good five minutes before he comes galloping by; the pair look great. Pete is riding rather deep in the saddle but relaxed, with his hands down and the horse simply cruising along. Good horsemanship does stand out; there's plenty of the other here, too. After Pete comes by the second time, he eases Thunder Clouds through his paces to a standstill, turns him around, and brings him back to the gap. He exchanges a few words with the girl who works on the gap, and then he departs.

I watch training for another twenty minutes, exchanging pleasantries with a few more horsemen, then leave to start visiting the barns. I have three horses I want to check on that are being advertised on my site, to make sure they are still here. I have two inquiries to advertise horses, including the one from the trainer I had just talked to at the track, so I need to take care of that. I also need to visit Pete's barn. I want to do that.

Checking the three horses is the easiest task. I know which barns and stalls they are housed in. I wander over to each of the barns, seek out a person who knows each of the horses and check up on them. All are accounted for. I chat with their connections a little, and provide any updates on activities. February is a tough month for placing horses, but March and April typically are not; more people are thinking about their summers and horse projects. I try to convince people to just hang in there a little longer. I know the pressures they are under; the racing secretary does not like horses in stalls that are not running. The more horses he can get in a race, the higher the betting handle, and the more money for the racetrack. That is the math with which he operates.

I stop by Jim Johnson's barn. He has an entire barn to himself – forty horses. He has one of the two horses I was asked to advertise. He's the biggest trainer on the backside at Missionville, in terms of number of horses, and generally runs second in the trainers' standings behind Mike. He's a claiming trainer, like everyone else here, but once in a while he will have a horse he decides not to drop to the bottom level, and tries to find a home for it. I guess there is a softer side to the old guy; I think he's in his eighties now.

"Hi, is Mr. Johnson around?" I ask the groom who is closest to the end of his shedrow.

"He's in his office, at the other end of the barn."

"Thanks."

I walk down the shedrow behind a couple of horses being led around by their hotwalkers. I knock on Johnson's office door.

"Yes, come in."

"Hello, Mr. Johnson, it's Amanda, I run the rehab website." That's how I refer to myself when I want to make a quick introduction and not waste anyone's time.

"Yes, thanks for coming over. I appreciate it. He's in stall 39, just around the corner. His groom, Javier, will help you out."

"Thank you, I'll keep you updated." I head to stall 39 and find Javier.

"Javier?"

"Si?"

"I'm here to take pictures of Painted Pretender for Mr. Johnson. Could you bring him out for me please?"

"Of course." Javier brings the horse outside the barn and I take photographs and video quickly.

I repeat the same routine for the trainer who I saw at the gap this morning. Simple stuff, which might help a horse. This afternoon I will add both horses to the website and promote them to the online communities I frequent. Five minutes later, I'm in Pete's barn.

"Hey, Pete." I'm a little nervous, which is not like me at all.

"Hi, Amanda. You make Saturdays better." Well, that calms the nerves.

"Can I take a look at Thunder Clouds? How's he doing?"

"Sure, he's on the wash pad. Alfie is hosing his right front leg. He's doing well, he just has an old injury we need to work with. He galloped well today."

"He looked good, Pete, both of you." I guess I shouldn't have added the second part. I wander over to see the horse, which is standing still, head down in Alfie's left hand, while Alfie directs the hose with his other hand to the horse's right ankle.

"Nice to see you, Amanda." Alfie's always polite.

"You too, Alfie. Horse looks good, happy."

"He is. Nice classy horse; not too many of these guys around."

"No, you're probably right. I hope you do well with him."

"Yes, it'll be good for Pete." Alfie continues hosing as I watch for a minute or two. He's a very gentle looking horse. You'd almost imagine a young child could ride him. I went over to the stall Pete is in.

"Pete, any word on Sarah's old horse, Spicy Lemon?"

"I chatted to Jorge a few days ago. He likes the guy but says he might have a weakness in behind somewhere. They hadn't ridden him at that point. He's been to the track the last couple days but I haven't caught up with Jorge since."

"Please could you keep checking on him? I was at Sarah's the other day, and she's still really upset."

"Of course. If I see Jorge later today I'll ask him; if not, very soon. He won't be racing for a couple of weeks at the earliest, so there's a little time."

"Thanks. Hey, do you know a horse called Harbor Lights?" I want to know if Pete knew who one of the horses was that we identified the other day at the auction. Pete thought for a minute.

"I think he's the horse that was vanned off last week after one of the races. Pulled up lame. Hope he's going to be OK, but you never know. Why?"

"Nothing, he just came up in a conversation with Sarah the other day."

"Oh, hope it wasn't her horse – that would be another tough break."

"No, it has to do with something else." I didn't want to share what I know, not yet.

"Cool. You busy this weekend?" Is he really asking again?

"No, quiet as usual." Is that a good enough opening for him?

"Can I take you out to dinner?" Yes, it is.

"Sure, why not. I mean, yes, that would be nice."

"Great. What's your address? I'll pick you up at seven?"

"Seven works. I'll text you the address."

"Perfect." I head out of the barn. As I walk over to the kitchen I text Pete my address. I then call Sarah and it goes to voicemail.

"Sarah, it's me. Thanks for a great night the other night, although work the next day was painful. I just spoke to Pete, he's keeping an eye on Spicy, his groom is Jorge and he says he's a good guy. I have a date with Pete tonight. Catch you soon."

It has been a long time since I've been on a real date. The friends I used to have were always trying to set me up with their friends, their boyfriends' friends, or their brothers. I would date a few of them once or twice and would get bored. Mostly they were career guys, obsessed with making promotions at work and doing better than their colleagues; frankly, they were very dull.

Many of my friends have now moved on from Missionville; work around here is tough to find since the mine closed down, and other related services moved away. Some friends have gone to Philadelphia, some up to New York. I've actually been headhunted once or twice for jobs in New York in investment banking and private wealth management. I couldn't think of a worse lifestyle – work all hours, make loads of money, but have no life to enjoy it all.

Down here I do all right. I'm well respected in our community, but I crave the ability to make a real difference, which is what I'm trying to do with the racehorses. The track here could be a good thing, but for now it's not, far from it. Not since Harry took it on in the late 1990s. At the time it was a curious purchase. The track was losing money and many assumed it would close down. When Harry purchased it people were excited – it was a lifeline for the local horsemen. But more than fifteen years later, the backside is grim, the horsemen go through the motions to keep their heads above water, and only Harry seems to do quite well.

Pete could be a good thing for me, but honestly I don't know. He has made some poor choices in the past, but he seems to be a good person underneath. We had a good time watching the race last week. He's attractive, good at what he does, and he's definitely not boring.

I go for a modest look: medium-length skirt, black tights, black leather ankle boots, a blouse, and leather jacket, with a hint of make-up. I'd already shaved my legs and plucked my eyebrows. Time for a quick glass of wine while I wait for Pete.

Minutes later, a car pulls into my driveway and shortly after Pete knocks.

"Hi, Amanda. Wow, you look lovely!" A good start.

"Thanks, Pete, you look pretty decent yourself." Pete has gone with a smart but dressed down look. Jeans, shirt, and sweater. He is cleanly shaven and looking very sharp despite his unruly mop of hair.

"Let's head out. Anywhere you prefer?" Pete inquires.

"Not really. I was hoping you would decide."

"Great, how about a quick drink at Jessup's before dinner at Zucchini's? Sound reasonable?" I would rather have gone straight to the Italian restaurant but I could live with it.

"Sure. Sounds like a plan." We head over to Jessup's.

"Budweiser and a glass of white wine?" Charlie asks.

"Thanks, Charlie," Pete says as I nod.

"Are you staying for a bite? Tables are getting busy."

"No, just a quick drink, then we're off for dinner."

"Good. Here you go." Charlie hands us our two drinks and we retreat to a table.

I'm not sure if I could see myself as a local here, but in Pete's company, it's fine. Pete knows a lot of people in the bar, so maybe this is just a way for him to feel good ahead of our dinner. Anyway, it doesn't take us long to finish our drinks.

"I booked a table for eight. We're a little early, but do you want to head out?"

"Sure."

Dinner at Zucchini's is terrific. For a smallish town like Missionville, this Italian restaurant is excellent. The one downside of not dating too much, or of not having a partner, is not having the opportunity to eat at places like this. Pete had made a great choice.

We spend most of the meal learning more about each other. Our upbringing, our parents, things that have impacted our lives. Pete is really easy to open up to, non-judgmental, and didn't make me think it was a kind of competition. He is far from the usual dates I've had.

His story seems to be one of lost focus, but he is very upfront about it. He wanted to be a leading trainer on the big circuits and believes he has the horsemanship to pull it off. When he was younger, he was naïve enough not to know any better. Now he's come to the realization that it takes more than horsemanship to succeed in the racing business; it also takes a bit of a hard edge. Maybe even a willingness to compromise your integrity from time to time. The more he talks about it, the more I realize that while I don't like what I'm hearing about racing, it is not too dissimilar to banking, business, and other walks of life. Those who are truly successful are often those who are most ruthless, rather than those with the most compassion. I guess this is part of the reason why I turned down offers to work in New York.

After two hours of talking, eating, and drinking wine – actually Pete only had a couple of small glasses of wine, while I finished the bottle – Pete pays the bill, and we leave. He drives me back to my house. What next I wonder? The guy has really grown on me, I haven't been with someone for a very long time whose company I enjoy, but what's the next move? Will Pete come on to me, or will he wait for a signal from me. I know in this world in which we live, the guy should make the move. But maybe things are changing. Pete had asked me out, so he must be interested. We'd had a great time, I think. I hope he doesn't just drop me off and leave. We pull into my driveway.

"Here we are." Should I ask if he wants a coffee, or a night cap?

"Thanks, Pete. It was a wonderful evening. It's been a long time since I've dined out like that. Do you want a nightcap before you head out?"

"That would be nice."

CHAPTER 8

PETE, WEDNESDAY

SINCE I'VE HAD THUNDER CLOUDS FOR NEARLY TWO WEEKS now, it's time to give him his first workout. This will give me a good handle on how the horse is doing. He's trained fairly well in his gallops, we've been hosing his leg every day, and I've been doing it up in a good sweat to help draw out the extra filling. The ankle is far from perfect, but it's the best I can do for now.

Alfie arrives right at seven o'clock.

"Longman will be here at break time to work Thunder Clouds."

"Not a good idea, boss." Alfie was a very good jockey back in the day, he knows his stuff, and he knows everyone on the backside.

"I know, but Ray is on at me about it. He says Longman called him up."

"Not a good idea, boss," Alfie repeats.

My relationship with Ray is beginning to deteriorate. This is how the racing game works. You train horses for someone for a while, you hope it lasts forever, but it seldom does. You do what you think is right for your owner and your horses, and unfortunately sometimes they're not the same thing. This is one of those cases. But I am bargaining from a weak position. If Ray pulls his horses, he'll have five other trainers begging him to hire them. I have to tread carefully and pick my battles.

I go about training my other horses – Ray's other horses. I want to get three out this morning before the break, and then need to get ready for Thunder Clouds's workout.

Over the last few days I keep drifting back to my Saturday night date with Amanda. Some of it surprised me, some of it really excites me. Is she for real, in the sense that is she really someone who could like a guy like me? She's gorgeous. I don't think I've seen anyone with such a beautiful smile. She's unusual, which I also like. She's her own person, which is the proverbial trifecta as far as I'm concerned. But it's hard to believe she would want to be with a 'racetracker,' as I have become over the last few years. Sure, if I'd gone the path of being an accountant, I would likely have been pretty successful, and had relationships with women like Amanda, but I didn't and I'm different. Oh well, no need to sweat it, Saturday can remain a fond, if expensive, memory, and we shall see what tomorrow brings, or at least what next Saturday brings, I hope.

At break time, Longman strolls into my shedrow.

"Horse ready, Pete?"

"Sure, Alfie's walking him."

"I assume he's going a half?" A half-mile at near to racing pace.

"Yes, usual type of first work after a race, an easy half a mile in fifty." I was looking for a time in about 50 seconds, which should be easy for Thunder Clouds.

"OK, Pete."

"Jake'll pony you. Take him back to the wire. Gallop him around to the half-mile pole."

"Sounds good."

I give him a leg up on the horse, Jake is waiting outside the barn and we walk up to the track.

"Jess, Thunder Clouds, half-mile." Jess will signal to the clockers to time the workout and make it official.

Rather than wait at the gap to watch, I walk over to the far side of the track so I can clock Thunder Clouds myself.

When I get to my position on the far side of the racetrack I can see Thunder Clouds and Longman, with Jake and his pony, waiting at the wire. Longman is adjusting his irons and is fiddling around a little. Then they turn and move off gently into a gallop, with Jake upside to keep them steady and calm. Thunder Clouds looks great. You can tell he has done this many times.

They round the turn by the gap and come through to the three-quarter pole. Longman is shifting around a little, making Thunder Clouds a little more attentive. Jake and his pony then start to drift wide as Longman points Thunder Clouds to the inside rail. The horse really starts to lengthen his stride as he crosses the half-mile pole. I click my watch.

For the first eighth of a mile, he moves very easily across the dirt track, and is very relaxed. Longman's doing a good job. 12.6 seconds, perfect. The next eighth of a mile is more of the same, and he notches the first quarter in a little over 25 seconds, perfect. Then something happens. Thunder Clouds's tail swishes and he appears to jump a little, and he really starts to motor. He comes around the turn running way too fast; click, 36 seconds for the 3/8ths. And now he is really rolling down the lane. He crosses the wire in 47 seconds flat.

Three seconds too fast. I'm furious.

This is not the type of work I was looking for. I watch him gallop out, he goes the extra eighth of a mile in another 12 seconds before he starts to ease back. Jake, who is waiting at the three-quarter pole, realizes he's in the wrong position to catch him and moves off at speed to head to the three-eighths pole.

Then I see it. Longman drops something to the dirt. The bastard had plugged him in. He had given Thunder Clouds an electric shock.

A few minutes later they return to the gap, Jake and the pony alongside Longman and Thunder Clouds, who's blowing very hard. His eyes look like they're about to pop right out of his head.

I'm livid.

I see a smirk on Longman's face. I say nothing as we walk back to the barn. Jake lets Thunder Clouds and Longman into the barn and departs to go and pony someone else. Longman brings the horse into his stall. I glare at him.

"What the hell do you think you're doing?" I couldn't hold out any longer.

"What's the problem? He worked great. He should win next time, for sure."

"You bastard, you plugged him in."

"What do you mean? Easy work, easy half-mile as you asked."

"That last quarter he was running way too fast. You shocked him."

"Pete, chill out. I'll swing by next week to see how he's doing." Longman walks off.

"Alfie, walk him an extra thirty minutes please. We have a big repair job on our hands."

"Sure, boss." Alfie didn't need to say anything else, he was right.

An hour later, my phone vibrates. It is Ray.

"I see the big horse worked." He sounds positive.

"Yes, Longman worked him as you asked."

"Good, nice fifty and change, just what he needed, right." I was not sure I heard that right.

"Sorry, Ray. I missed that. What did you say?"

"I've just been looking at the clockers' report online, it has him down at 50.2, the 5th fastest half-mile for the day." I don't understand, would the clockers really get it that wrong or is something else going on?

"He's cooled out now, Alfie is hosing the leg, let's hope he stays good." I want to change the subject.

"Sounds good." Ray clicks off. Is Longman working with the clockers? What's really going on here?

An hour passes. I'd busied myself mucking a couple of the stalls and grooming my horses. I was poulticing Thunder Clouds when Jake stops by.

"Hey, Pete. The guy worked well."

"Too fast Jake, you saw it. I think Longman screwed me. But whatever."

"He worked fast for sure. Any chance you've got my pony money?" I now owe Jake thirty dollars.

"Sure, damn, sorry. I meant to get you that other twenty at the beginning of the week." I pull out three tens from my wallet and hand them to Jake.

"No worries. I know things have been tight for you."

"No kidding, this is turning into a month from hell."

"I could fix you up, if you want to make some extra money. Weekend work, when the track is dark."

"Really? Like what?"

"My guy always needs drivers, shipping horses. Reliable people."

"Shipping horses to where?"

"Canada. The slaughterhouse."

"Jake, you know I can't do that. Shit, things aren't that bad yet."

"What's wrong? You wouldn't be killing the horses, they might as well be dead already. You'd just be getting them up there and if it's not you, it'll be someone else. It's five hundred dollars a round trip, plus expenses."

"No way I could do that."

"You would be up and back over the weekend, train your horses on Saturday, ready to train again on Monday."

"Thanks for the offer, but I'll keep doing what I'm doing."

"No worries. If you change your mind, I can hook you up." Jake goes up the shedrow to Mike's.

Have things really gotten so bad I would have to consider something like this? There's no way I could do it and see Amanda, nor do it and sleep well at night. Damn, today is just another bad day. I've been screwed by the track and offered a job with a kill buyer.

CHAPTER 9

AMANDA, SATURDAY

ANOTHER SATURDAY MORNING AT THE RACETRACK. I'm excited to be here, and not just because I will be surrounded by horses. It's been a week since I've seen Pete, and I want to see him again. It's confusing that we haven't communicated since our date last Saturday, but I'm not going to stress about it. You can tell when you have a real connection, and I can tell that Pete and I are good together.

After grabbing my coffee from the track kitchen, and heading out to the track, I relax and enjoy watching the horses run through their exercise routines for an hour. I chat to three or four horsemen who are on the rail watching their charges and catching up with their colleagues. Jake is out here a couple of times during the hour, ponying one horse without a rider, and ponying another with a rider. I have to admit, Jake is a good horseman. He seems to have a nice way of settling down the horses he leads around. He does it with instinct, rather than effort.

Just before I was about to leave the gap and wander the barns, Pete comes out on one of his horses.

"Hey, Amanda. Are you stopping by?"

"Yes, I would like to see the old horse if that's OK?" I'm actually more concerned about Spicy Lemon, but don't want to say that in front of others.

"Yes, anytime. If I'm not there, you know which stall he's in."

"OK, thanks." Pete moves off, jogging in the direction of the wire. I wait and watch until he leaves the track.

I visit four barns, two visits are to check on horses I'm advertising. Both horses have been on my site now for a month, and I need to reassure their connections that I am doing all I can to help get them placed. They listen, they tell me they understand, but they are under pressure to replace their horses with runners, or lose the stalls. The usual problems that I know only too well. The third barn is to see a new horse I will be listing this afternoon. Finally I wander over to John Swank's to confirm that Rocket Road has left for his new home in Ohio.

"Is Mr. Swank around?" I ask a groom in John's shedrow.

"Si, he's in the next stall." I move up one stall.

"John, Rocket Road, did all that work out?"

"Yes, you don't know how grateful I am. He left yesterday, actually. The lady came herself to pick him up. She seems very nice, and very competent."

"That's great. I'll follow up with her, and get back to you with any updates I hear."

"Thanks, I have something for you." John walks over to his tack room and comes out with a bottle of wine. Does he know of my weakness?

"Here you go. It's something small I know, but really, you saved us here. That horse has been very good for me, and I couldn't have found a home for him without you," John says, handing me the bottle.

"John, there's no need, but I'll take it of course. Very glad things worked out for you." I leave his shedrow and head over to Pete's.

On my way across the backside, I run into the racetrack chaplain, Shawn, also doing his Saturday rounds.

"Amanda, good to see you as always. I'd hoped that I would run into you soon."

"Nice to see you. I hope all's well."

"Yes, very good. I had a lot of great feedback on the new program we ran together." Shawn is referring to a new intro-banking course I designed for backstretch workers. It is based on a similar program we have been offering for a little while now. We conducted the new program a month ago; it was a fun project.

"Great. I enjoyed doing it. If you need anything, I'm always happy to help."

"Was hoping you might say that. I've had a few more inquiries now the word's gotten out. Any chance you have time to run another course? We could run them on Saturday lunchtimes again?"

"Of course. You know I can do that for you. Call me and we can arrange it?"

"Thanks, Amanda. I will. Maybe sometime in April and May?"

"Absolutely." I like Shawn. While I won't profess any religious affiliation, Shawn does a great job of providing religious counseling to backstretch workers here at Missionville. He's also sought out resources to make backstretch workers' lives more manageable. There's a well-attended Alcoholics Anonymous meeting every Wednesday night, for example. I am his financial services person; we've worked together to provide a straightforward bank account for workers who only want a service to deposit their cash and checks, and to wire money to other accounts. This latter service, which is new, is very important for some of the Mexican workers that are here at Missionville; they want to send money home directly to their families. Traditional wire services take a big commission; I worked with my bank to reduce the cost of the service for these guys. Shawn also has an exercise rider, from Jim Johnson's barn, teach backstretch workers how to use computers and access the internet. It's all good stuff for the community at the racetrack.

I wander into Pete's shedrow. Alfie is hosing Thunder Clouds's leg.

"Hi, Alfie. Is Pete around?"

"Amanda, nice to see you. Yes, he's in the tack room, I think." I enter Pete's tack room where he is cleaning bridles. Hairy is snoring away in the corner.

"Hey, Pete. How's things?"

"Good to see you, again. All good. Thunder Clouds is being hosed."

"Yeah, I saw Alfie. Any word on Spicy?"

"Ahhh. Yes, I caught up with Jorge a couple of days ago. They've galloped him a few times. They like him. Jorge still thinks something's wrong with one of his hind legs, but he's working on it. He should be breezing on Monday or Tuesday; first workout since the claim."

"Thanks, I'll tell Sarah." So far this seems rather like a business exchange. What about last Saturday night, I wondered.

"You busy this weekend?" Pete asks. Is this the opening?

"No real plans yet." But I would like to do something.

"Can I pick you up, same time?"

"Yes, why not. Would be fun to do something." I try to remain non-committal.

"OK, great. I'll be at your place at seven." Phew. I walk out of the tack room and head back to my car. On my way I leave Sarah a voicemail.

"Just spoke to Pete. Spicy should be breezing early next week. They're working on his hind end a little, probably figuring out what you know about his back end issues. Jorge says they like him." I hang up. I didn't stop by to see Sarah this week after I went to Owenscreek on Tuesday, but I was planning on visiting again soon.

Time to get ready for our date tonight. Last Saturday was a revelation for me. We had a great meal and great conversation. That conversation continued late into the night at my house, over a couple more bottles of wine. Pete is so easy to talk to, but he also seems a little shy. It took him a few hours before he made any kind of move on me. Nothing aggressive, just a long, slow kiss. He was so gentle, and very attentive. The entire night was simply wonderful. Things moved forward, I think he could tell I wanted more, much more. We just stopped short of making love. I was used to expensive meals and dull conversations from my dates, with the presumption that this bought my date more from me, as if I was a cheap piece of meat. Pete is different. He's far from dull, and far from presumptuous.

I'm curious what he has planned for tonight, and I also am hopeful that after our date tonight we might have a more normal relationship and communicate throughout the week. But we shall see. I've never been good at dating, but I've also never felt like this about a person, regardless of his flaws. I'd decided not to share these feelings with Sarah, not yet anyway. I know she's not Pete's number one fan, but I hope I can convince her otherwise.

I dress in a nice skirt, black stockings, and garter belt, I wear a blouse over a half-cup bra, adding a simple red sweater. After applying a hint of make-up, I am dressed for the night. The last thing I need to do before Pete arrives is to tidy my bedroom and make sure the house is presentable. I also place a couple of extra bottles of wine in the fridge.

When Pete's car comes up the driveway, I feel butterflies in my stomach. I'm becoming a nervous wreck; this is ridiculous.

The doorbell rings. I open the door and Pete is standing there, looking great. His blue eyes look right through me. I'm willing him to grab me and kiss me passionately.

"Ready?" Pete offers instead.

"Yes, all set," I mumble back.

"Great, let's head over to Jessup's, and then head out from there." I feel a tinge of disappointment.

Jessup's is pretty busy when we arrive. I guess racetrack people go out early. Charlie pours my wine and gets Pete's Budweiser, and we head over to a booth.

"You look lovely, Amanda, thanks for coming out again." Not a bad start.

"Glad to be out, Pete. I really enjoyed myself last weekend." I want him to know, I don't want to play games.

"I did too." Pete moves his hands across the table and hold mine, for a small moment. It makes me tingle. "How was your week?"

"Not too bad. I helped place a horse from my site. So that was a good thing. One of John Swank's geldings."

"Rocket Road?"

"Yes, do you know him?"

"Sure, John's had the horse for a long time. Nice to hear he found a home. Where's he gone?"

"To a lady in Ohio."

"Great job, we should celebrate." Pete goes to the bar and gets another round of drinks, even though I've only finished half my glass of wine.

"What about the rest of your week?" Pete asks when he returns. He seems determined to understand how things are for me; that can only be a good thing I guess.

"Not bad. I went to Owenscreek on Tuesday, the sale was pretty much like the week before, a few Thoroughbreds, only fifty or so horses in total. I didn't stop by Sarah's on my way back, decided to avoid another week day hangover!" I'd told Pete about my long night with Sarah, he'd seemed rather amused by it.

"What about your bank work. All good?"

"Yes, a quiet week. We're still struggling to maintain the number of branches we have. We're going to consider a reconsolidation plan; a consulting firm is sending some people out to take a look."

"Wow, that doesn't sound too good?"

"It's life in these smaller towns. You know how it is." Pete does know, and it is nice to talk to him about some of this stuff. And we did, for a few more minutes. But now I want to know how Pete's week has been.

"Ugh, where to start. Honestly this has been a week from hell, on top of another bad week. Let me grab a couple more drinks." Pete heads to the bar again. No hint that we're going anywhere else. A few more drinks and we won't be able to move on. Pete returns, a Budweiser and glass of wine in hand.

"I worked Thunder Clouds this week, on Wednesday," Pete begins.

"Oh good, how'd it go?"

"It was a disaster." Pete drinks his beer quickly.

"Why, is the horse OK?" Thunder Clouds had seemed OK when I saw him this morning on the wash pad. Pete takes another long swig of his beer.

"They screwed me, Amanda. Longman, Ray, and the clockers."

"What do you mean?" I'm confused, which is not too hard given I am still a bit of a novice around the racetrack.

"It was Thunder Clouds's first work since we claimed him. Always, the first work after a race, I want a half in fifty seconds, or slower. I just want to see how the horse is." Pete takes another swig of his beer.

"Longman knows this, any jockey who's ridden for me knows this."

"Why was Longman on your horse? I thought Emma rode most of your horses." Pete takes another swig.

"Ray's been insisting, after we got beat with the filly. He wants Longman on him, Longman was on him the last time Thunder Clouds won a race. Are you ready for another?" Pete was referring to another glass of wine, and I wasn't.

"Not yet."

"I'll be right back." Pete heads to the bar. I'm starting to get a little nervous. What I had hoped would be a quiet evening that would pick up when we return to my house is starting to look like something else. Pete returns.

"Longman worked Thunder Clouds in 47 seconds, 3 seconds too fast." It sounded like an error, which could have consequences, but nothing to get steamed up about, and Pete is getting fiery.

"He worked really nicely for the first part, right on the money, 25 seconds. Then he accelerated quickly. The bastard plugged him in." Pete is fired up now. "I wondered why Longman was in my barn a couple of days after I claimed Thunder Clouds. I wondered why the horse hasn't won since Longman last rode him. Once a horse gets used to being buzzed, they only run for the battery." This is all sounding very ugly to me. I feel bad for Pete, but I'm also seeing Pete start to deteriorate a little. Maybe he just needs to unload.

"Anyway, that's not all of it," Pete continues. "The clockers reported a fifty second work. So either they're blind – and I know they're not because they're usually spot on – or they're working with Longman." It sounds like a conspiracy theory to me, and I don't really understand why the clockers would want to do something like that, but again, I don't know all the ways of the backside.

"Ray called me up after the work. He was delighted. The first good words he's spoken to me since the filly got beat. Ready for another?" I decline, and Pete goes to the bar.

The evening is not going according to plan. I feel sorry for Pete. He's obviously in a bad situation with his owner, and he cares for his horses, but he is letting it all take control of him. He downs a couple more Budweisers as he relays more stories of why things are not good for him right now. I sit and listen, but by now I've stopped drinking completely. There is no hint of us going anywhere else to eat, Pete seems to want to stay at Jessup's and get drunk. Had I really misread this guy, or is there something else going on?

At ten o'clock, I go to the bar and ask Charlie if he has a number for a local cab service. He hands me a card. I call a cab and leave Pete behind. He's drinking himself into a stupor. He's found a couple of racetrack friends to share his misery. I feel terrible; whether it's because I really thought this guy was different and had excited me, or whether it's because I'm leaving someone to deal with his own sorrow, I don't really know. Whatever the reason, I want out.

At home, I open the fridge, pull out one of the bottles of wine, the one that John Swank had given me this morning, and decide to have my own little pity party.

CHAPTER 10

PETE, MONDAY

WHEN THINGS GO WRONG, THEY TEND TO GO WRONG in bunches. Last week's workout with Thunder Clouds was a disaster, and while the horse seems to have recovered from the experience, I really don't know what to do next with him. It's time to start looking at the condition book and find a race for him, then plan his training schedule accordingly. I really don't want Longman back on him, but Longman seems to be more in control of the situation than me. If I put Emma on him, I'm sure Ray will pull his horses and I would need to figure out another livelihood. Not that this is much of one right now.

The filly who was just beaten has been training nicely since her narrow loss. I've been able to persuade Ray to allow Emma to continue to ride her, a small victory for me. We really do need to win with her next time.

The biggest screw up by far was my Saturday night date with Amanda. I had really been looking forward to hanging out with her. She looked gorgeous when I picked her up. I just totally blew it. It was almost a relief to have someone to talk to, to confide in, regarding the Thunder Clouds debacle, but once I got going, I just kept going. Amanda let me unload, but then the Budweisers started flowing. Sure enough, by the end of the evening I was hammered, and Amanda was long gone. I can't imagine I can recover from that.

And then there's the money issue. Ray always pays his bills, but he's usually a month late. I need to pay the feed and straw bills on time, and cash flow always gets tight when I haven't had a winner for a while. And it's been a while now.

"Hey, Pete. All OK?" asks James, the vet, doing his rounds during the track break.

"Sure. I may have a runner later this week, Friday. If he gets in, can you swing by Wednesday and Thursday for a pre-race?"

"No problem. Usual – Bute and Banamine?"

"Yes, thanks." James walks down Mike's shedrow. I watch him duck into a stall with a syringe in his hand. That horse is due to race tonight.

PART 2:

ONE WEEK LATER

CHAPTER 11

PETE, MONDAY

I NEED TO GET MY ACT TOGETHER. LAST WEEK WAS ANOTHER bad week at the track, bad runs seem to last forever. The gelding I raced on Friday night appears to have lost some of his edge. He finished in the middle of the pack, which means we lost money. I'll need to drop him to the bottom next time, or risk getting stuck with him. Ray was annoyed with the race, because Emma was aboard. She's ridden him in each of his races we've had him, and she's done well with him before. Her ride on Friday was not one of her best, but honestly I don't think Shoemaker could have won on him.

Anyway, I need an additional way to make some money, to keep me afloat. It has to be, just for the time being.

Amanda had been by the barn on Saturday, as usual. But it was not like her visits in the previous weeks, obviously. She asked me some questions about Thunder Clouds, who does seem remarkably resilient after that first workout. I worked him again last week, with Longman back in the saddle. We hardly communicated, but he did work Thunder Clouds perfectly. I guess Longman just needed to buzz the old horse once, just to remind him. Anyway, we'll have a race for him in a couple of weeks. I told all this to Amanda, who listened without really responding. She then asked me about Spicy Lemon. Sarah Lester is still very upset about the situation, and honestly, I understand. But that's racing, and she knows it. Jorge had updated me on the horse: they are working on one of his hocks, and think that they'll have him in good shape for his next start. He's also worked a couple of times now, under Longman, and Jorge reckons he's training well. All this, I relayed to Amanda. She then left the barn. I didn't see any reason to ask her out and get rejected. It's frustrating though, we had a real connection. I know we did. But I blew it.

I've finished training my three horses for today, the fourth is only walking after his race last week. But I need to hang around to catch up with Jake. His morning routine means he usually returns to Mike's shedrow after finishing up all his pony chores, and before long, Jake appears at Mike's end of the barn. I wander over.

"Jake, when you've got a minute, can you stop by my tack room? I want to run something by you." The conversation we are about to have needs some privacy.

"Sure, Pete. Just need to catch up with Mike about plans for tonight's races, then I'll come look for you."

I walk back to my tack room where Hairy looks up at me, as if asking if it's time to head over to the kitchen. He then lays his head back down when he sees me start fiddling around with the tack, killing time ahead of a difficult conversation. Five minutes later, Jake strolls in.

"What's up? Are you looking for a place for the gelding that ran last week?"

"No, not yet."

"Well if you do, you know where I am. Seemed to run a muddling kind of race, but maybe you can drop him down one more time." Jake's right about his race, he ponied the horse for me, so no doubt he watched.

"It's something else. That conversation we had a couple of weeks ago." I struggle to bring myself to flat out ask him.

"Oh, OK. You might want some work?"

"Yes. Things are very tight. I need to make some quick cash just to get my head above water."

"No problem. I can sort you out."

"Remind me again what it all entails?"

"All you need to do is show up at Tom's farm on a Saturday. Drive up to Canada and drop off a load of horses. Stay the night and head back on Sunday, dropping off the truck and trailer. Five hundred dollars plus expenses."

"Have you done it?"

"Once in a while, when Tom's in a pinch. It's straightforward, and doesn't mess with our training and racing since it's weekend work."

"It's tough for me to do it, but I don't see any other way to get some of my shit sorted out." I realize I want Jake to rationalize it all again for me.

"I get it. People have different opinions about horse slaughter. The reality is, the horses you'll haul will have to be shipped by someone. You're not adding to their demise. You could almost argue that you're making their last days better, if you drive well, give them a pat." OK, I understand the first part of Jake's logic, but he's stretching it a little with the second part.

"How would I get started?"

"If you think you're up for it, head over to Owenscreek for the sale tomorrow. Call me when you get there, and I'll connect you with Tom. He might get you started this weekend, or it might be some other weekend. But it'll be soon, he always needs reliable drivers."

"OK, thanks. Keep this between us, will you?"

"Of course. You don't need to worry about me." Jake heads out of the tack room.

"Come on Hairy, let's see if Alice has a treat for you." I need to get out of here, get a sandwich and go find somewhere I can get some fresh air and spend time with my dog.

CHAPTER 12

PETE, SATURDAY

TODAY IS GOING TO BE A LONG DAY. I WANT TO GET FINISHED at the barn early and head out, but I need to arrange for coverage for tomorrow. I go to see Jorge.

"Jorge, are you off tomorrow or working?" Mike gives his grooms every other Sunday off. It's their one day off over a two-week cycle, which is actually quite generous on the backside.

"Si, Pete. My Sunday off is this week."

"You want to make some extra cash?" It's unlikely that Jorge would have much planned for his day off. His family is back in Mexico. He's probably just going to hang out tonight and drink a few extra beers with friends here. That's the routine.

"Sure. What do you need?"

"Can you help Alfie tomorrow, pick up the stalls while he walks my horses? Fifty dollars, a couple of hours. I'm heading out of town for the weekend."

"No problem. Seven thirty OK to start?"

"Seven thirty's great. Will have the cash for you on Monday."

"Sounds good. Enjoy your weekend." Not likely.

I return to my shedrow and Amanda appears. Shit, I kind of wanted to avoid her completely today, but I guess that was unlikely. I hope she didn't see me at the auction on Tuesday. I tried to stay completely out of the way, but I did observe her looking at the Thoroughbreds at the back of the barn.

"Hey, Amanda. Nice to see you." I still have feelings for her, strong feelings, but I'm going down a different path, so I don't want to push it, not now.

"Pete. How's the old horse?" Well, it seems Amanda isn't up to small talk either, straight to business.

"Thunder Clouds is doing well. He'll work one more time next week. I should have a race for him in about two weeks. I have one or two picked out."

"That's good. How are his works?" No doubt she's inquiring after the episode at Jessup's.

"He's worked one time since, and it was much better thankfully. No dodgy stuff from Longman."

"Longman rode him again? I thought you'd make a switch?"

"Unfortunately it's not as simple as that. Longman will be riding him in his next race; my hands are tied."

"Any updates on Spicy Lemon?" I guess I should have asked Jorge when I just saw him, but my mind was somewhere else.

"I think he's good. Honestly I don't have any more updates. I'll ask next week."

"OK, thanks. Look after yourself." With that, Amanda leaves the barn. Damn, how could I have screwed that up?

Alfie is finishing up hosing Thunder Clouds.

"Alfie, I'm heading out of town for the weekend. Jorge is going to help you, he'll get the stalls done. Can you feed them and walk them as usual? Just pull off their bandages and leave them off for the night."

"Sure, boss. No problem. Will get them fed when I arrive at seven, then start walking."

"Perfect, Jorge will be here around seven thirty."

"Sounds good. Enjoy your weekend." Not likely.

I head out to Tom's farm, which is about twenty miles north of the auction at Owenscreek, a little over an hour's drive from Missionville. It gives me too long to sink into my thoughts: Am I really prepared to do this, drive a truck full of slaughter-bound horses to their final destination? Could there be any justification for me to do this? Christ, this training career has not turned out to be what I had hoped it would be. My conversations with Amanda have made me realize how far off the mark I've fallen, but I have still tried to do the right things for the horses, most of the time. This may be a step too far.

Visiting the auction on Tuesday in Owenscreek was a wake-up call. I obviously knew about the auction, but like most horsemen at the track, I had never been. It's always easier to avoid something, by simply avoiding it. We don't like to talk about slaughter, regardless of whether we think it's necessary. We train horses for the most part because we're horsemen, we like horses. The disposal of horses is simply a necessary evil. That being said though, there are a few trainers at Missionville who aren't really horsemen, and I'd put Mike in that group. He's living proof that you don't need to know much about horses to be a successful trainer. What you need is the backing of a big owner, and maybe some questionable ethics too. But I digress. How have things gone so badly wrong for me? How have I let myself get into a situation where I have one owner who's calling all the shots over my small string of horses, and now I'm prepared to work in the slaughter trade? How had I let Amanda down, the one bright spark in what has been a tough last month or two?

I pull into the driveway of Tom's farm. There are horses everywhere. They're turned out in small paddocks. Each paddock has about ten horses standing around a large round bale of hay. I bet I could count more than a hundred horses of all shapes and sizes. I guess this is where Tom keeps his horses before they're shipped to Canada. It's depressing to think that they each have a death warrant, but that's the reality. They're the walking dead.

There is a truck and trailer, backed into a large barn. Horses are inside the barn, loose. This looks like Tom's system for loading horses. Get them in a large, contained area, and then herd them into the truck. It makes sense, that's how they would do it with other livestock.

I spy Tom, walking across his yard.

"You're a little early, Pete, but that's fine. We'll be loading the horses in about twenty minutes. Just need to get the paperwork ready." Tom heads off to his house, which is adjacent to the barn full of nearly dead horses.

I walk over to the barn to take a closer look at the stock. There are thirty of them. A few working horses, which have worked their last days. It's a pretty mixed bag of horses all told, but all a good weight, and for the most part, they look pretty healthy. There are also a half dozen Thoroughbreds. I pull out my phone, and quietly take pictures of each. I'm not going to turn their lips. I don't want Tom to wonder what I'm up to; I need the five hundred too much. But I just figure I should see if I can identify them visually, later. After a short while, Tom emerges from the house.

"Are you ready, Pete?"

"Yes. Horses all look good and healthy."

"That's how the slaughterhouse wants them. I get more per pound that way."

"Do you buy them like that?" Am I inquiring too much? Maybe I should just get on with the job.

"Sometimes. Some horses ship the week I buy them. Some horses will spend a month or six weeks here, fattening up." Tom hands me some paperwork.

"You'll need this when you cross the border, and you'll need these other forms when you arrive at the slaughterhouse." Tom hands me a second set of forms. "All's in order. Let's get them loaded up."

We herd the thirty horses onto the trailer. I haven't seen horses being loaded like this before, and you can imagine how skittish some of them are, but we get it done, and shut the back of the trailer.

"Now no one should need to open this trailer until you get to the slaughterhouse. It's about a ten-hour drive. The border guys will look at the paperwork, but won't need to visually inspect. You're good to go." And that was it. I'm about to take my first trip to Canada, and it is to deliver live horses for slaughter.

CHAPTER 13

AMANDA, TUESDAY

I DRIVE DOWN SARAH'S DRIVEWAY. IT HAS BEEN THREE WEEKS since my last visit, and I really want to catch up. If it means staying the night, and suffering a little tomorrow, so be it. Sarah is a friend, and I need to hang out with someone after the Pete fiasco. I enter her house through the kitchen door.

"Hey, Sarah, sorry I'm a little late." I was planning to be here around three o'clock, but the auction ran a little longer today; more horses were sold.

"Very good to see you. Coffee?" Sarah puts some coffee in the coffee machine. "How was the auction today?"

"It was a little busier than it's been for the last few weeks. About seventy horses went through. Tom and Fred bought about half of them, as usual. Only three Thoroughbreds, so I guess that's good." Sarah hands me a cup of coffee.

"Do you want to look them up? Though I need to go out and get the horses in pretty soon."

"That's OK, I can do it all later in the week. I've not much else to do in the evenings." Not sure why I needed to add that, but Sarah knows very well that my personal life is a little bit of a disaster.

"Oh, I've got some news for you. I had a horse running at Missionville last night."

"How did you get on?"

"She ran fourth, the maiden I have that's still learning. But that's not the news. Your guy, Pete, he's missing."

"What?" She has my attention.

"Yes, I overheard someone from Mike Franks's barn, they had a couple of runners last night. Jorge, a groom of his, was saying something to someone else about Pete disappearing."

"Missing in what way?" I'm flustered. I'd seen Pete at the auction last Tuesday, and had planned to ask him about it, but haven't yet; I'm still too mad at him.

"Apparently he left the barn on Saturday at lunchtime. Told his guy, Alfie, he would be back first thing on Monday. Had something to do on Sunday I guess. But by Monday night he hadn't returned."

"Damn, sounds pretty uncharacteristic of him." Is it? I don't really know.

"I know you like him, Amanda, I should have called you last night, but I knew you were planning to come over today after the sale."

"Yes, no worries. We've had a bit of a falling out anyway."

"Well, anything I can do, let me know." We both finish our coffees and head out to the barn to get the horses in and readied for the night.

It is another pleasant evening, hanging out with Sarah. We basically repeat my last visit. The conversations bounce around from her continued stress with the Spicy Lemon situation, to my poor judgment as far as Pete is concerned. Or at least that is Sarah's opinion, and while I don't argue, I'm now curious about what might have happened to him. We also talk more about the auction situation, and what we could potentially do to reduce the number of horses that go to slaughter. Sarah also has an idea about how to expose the slaughter pipeline for some of its illegal practices; that's the kind of stuff we've wrestled with frequently over the last couple of years, without getting anywhere.

The conversations require three bottles of wine, and a lovely lasagna dish. It's good to be at Sarah's again. She is really my only friend who's remained in the Missionville area. Throughout the evening, though, I have something else on my mind – what's happened to Pete. I text him before we eat.

"Pete, it's Amanda. Can you call me as soon as you get this?" No response.

I send a second text much later in the evening, "Just let me know you're OK." Again, no response.

CHAPTER 14

PETE, TUESDAY

IT'S TOUGH TO ADMIT YOU HAVE FAILED. FIFTEEN YEARS INTO my career, and I start shipping horses to slaughter. That's failure. I take another swig of my Budweiser.

I'd made a bargain many years ago with my father. I could do whatever I wanted to do, as long as I went to college first and got a degree. He was adamant about that. He assumed that whatever I do in life, it's smart for me to have a college degree to back me up. I think he was also hoping that four more years of studying would be enough to sway me into a career away from horses. I did go through the motions of trying to seek an accounting position after graduation, but my efforts were half-hearted at best. It was too easy for me to fall into the life of the racetrack. My father never wanted me to follow my passion, something my parents had accidently nurtured when I was very young. I take another swig of my beer.

My father was a very successful accountant, working out of Philadelphia. He started with nothing. He ended up establishing his own firm, later in his career, and hoped that I would join him, to continue to grow the business. He'd tried to get me to intern with him during my college years, I found excuses not to join him, wishing to maintain a level of independence.

Sadly it ruined our family relationship. I rarely see my parents anymore. They are still in Philadelphia. Father is now retired; he sold his business.

And I'm still trying to prove my independence. Silly really, but resisting my father is what's driven me over the last several years.

And now this, stark evidence that I have failed.

I receive a second text message from Amanda. I take another swig of my beer.

CHAPTER 15

AMANDA, WEDNESDAY

I LEAVE SARAH'S AT AROUND SIX IN THE MORNING. MY HEAD is pounding. I guess what I could do in my early twenties is just harder to do in my late thirties.

I'm going to call Shawn, the racetrack chaplain. He's the only guy on the backside of the track that I have a phone number for, except of course Pete. When I called Pete's phone first thing this morning it went directly to voicemail. Any other time I've tried to contact Pete, he's always answered – I'm getting more concerned. Anyway, I figure I'll call Shawn after I get to my house, shower and I'm in a more human state.

I arrive back at my house in good time. For the entire drive I couldn't get Pete out of my head. I would bounce between the strange last evening we had at Jessup's where he seemed to be hell bent on getting drunk, while talking conspiracy theories about his horse, to the wonderful evening the weekend before, where we stayed up for most of the night. I guess his behavior could best be described as erratic. Disappearing, when he has animals that depend on him, only makes his behavior seem more bizarre. Should I care? Should I just leave it, and wait until Saturday to see what happens? I guess that's the rational thing to do, but that's not my style.

I get into my shower and blast it as hot as I can bear it. It makes for the same feeling I get from a good sauna. I want to let my pores open up and sweat out some of the alcohol. I stand in the shower for a good ten minutes, gently soaping myself. The whole time, I keep replaying moments with Pete, the good moments, the moments watching him ride horses, and his weird behavior that last time at Jessup's. I stay in the shower until I can't stand it any longer, and then when I step out, I nearly faint. But I don't. Five minutes later I'm dried off, and still in my towel when I dial Shawn's number.

"Hi, it's Amanda."

"Hey, Amanda, great to hear from you. No dates planned yet for the banking program."

"That's not why I called. Do you know the trainer, Pete Wright?"

"Yes, sure, I know Pete."

"I hear he's gone missing. Left a couple of days ago. Do you know anything about that?"

"I haven't heard anything. Let me stop by his barn a little later, and I'll call you back."

"Thanks. I'd appreciate it."

"No problem. Anything for you." Shawn hangs up.

I dress, apply some necessary make-up, and head out to my day job. As I enter the bank, my phone rings.

"Shawn, did you hear anything?"

"He's still missing. Apparently he left on Saturday, and made a plan for Sunday with Alfie, his hotwalker, and a groom of Mike's, Jorge. They assumed he'd be back on Monday, but it's now Wednesday and there's no sign of him."

"Thanks. Any chance you know where he lives?" Pete had always come to pick me up, I've never been to his house.

"I don't, Amanda, but I could try to find out. I'll call you later if I hear anything, or get his address."

"OK, thanks." I hang up. My head is still pounding, and I feel that typical disorientation you get when you are truly hung over. I also have an ominous feeling about Pete. I really want to know what he's up to. I'll swing by Jessup's after work; Charlie may know something.

My work day moves incredibly slowly. I really didn't have much to do today, which makes it worse. When I'm busy, my day flies by, but not being busy *and* hung over makes it a doubly slow day. Unfortunately I wasn't in the right frame of mind to tackle some of our longer-term projects like our consolidation plan. That's what I'd normally do on a quiet day. I did manage to use my lunch break to look up the lip tattoos of the Thoroughbreds I'd seen at the sale yesterday. Three more horses, now doomed. Two of them raced last week.

Five o'clock finally, which couldn't have come any more slowly. I walk out to my car, and go straight to Jessup's. If I go home first, I'd struggle to leave again.

Ten minutes later I walk into the bar. When I came here the first time, I was very hesitant, here to see someone I hardly knew. But now I have a purpose and am seeking answers about that very same person.

"Hey, Charlie, have you seen Pete?" Charlie nods in the direction of the far corner. There he is, hunched over a bottle of Budweiser.

"He's been here most of today, and the last two days. Something's up with him. He's not his usual self."

"Thanks, Charlie. Glass of wine please." Hair of the dog and all that.

"Sure. It's on the house if you can get Pete to leave."

"Thanks, that's what I'm hoping to do." He hands me my wine. I walk over to the corner table and sit down. Pete looks up. He looks like a zombie. His blue eyes stare right through me. He takes a swig of his beer.

"Pete, I've been trying to contact you." He looks at me again.

"Pete, what's happening, what's wrong with you?" He takes another swig of his beer and looks away. I sip my wine.

"Pete, talk to me. You've not been at the track for four days." Still no response.

"Pete, people are worried about you. I don't get what's happening. I saw you at the auction last Tuesday." Pete registers, I've got to him.

"I don't understand what's been going on lately. First you get drunk in front of me. Next I see you at Owenscreek. And then you go missing. Shit Pete, I thought we had something." Pete looks like he's about to say something, but doesn't.

"Pete, listen to me, I don't know what's going on, but if I can help you, I will."

Pete looks up again, and says, "Amanda, I'm a complete train wreck. I took a truck to Canada, and dropped off thirty horses at the slaughterhouse in Massueville. All to make a few bucks to try to pay some bills so I could carry on my miserable existence as a trainer." I struggle to comprehend what he is saying.

"You saw me at the auction, because I was there to meet Tom, get a job." Christ, this isn't good and not what I was expecting.

"I watched horses being unloaded at the slaughterhouse. All healthy looking, all relieved to get out of their ridiculously cramped trailer, expecting something better. All. Now. Dead. But I got my five freaking hundred." Pete is completely unravelling.

"Pete, it's OK, I get it." I don't, but what else could I say?

"Get what? That I'm a horse killer? That's what I am, Amanda, a freaking horse killer. I need to add that to my resume."

"No, Pete. We all have to make choices, based on our circumstances. Sometimes the choices we make are wrong, and we have to live with that. But we learn, and don't repeat the mistakes." Shit, I was talking as if someone had made a business error at the bank that we could fix, and we wouldn't repeat. But this is very different, lives were lost.

"You were the one bright spark of my sorry life here, I screwed that up. Now I've gone and done this. My owner is an ass. I'm just screwed any which way I look at it." It does seem that way, but I need to put on a strong front and sort this situation out for the now, for this moment. In the next few days, we can worry about the consequences, the bigger picture.

"You haven't screwed anything. I was very disappointed about our last night here, but that's because I really like you. We can be good together, let me get you out of here so we can be together." Was he buying it, could he think that I could really be with him, given the circumstances?

"No way. You're way out of my league. I just need to be left on my own."

"OK. You disappointed me, big time. Now I see you for the low-life you are. Here I thought I could come out and try to help you, but if you want to wallow in your own worthless company, then I guess I need to go and pay for my wine." I'm not very good at these types of conversations. I really do want to get Pete out of here. I hate failing at anything. And there's still a piece of me that cares for him.

"Pete, please, I'm sorry. Can I take you home? Where's Hairy anyway?" I had Pete's attention again.

"Hairy's at home. Shit. I need to feed him. Shit, Amanda, just get me the hell out of here." Pete stares right at me. I'm relieved, but I really don't know what to do next. I glance up at Charlie, who comes over.

"Charlie, any chance you can help us get to my car?"

"Sure. Pete, c'mon, time to go." Fortunately Pete doesn't resist, and Charlie is able to get him out of the bar and into my car.

"Thanks, Charlie. Drinks on me next time." I drive away.

CHAPTER 16

PETE, THURSDAY

I NEED TO GET MYSELF TOGETHER. SIMPLE STEPS: FIRST, GET to the barn. I've let people down, not least, Alfie. But I knew he'd manage things for me. He's been very good to me over the years.

Amanda had gone out of her way to get me out of Jessup's last night. I'm not sure she's for real. She was part of the reason for my self-destructive journey, just realizing how I've screwed things up with her. Anyway, she got me home, made me some coffee and forced me to drink it, and then some more. She made me come with her to walk Hairy, get some fresh air under the street lamps. We talked, just about stuff. Then she put me to bed. She was still there in the morning, at five, to wake me up and make sure I headed here to the barn. What kind of person does that for someone like me?

I feed my horses. They seem pleased to see me. I guess they're happy to see anyone who's got food for them at their feed time. I wash out their water buckets, smashing the thin layers of ice that have accumulated over night. All the horses are clean legged, no bandages. I spend some time checking on them, making a couple of mental notes of what to look out for later in the morning. Mike's people start arriving in the barn. Jennifer and a couple of others acknowledge me when they see me. They had noticed my absence.

Alfie arrives at seven, as usual.

"Hey, Alfie," I say, rather sheepishly.

"Hey, boss. Glad to see you." Always a good guy.

"Sorry about the last few days. No excuses."

"No worries, boss. I managed. Jorge helped me out after he was done at Mike's. Horses are fine. A couple of people stopped by looking for you."

"Thanks, I'll swing by and see Jorge later." I go to the tack room, Hairy follows me and settles into his usual spot. I get my first set of tack and go to Thunder Clouds's stall. Galloping the old man first thing will be a nice way to try to get the last few days out of my head. Five minutes later I'm at the track.

"Hey, Pete," Jess says.

"Jess, good to see you."

"Good to see you. You had us worried."

"Thanks. Just needed a few days is all."

"We can all use those sometimes. The old horse looks glad to see you back."

"I hope so." I wasn't really sure how to respond. Jess is a good-hearted person.

We jog off back to the wire. Thunder Clouds trains nicely. I repeat the routine with two of my other three horses, before the track break. Coming back to the barn on my third horse, James is waiting for me.

"Good to see you, Pete." I guess I'll have to get used to that statement for the rest of the morning.

"Thanks. All good today here, I think. May need you in a couple of days for a pre-race. Need to sort out what I plan to race." I'd gotten behind at looking at the condition book. Ray will be on to me if we don't have a runner soon.

James walks up Mike's shedrow. I keep my eye on him; I'm becoming more curious now about his routine at Mike's. And sure enough, he goes into a stall of one of Mike's runners for tonight with a syringe in his hand. Damn, this cheating is becoming more and more obvious.

I get some tack for my last horse, the filly. I'm tacking her up when Shawn, the racetrack chaplain, stops by. He's one of the nicest guys on the backside, always trying to improve the lives of backstretch workers. I figure he wants to see Alfie.

"Hey, Shawn, good to see you."

"Good to see you, Pete. Is everything OK?" Had he heard I was missing?

"Yes. Just took a few extra days off."

"OK, that's good. I had a call from Amanda yesterday. She seemed pretty upset about your disappearance."

"Yes, she caught up with me."

"Good. She's a terrific woman."

"Yes, almost too good."

"Look after yourself. You know where I am if you ever need anything."

"Thanks. I will." If Shawn is looking to help me out, word's really got out that I'm in trouble.

The filly trains well. It just goes to show, a trainer can be completely missing for a few days. The horses don't get trained. When he returns, they're all better than ever. I guess that's the silver lining of the last few days. But it is nice to be back in the barn, among my horses, although the guilt over the trip to Canada still lingers. Drinking for a few days afterwards only added to the feeling of misery.

The one guy I'm not looking forward to seeing is Jake. He knows where I went over the weekend. Obviously he doesn't know where I've been over the last few days. But it's inevitable that I would see him this morning, and sure enough, he arrives in the barn just as the track closes for training for the day. He comes straight down Mike's shedrow, seeking me out.

"Hey, Pete, you OK?"

"Sure, Jake." I walk into my tack room, Jake follows me.

"How was Canada?"

"Cold."

"You know what I mean."

"I did the trip. Got my money."

"Yes, Tom said you brought the truck and trailer back OK. All was good. Just not seeing you for a few more days had me worried."

"I just needed a break. No worries." Wasn't worth sharing my feelings with Jake, not right now.

"Well, as long as you're OK."

"I'm good."

"You've got my number; if you want to do another trip, let me know. Tom's good with you. He likes you."

"Thanks." I can't imagine being so low that I would do that again.

I need to swing by and see Jorge. He'd really stepped up to help Alfie while I was away. But there is also something else nagging me. One of the horses I shipped looked like the horse Jake picked up off Jorge a few weeks ago. I want to confirm if that is the case.

I stop over to see Jorge, on my way out of the barn, Hairy in tow.

"Jorge, thanks for helping me out."

"De nada, Pete. Always help you if I can."

"I appreciate it." I hand Jorge a hundred dollars. "Is that enough?"

"Si, that's plenty." I take out my phone, and pull up the photo album and sort through the pictures until I find the one of the horse I thought was Jorge's.

"Jorge, your horse that Jake picked up from you, just before you got Spicy Lemon."

"Speckled Hen?"

"What happened to him? Where did he go?" Jorge looks at me, wondering why I'm asking I guess.

"He went to farm, for six months I think. Bad ankle, needed time. Should be back late summer." I hand Jorge my phone.

"Is that Speckled Hen?" Jorge looks at the image for a little while.

"That's him. You seen him?"

"Jorge, I'm sorry, he went to slaughter."

Jorge stares at me, I see moisture appear around the edges of his eyes. He really did not know.

CHAPTER 17

JORGE, THURSDAY

(TRANSLATED FROM SPANISH)

I KNOW IT. I TRY NOT TO KNOW IT, BUT IT MAKES SENSE. Jake picks up too many horses from us. They can't all be going to farms and rehab. We rarely get horses shipping back to us from the farms - one or two maybe. I am here two years now, and the only new horses we get are the ones we claim, or the ones boss buys from Churchill Downs at the end of their meets. We claim a lot of horses, so we have to make room for them.

Mike's job is good, if you look the other way. I am paid well, cash too. I can send money back to Mexico every second week. Soon I am able to build a house for my family. Soon I will return to Mexico for good. Ten years in America, two years at Missionville. I really want to go home. I love my horses, but I can't keep doing this and still love horses. Soon I will leave.

PART 3

CHAPTER 18

AMANDA, SATURDAY

TO SAY THAT THIS HAS BEEN A BIZARRE WEEK UNDERSTATES things. But the art of handling this kind of stuff, I find, is to simply carry on and do what you normally do. Saturday morning, that is to head out early to the racetrack. I'm not sure what the day will bring, particularly how things will be when I see Pete. I don't want to avoid him, I do want to get updates on Thunder Clouds and Spicy Lemon. I am guessing that both must be getting close to their next races.

I head up to the track after getting my coffee from the track kitchen. There is the usual gathering of trainers, watching their horses going through their paces. This hour in my week is one of my most enjoyable, despite the chilly temperatures, or perhaps even because of the cold, which seems to amplify all the sounds of the horses and humans.

Jake comes onto the track, ponying a horse without a rider. I wonder if it's Jake who had gotten Pete a driving job with Tom. It almost certainly has to have been him, but I haven't asked Pete.

"Amanda, always good to see you on a Saturday." He's probably referring to the fact that he doesn't like seeing me on a Tuesday.

"Nice to see you too." He moves on. That's about as much of an exchange as we usually have. I spend the next thirty minutes or so chatting with a few trainers and enjoying the scenery, then Pete enters the track. I was getting a little worried he might have disappeared again, we haven't spoken since he left for the track on Wednesday morning. Pete stands his horse in, and exchanges hellos with the girl who works at the gap. Then he sees me.

"Hey, Amanda. Can you stop by the barn later?" An invitation, but we have moved beyond the idea of a relationship, I think. Perhaps Pete just wants to explain some stuff. Anyway, I want those horse updates.

"Sure, Pete. What time's good?"

"Any time after nine thirty. I should be all done training by then."

"I'll be there." That's settled. I have a little over an hour and a half to kill.

After I leave the track, I go on my barn tour. Today I have two barns to visit, to check up on a couple of horses and relay a bit of good news to one of the trainers.

On a day like today, when I have extra time to hang around, I visit a few extra barns that don't have horses that I advertise. I just introduce myself, and let those horsemen who will listen know a little more about what I do. That's the hardest part of this work, if you can call it work. Meeting new people, trying to convince them that I am legitimate and can help their horses. The backside is generally skeptical about us 'rescue folks.' And to some degree, they have a point. There have been occasions when a trainer has given a horse away to a 'good home,' only to see the horse get neglected. It makes them all a little gun shy. I can only be successful if I dispel these types of concerns.

I see Shawn leaving one of the barns I'm heading toward.

"Amanda, good to see you on your Saturday rounds."

"Thanks, Shawn. I found Pete."

"Yes, I heard you rescued him, I guess kind of like you do with some of these horses." Shawn smiles.

"Not sure if that's how it was, but I'm glad to have helped."

"I stopped by to see him on Thursday. I'm glad he's back. Will catch up with you soon about dates for the banking program."

"Great, I'm very flexible so just let me know."

I arrive at Pete's barn right at nine thirty, and true to his word he's in the barn, jumping off his last horse. He looks pleased to see me.

"Very good that you're here." Pete seems a little off his game. But maybe that's alright.

"I could say the same. I'm glad you're here."

"Look, the last couple of weeks have been a disaster, but I've spent a lot of time thinking these last couple of days." Interesting, maybe.

"Can we get together later? Promise I won't get drunk, just friends talking." I hadn't been expecting this, so I'm not sure the best way to respond. Saying no seems petty, if I don't have a real excuse, which I don't.

"Sure, why not?" There are probably several reasons why not, but I don't want to push it.

"Great. Harry's horse runs in the Wood Memorial today, maybe we can watch it together?" I suppose that's as good a reason as any to get together.

"Sounds good."

"Want to come over to my house, hang out with Hairy too?" Do I want to do that, is that a little too intimate, or is it better than going back to Jessup's? I guess Pete's it is.

"OK, I'll come by about four thirty. What time's the race?"

"Race goes off around six, TV coverage begins at five."

"Can you catch me up on Spicy Lemon and Thunder Clouds later?"

"Sure, I'll check in with Jorge before I leave the barn this morning."

"OK, see you later." I hadn't expected to make arrangements with Pete for later in the day, and I really don't know how I feel about it. But I suppose there's no harm done by hanging out for a little while and seeing where our conversations lead us.

I arrive at Pete's a little after four thirty. I knock on his door. Hairy starts barking.

"Hey, Amanda." Pete lets me in. Hairy is wagging his tail like his life depends on it. I give him a pat on his head. He really is a scruffy looking thing with his long, shaggy, wiry coat.

"I've got a bottle of wine in the fridge for you. Snacks are out by the TV. Take a seat. Are you ready for a glass?" The place looks very nice.

"Sure, thanks." Pete comes from the kitchen with a glass in hand. I don't see his usual Budweiser.

"You not having anything?"

"A little later, still recovering from my short vacation I guess." Pete seems pretty casual about it all.

"I'm sure I would be too." Anyway, it's good to see Pete sober and clear thinking.

"This is why I wanted to get you over here." Uh oh?

"The last few weeks at the track have been tough, and last weekend was a serious mistake." He's right on that score.

"There's not much reason for me to go on training. I need to find something else to do. I know that." Interesting, but I'm not sure switching to be an accountant at this stage in life is any holiday.

"But I figure before I make a move, I can be useful." Useful, what does that mean?

"I mean, the track sucks, we know that. Things aren't right, and the connection to the kill auction only makes things worse." He is talking sense. "I think there are other things going on at the track, and I'd like to try to do what's right before I leave." What other things? I wonder.

"Go on, I'm listening."

"Mike's vet, James, I use the same vet. I think he's cheating with Mike. Actually, I know they're cheating. I just need to prove it."

"How do you know?"

"I see James going into some of Mike's horses' stalls on race day with a syringe. It's illegal. He can't do that. I don't know what's in the syringe, and why they've never had a positive, but I know it's happening." This stuff is out of my league. Sarah would get it, but I don't really know the rules.

"OK, so we could try to figure this stuff out. Not sure how." I take a swig of my wine. The broadcast for the Wood Memorial is just starting on the TV. Then I have an idea.

"Pete, I'm no expert on all this, but I'm interested in what you're saying, and helping in any way I can to improve the racetrack. Can we discuss all this with Sarah Lester?" Sarah will know what Pete's talking about, and she might have some ideas. It would also be good to get Sarah and Pete together, so she can get to know Pete for who he really is.

"Yes, I was thinking that connecting with Sarah would make sense. Can you set it up so we can all get together?"

"Sure, how does a Tuesday evening sound to you, at her farm?"

"That works for me. I won't have any runners this Tuesday, so if you could make it for next week, that would be great."

"I'll call Sarah tomorrow, then text you to confirm."

"Perfect." I take another swig of my wine. I wasn't expecting any of this, but it might be interesting. Pete seems to be a person on a mission. I like that.

"Obviously the trip to the slaughterhouse was a one-off gig. I can't do that again," Pete says, trying to explain himself.

"Let's chat about that on Tuesday with Sarah too. Maybe it would be useful if you worked for Tom a little more?" Having an insider working in the slaughter trade might provide us some answers that we really need to end the practice.

"I don't know. That was a nightmare. One of the horses on the trailer was a horse Jorge had before they claimed Spicy Lemon. I showed Jorge a picture. He had no idea."

"You took pictures of the horses? Where?"

"While they were still at Tom's place. The Thoroughbreds."

"Can I see them?" Pete pulls out his phone, fiddles with it a little and hands it to me.

"Just scroll backwards." Each was a Thoroughbred, all healthy looking.

"So one of these was a horse of Jorge's, most likely shipped to Owenscreek, but not available for sale. Straight to Tom's kill pen. Do you know who the others are?" I'm impressed he has pictures.

"Not yet, but I'm guessing one of them is Harbor Lights, the horse that was vanned off a few weeks ago. I plan to go to his trainer and show him the pictures, but I haven't gotten around to it yet."

"Ugh. Racing can be brutal. I know Harbor Lights was at Owenscreek. Remember, I asked you if you knew the horse? I'd identified him at the sale." This is the really ugly side of the sport for sure. It is interesting though that Pete seems to have had somewhat of an awakening over the last couple of days. I like that. I like that very much.

"Ready for another?" Pete asks, pointing to my wine glass.

"Yes, thanks. Any updates on Spicy Lemon?"

"I asked Jorge. He thinks he'll race within the next ten days or couple of weeks. One more workout. Says the horse is doing well, his hock issue seems to be under control."

"Great. If we meet up with Sarah on Tuesday, you can give her a direct report. She'll appreciate that."

"I will. Thunder Clouds is doing well too. Of course I'm now of two minds regarding what I should do with him. I called Ray this morning and told him that the horse is a little off on the old ankle."

"Bummer, what happened to it?"

"No, it's fine, it's old, but fine. Just wanted to buy some time, so we didn't have to run him yet."

"Was he upset?"

"No more than usual. He'll fire me soon anyway, I think. But while I'm still training for him, I want to help figure out what's really going on in that barn with Mike's runners."

On the TV, the horses are in the paddock for the Wood Memorial. I'm starting to enjoy myself, intrigued by Pete's new found spirit. The wine is going down well too. I take a side plate and fill it with cheesy nachos.

"So can Harry's horse win this race?"

"Dancer's Foil will be the favorite, I think. But it'll be close. Northern Peaks has been running well in Florida this winter, and just shipped up to New York this week. They'd planned to run him in the Florida Derby, but for whatever reason, decided to come north."

The runners are heading down to the start. It is a small field of horses, and this will be their last race before the Kentucky Derby, if any of them line up for the big race. The commentators are saying how it's really a race between the top two horses, the rest of the field just doesn't have the same caliber of form. Harry must be pretty excited. I can only imagine how he will react if he wins. More high-fives, more people trying to avoid him.

The horses are loading into the starting gate.

"Here we go." Pete looks pretty excited. He is passionate about the sport that seems to have left him behind.

The horses break from the gate. Jose Figuaro, back aboard Dancer's Foil, tucks him in in fourth position, behind the early speed of the race. Northern Peaks is two more horses behind him, and sitting in last place in the field of six.

"Nice. Again, too much early speed. Race should set up well for the top two." Pete ends up being right, as the top two horses make their moves coming around the final turn, and head down the lane, neck and neck, a wide margin ahead of the remaining four.

"C'mon Dancer's!" Pete wills him on. They really hook up in a head-to-head battle, with neither horse backing down. They flash across the wire. I can't separate them.

"Close. What do you think?" Pete asks.

"Too close." I'm still watching the TV screen. Dancer's Foil pulls up quickly.

"You think he's OK?" I ask Pete.

"No, something's wrong. He's not putting weight on his left front."

"Shit, after such a great effort." The TV announce Northern Peaks as the winner, a nose in front of Dancer's Foil. There is no further mention of Harry's horse.

It's a bad ending to what has been an unexpectedly good afternoon.

"More wine?" I should go, I don't want to give Pete the wrong impression. But the reality is, I don't really want to go, and I don't have any reason to go.

"Sure. Damn, that's tough on Harry's horse."

"We can look online later if you like. Someone will report what happened to him." Later? How much later should I be staying? Pete opens a Budweiser for himself, I assume his first for the day.

We continue chatting throughout the evening. Pete's new conviction is clear, he wants to make an impact. He has thoughts on what is going on at the barn, which we plan to discuss with Sarah. He also recalls the fiasco around Thunder Clouds's first work for him, but this time he is very level-headed. I continue to drink wine, while Pete sticks mostly to water.

We check online about Harry's horse. It appears that he blew his left front ankle, which might require surgery and a couple of months away from the racetrack. Harry will be shattered, not because the horse is hurt, but because he won't be able to go to the Kentucky Derby. Northern Peaks is now the favorite for the big race.

Pete orders a pizza delivery. I drink a little more wine. I stay the night. It turns out to be a very good evening.

CHAPTER 19

PETE, MONDAY

I'M DETERMINED TO MAKE SOME KIND OF DIFFERENCE around here. I know I won't be training for Ray for much longer, but for that short while I need to focus on other things that are happening. I know something is going on with Mike's horses, and my guess is it's mostly the horses that Mike trains for Harry. I know that James is involved. I know that Longman plugs horses in. And I know the clockers are corrupt too. Maybe there's more.

Saturday night was a good night. I enjoyed spending time with Amanda again, this time sober. Hopefully we'll get together tomorrow at Sarah's and come up with some plans. Today, I want to get my horses trained, and I want to chat with Alfie and Jorge a little.

I have all four of my horses to gallop this morning, so it's going to be a pretty busy day. But that's how I like it. Plenty to do. I get Thunder Clouds ready, first.

When we get up to the track, just after it opens, there are already horses out working under the lights. It's a typically busy Monday morning on the racetrack at Missionville.

"Hey, Pete, good to see you this early in the week." Jess is being a little funny, but I don't care.

"Thanks, Jess. Always good to see you, any day of the week." I smile. I jog Thunder Clouds back to the wire. His whole training routine is very straightforward, and the old horse feels pretty good. It's nice to know that

I won't have to worry about running him for a couple of weeks; but I won't be able to hold Ray off for too long. Anyway, screw Ray. He's just a reason for me to stick around here for a few more weeks; soon I'll be gone, and Ray will just be a sour memory.

After I finish training Thunder Clouds, I bring the old horse back to the barn and into his stall. I strip his tack and hand him off to Alfie.

"Hey, Alfie. Longman, what's the deal with him?"

"You know, he's a battery jockey. Always has been."

"I know he plugged in this fella when he worked him the first time for us." I give Thunder Clouds a pat.

"He just needed to remind the old guy. Sure as shit he'll do it in his race, just like he did last time he won on him."

"You think?"

"That's what he does. He'll do it on Franks's horses, no problem. Always wants to work them first. Won't buzz a horse in a race unless he's tried in a work."

"Did you do that when you rode?"

"No, boss. No. Longman's no good. He's the only one who'll do it here. Everyone knows. Stewards know. No one wants to care."

"Why? What do you know?"

"I live here. I hear things. I know. I've been around forever. Longman rides for Franks first call, and on all Harry's horses. The guy owns the track, who's gonna argue?" Alfie is making the connections that I knew. But he makes a good point, who stops Harry?

"Anything else I should know?" I walk around the shedrow with Alfie and Thunder Clouds.

"Watch your vet." Alfie stops at a water bucket so Thunder Clouds can take a drink. So Alfie knows James is up to something. Alfie's here every day, just walking around the shedrow. He wouldn't miss something so obvious as a vet going into the stall of a race-day runner.

"Thanks." I leave him to continue his walking routine. I tack up my next horse.

If Alfie knows what's really going on, you have to wonder who else knows, and why no one has tried to stand up and stop the corruption, or whatever it's called. Should we really just accept the status quo? Should we just put up with it and take our victories when we can? That's exactly what we do. I head out of the barn on my filly.

All morning my head spins with what is going on around me. How naïve I've really been to assume I could compete in such a wretched environment and win. But that's what I've been trying to do for the last ten years. Shit, I could have gotten out much sooner if I'd seen the light. But I guess it's never too late.

After I finish riding my four horses, it's time to clean them up and wrap their legs. My phone vibrates with a text message.

"We're on for Sarah's. Meet us there after 5pm tomorrow x."

I tap a reply into my phone, "Will do, look forward to it x."

Sweet. I am curious to meet Sarah. We know each other. We've run horses in the same race from time to time, but we never really chatted or spent time together. Honestly, I think she thinks I'm a bit of a low-life, but maybe I've misjudged her over the years too. She has seemed to be a little clueless in terms of how she places her horses in races. She doesn't win too often, and when she does win, it's usually a big payout at the windows, which is a sure sign that the win was a fluke. Anyway, tomorrow could be very interesting.

After I tidy up my shedrow, I head over to Mike's to see Jorge. I want to get another update on Spicy Lemon for Sarah.

"Jorge, que pasa?"

"OK." Jorge seems a little off form. He's usually always upbeat.

"You OK?"

"Si." Not convincing.

"How's Spicy?"

"He's OK. No problem. You keep asking. For that trainer, Sarah?"

"She's worried about him."

"De nada, I understand. Spicy's doing good. One more work this week, then race."

"Thanks."

"Pete, is all OK?" Jorge is quizzing me now. Our conversations are usually me asking the few questions, Jorge answering, that's it.

"Things are OK, no bueno." I want to be honest, since Jorge's always been good to me.

"Si, things are no bueno." What is Jorge referring to, I wonder.

"You've been here a while, right?"

"Si, two years."

"Good job?" I want to push a little, but I don't want to shut Jorge up either; he could be an ally.

"Money's good. That's it. Other stuff, no bueno. You know." I know he's still upset about that horse of his, Speckled Hen. But is there more?

"You guys win a lot of races." I try changing track a little.

"Si, sometimes we shouldn't." Bingo. Jorge does know something.

"I've started to wonder. You're a good guy. But some of these races, you shouldn't be winning." We're at an end of the shedrow, thankfully out of ear shot from anybody.

"Si. Is simple. The vet, and Longman. One or the other, sometimes both. Mostly Harry's horses." So Jorge knows. Others must know.

"Thanks. I figured." Time to back down now. I don't want to do anything until meeting Sarah and Amanda tomorrow.

"No problem, I help." I'm curious what Jorge means by that, but I don't push it.

"Thanks, see you tomorrow."

CHAPTER 20

AMANDA, TUESDAY

SATURDAY EVENING WAS NOT WHAT I'D PLANNED, nor expected. Pete seems like a different person. I hope that it's not just another swing of his erratic behavior; maybe this is his new normal. I like Pete's new sense of purpose. If it's for real, then I think we might have a shot at doing some good stuff together. I know I shouldn't have stayed the night, but then again, who's judging me? Staying the night was the right thing to do at the time. And Pete was wonderful. It's been hard to get him out of my head the last couple of days.

Work at the bank has become tougher over the last month or so. We've had a few consultants in from New York, which has understandably unnerved some of the staff. They know that you don't hire consultants because everything is going great, and they also know that big banks and online banking are crushing our community banking business. I need to try to keep the morale of the staff up as the leadership team and consultants figure out if we need to let people go and close branches.

Today, I need to visit a second branch before heading off to the auction. Visiting each of our branches at least once every two weeks has become my habit over the last few weeks, to try to keep everything on an even keel, and catch up with any work gossip. The second branch I'm visiting today is in Owenscreek, so I drive over to the town early, and do my work from there, before heading out to the auction, which is only down the road from the bank.

The auction is starting to get busier. As the quieter days of the winter months end, spring means more horses come through the auction. Also, a few more private buyers come to the auction to seek out their summer projects. One or two Thoroughbreds might get lucky today I suppose—I hope.

Upon arrival, I go through my usual routine, checking for Thoroughbreds. I discover only three, which is a good thing. Two are in one corral, together. With a bit of a struggle I get their lip tattoos. The other is in another part of the barn, in amongst a bunch of work horses. I get his lip tattoo too. There are no horses standing in Tom's kill pen. No horses from Harry this week, I assume.

I settle into the gallery, and see all the usual attendees, the two kill buyers, a few horse traders, and Jake. We avoid eye contact. In total, eighty-two horses go through the sale. It takes a little over an hour. Forty-three horses go to the two kill buyers, and I'm guessing about twenty-five go to private buyers, including one of the Thoroughbreds. The rest go to the horse traders, no doubt some of those will show up again here in a couple of weeks, or at one of the smaller auctions in the area – horses just getting shuffled through the system.

I arrive at Sarah's a little after three o'clock. Pete isn't due until five, which gives us some time to hang out and then feed the horses. I walk into the kitchen, where Sarah is getting some coffee ready.

"I'm curious to hang out with Pete."

"Yes, I think you will get along. Something really seems to have changed in him."

"I hope so, for your sake. I still can't believe he took those horses up to Canada."

"I admit, I was shocked. But it also seems to have had a real impact on him. Did I tell you he took pictures of the Thoroughbreds that were on the load?"

"Oh, no, I didn't know that. Interesting."

"He's got the pictures on his phone. We should ask him about them. He's already ID'd one horse, a horse of Harry's. Says Harry's groom, Jorge, was pretty upset about it when he showed him the picture. He thought the horse had gone for some rehab on an ankle."

"Huh. You've never identified Harry's horses at the auction, but sure as shit, they're there." Sarah is right of course.

"They must be the ones that are already in Tom's kill pen. The ones I can't get close to."

"Makes sense. I wonder why Harry doesn't want them identified?" Our conversation continues, but clearly this is the sort of chatter we need to have when Pete is here. We go out to bring the horses in and feed them. Sarah seems upbeat, but I know that the Spicy Lemon situation still weighs heavily on her mind.

I'm excited to see Pete again. I hope to see the same Pete I'd witnessed on Saturday. I find myself looking in the mirror in Sarah's feed room, just before Pete is due to arrive. I look decent, although I'm still in my auction outfit.

Right as we return to the house, Pete's car comes up the driveway.

"Hey, guys," Pete says, as he walks through the open door, a couple of minutes later.

"Pete, good to see you." It is good to see him, and he looks great. He gives me a kiss on my cheek. Nice.

"Sarah, nice to really meet you." Pete puts out his hand, and they shake.

"Nice to meet you, away from the racetrack."

"Yes, for sure. Thanks for letting me come over."

"Wine, beer or coffee?"

"Coffee for me," Pete responds.

"I'll take a glass of wine, Sarah." Time to unwind for me. I'm not planning on leaving tonight.

"Good, I'll join you with the wine," Sarah says as she makes the coffee and goes to get a bottle of wine.

"Pete, are you good for staying for dinner? I assume Amanda is, but I haven't asked either of you."

"That would be great, I appreciate it." Pete seems pretty relaxed and happy to be here. Sarah doesn't need a response from me.

"Good, then we have a long evening ahead to chat about what's really going on at Missionville and Owenscreek." Sarah puts the drinks on the kitchen table.

"Amanda tells me you made a trip for Tom?"

"Yes, I still can't believe things have gotten so bad I decided to do that."

"Things must be bad for you. There's no way I could even contemplate doing that." Sarah isn't making things too easy for Pete. "But it's interesting. You took pictures?"

"Not sure why I did at the time, but I was curious who the Thoroughbreds were. I figured they must have come from Missionville. Turns out, at least one of them did, and I think Harbor Lights was another one. I just need to confirm."

"You know, it could be good for us if you keep that driving job." Sarah makes the same suggestion I'd proposed on Saturday.

"Why's that?" Pete asks, clearly not thrilled about the idea.

"Two things really. You could help identify horses that we know go to kill. You can also look at the paperwork and see who's signing off that they're drug-free. Someone is signing those EID documents." Interesting, I hadn't thought of that. The EID basically states that a horse is drug-free, which isn't possible for a horse that has come straight from the racetrack. There's lots of fraud in this system. If we could get copies of the forms, ID the horses, and trace them back to their medical records at the track, we might be on to something.

"Do you really think I can do something that can make a real impact? Otherwise I would just rather not ever go back to Owenscreek, Tom's place, or the slaughterhouse." Pete had clearly been shaken by the experience. I guess he wants assurances that it would be worthwhile if he were going to do it again.

"Pete, we've gotten nowhere so far. We've never had someone working directly for the kill buyers or slaughterhouse who's been willing to blow the whistle. You could be that person. It won't be easy, but it might be worth it, if you've got the stomach for it." Sarah is pushing Pete. If Pete is serious about wanting to make a difference, this might be one way he could do it. Pete looks over to me.

"What do you think, Amanda? I know you brought it up the other day, so do I need to ask?"

"It's up to you. I couldn't do it. But if you could, I think Sarah's right, we could really blow up this slaughter business. At least for the Thoroughbreds."

"OK. I'll do it. I'll talk to Jake, and make an arrangement with Tom. I'll let you both know when my next trip is scheduled." Wow, that's settled, and a very good start to the evening. I reach for my second glass of wine, as does Sarah. She's also put dinner in the oven. Our conversation begins to meander and lighten up a little. Pete chats more about his upbringing and what brought him to Missionville. Sarah shares her stories of how she started breeding and training her own racehorses, along with her husband. She shares some of her and her husband's successes together, then how the 'bastard' screwed everything up with his affair with a work colleague. She talks about how tough it has been to keep the farm and breeding operation going, but how she's now in a good place with it all. Pete gives her an update on Spicy Lemon. The two are getting along like fast friends.

Sarah serves up dinner. It is delicious, as usual. The conversation then circles back to the problems we are facing at the racetrack.

"Pete, tell us what's going on at the track. I know Harry's no good, but I've never really understood what they're up to." Sarah had told me, time and again, that she knew they were up to no good, but she's never backed up her assertions with any substance. She wants to know what Pete knows.

"It seems to me there are two issues. The jockey they use, Longman, and the vet they use, who also happens to be my vet, James Norwood. And the clockers seem to be involved in some way."

"Does Longman use a battery then? I heard the rumors, I know his history," Sarah asks.

"Yes. He used one on my new horse, Thunder Clouds. I should've known better. Alfie reckons he does it on some of Harry's horses. Always works them first with the battery, then knows how they'll respond in the races. Apparently no one seems to care. When he worked my horse, the clockers reported a time three seconds slower than it actually was. A time I had asked Longman to work the horse in. All very fishy. I don't really understand the clocker connection, but the battery issue seems very straightforward."

"Yes, the clocker thing seems peculiar. But I wonder if they're planning a big bet or something. Wouldn't surprise me, using Vegas so as not to impact the track odds." Sarah knows her stuff.

"Maybe. I know my owner, Ray, bets in Vegas. Maybe he's in on it all too. I just don't know," Pete thinks out loud. But the betting angle makes some sense, at least in my limited understanding.

"What about the vet?" Sarah probes.

"Looks like James gives an IV shot to some of Harry's runners on race day. Only the state vet can give a race-day shot, as we know."

"Christ! How the hell does he get away with that? That's really risky."

"Simple. Track security doesn't come anywhere near our barn, making it nearly impossible for James to get caught."

"Wow, it still takes some balls to do something like that. I don't have security here, and I'd never dream of tampering with my horse on race day." Yes, I guess Sarah could cheat too, if she'd really wanted to. "I don't suppose we know what he's giving the horses?" she continues.

"No. And they never have a positive test, which would seem odd, unless they know what the track is testing for. Which, given they're Harry's horses, at Harry's racetrack, not too crazy."

"If we can identify what they're giving the horses, we might be able to do something. We probably need to contact the track investigator. He needs to be involved."

"I didn't know there's a track investigator? But if security isn't allowed near Harry's barn, what can an investigator do?" I ask.

"The investigator works for the state racing commission, not for the individual racetracks that are owned by separate entities. The investigator is independent of Harry. He's our guy – Steve Timmins. If it's OK with you Pete, I'll contact him tomorrow, set up a time to meet with him. Can you come along? He's based in Harrisburg."

"Sure. Anything to help."

So that's settled then. We'd come up with a plan for the slaughter situation, and a plan for the racetrack. I like that. Now time to enjoy the rest of the evening. A couple of glasses of wine in, I'm staying the night, as usual. I wonder what Pete has planned. He has Hairy at home, but I hope he's made some arrangements, just in case.

Pete goes to the kitchen to grab another bottle of Budweiser, only his second.

CHAPTER 21

PETE, WEDNESDAY

FOR THE FIRST TIME IN A WHILE, IT FEELS GOOD TO BE AT WORK. I figure that I can make some things happen, and I also have a horse in on Friday which I'm hoping will earn me some much needed money. My filly, Pink Slippers, is back in, and she is in an almost identical race that she ran in last time. Emma will ride her again. I'm hoping this will be a good race for all of us. The filly has been training very well. While it feels good to have a horse in with a live shot again, I'm more jazzed about what we discussed yesterday, quite late into the night. Sarah seems like a person who can get things done, she knows how things work. I can definitely see us working together. Our first move will be to meet with the track investigator. I'm looking forward to that. Amanda is special. I need to make sure I don't screw that up again. How she's stuck with me is crazy, she could really have anyone she chooses! Anyway, it's all very invigorating.

I ride my first horse, Thunder Clouds, to the track. The old guy is doing well. I think I've got a good handle on his ankle now, but the longer I can delay running him, the better for him. I turn him in at the gap.

"Hey, Pete. Not a bad morning," Jess says with her usual cheer.

"You're right, it's a great morning." That's probably not the response she was expecting, but it did really feel like a great morning. I jog the old guy back to the wire. We stand in for a little while, as we normally do, and watch a couple of breezers fly by. I remember, many years ago, wanting to look good on a horse. I thought style was the most important thing. You see this a lot with the younger exercise riders. Us more seasoned guys ride longer, with more balance, and much more patience. The breezers that went by, their riders are riding so short I'm not sure what they'd have done if one of the horses spooked a little, at speed. And it happens.

I ride my other two geldings before the break, just making the track with the second one. Both these horses are ready to be dropped for their exit race; the race I pick out to get them claimed. But these last few weeks have made me think about the claim and drop system. While it's good for Ray and me that we're not left with the horses when they can't run any longer, it's not good for the horses. Someone has to deal with that final decision – what to do with them after their racing career. I need to come to terms with that, and try to figure out how to handle it with Ray. It's another reason I know I won't be training for him for much longer.

Emma Sparks stops by, during the break.

"Hey, Pete. How's things?"

"Good, very good." Emma looks a little surprised by my enthusiastic response.

"That's great. Filly looks good in that race on Friday."

"She does. I'm hoping we can win with her this time, but as long as she runs her race, we'll be fine."

"Well I hope she wins for you. I'll see you in the paddock on Friday."

"Thanks, Emma."

I'm glad I've managed to keep Emma on the filly. I definitely don't want Longman on her. Pink Slippers is a little light-framed, on the small side. I just think she benefits from a soft approach, which is how I train her. Emma's got nice soft hands, and a very kind way with horses. She suits the filly. Maybe she should have won last time, and maybe Thunder Clouds has to pay the price for Ray's decisions, but at least this filly gets another shot. I go to my tack room to grab her tack, she's my last horse to train for the day. Hairy is blissfully snoring away in the corner.

Ten minutes later I'm heading up to the track, walking alongside another trainer, Hank Fredericks. Hank was the trainer of Harbor Lights.

"Hey, Hank. All good?"

"Pete, you know how it is. I'm down to two horses." Hank is a small trainer like me. But he doesn't gallop his own horses, and really, I'm not sure how he makes it at all here anymore. But he's always seemed a nice enough guy; he was a leading trainer back in the early eighties.

"Yeah, sorry about Harbor Lights. Haven't seen you since. Was it a bad breakdown?"

"It would have meant a few months off and surgery to get him back to the races. Just no way I could afford that, not the time, not the expense."

"Are you around later? I want to show you something?" I want to confirm I'd shipped his horse to slaughter.

"Sure, I've got nowhere to go. I'll be in my barn until lunchtime, then I'll be in the kitchen."

"Great, see you later." I walk onto the track and stand the filly in. I'm not exactly sure how to handle Hank. I'll show him what I think is the photo of Harbor Lights and also two other horses in case he has any idea who they are.

My filly trains beautifully. She really has matured into a nice progressive mare, and makes me think that she's improved a little from her last start. We walk back to the gap.

"Filly looks good, Pete."

"Thanks, Jess. I'm hopeful."

"You should be. Emma will win on her this time." It's good how some of the women try to stick together. Jess is a big fan of Emma Sparks.

"I hope so. But win lose or draw, I hope we run a good race."

"I'm sure you will. You've done a good job with her since the claim. I hope you keep her around." Jess knows I don't keep too many horses around for too long.

"See you tomorrow." We leave the track.

It takes me about an hour to get things finished in the barn, grooming my horses, working on their legs, and finishing up. Before I go over to Hank's barn, I want to catch Jake. I head over to Mike's shedrow to find him.

"Jake, any chance we can talk?" I want him to come to my tack room for a bit of privacy.

"I'll be over in a minute."

"Thanks." I wait in my tack room, and Jake stops by after a few minutes.

"I've been thinking, no harm done on my end, I should drive again. I need the money." I was trying to use Jake's argument that the driver doesn't kill the horses.

"Sure. Tom will be glad to have you back. I don't know how he's fixed for now, but he'll want to use you at some point soon. Is that OK?"

"That works."

"I'll text you when I've talked to Tom, let you know."

"Thanks. Just between us of course."

"Course Pete, no worries." Jake heads out of the tack room. I call Hairy, and we head to Hank's barn.

"Hank."

"Hey, Pete. What's up?"

"I hate to ask, I know things have been rough for you, but Harbor Lights, what happened to him?"

"I had to sell him. I needed the two hundred dollars. You know how it is."

"Sure, I've done it myself. Jake, I assume?"

"Yes, Jake picked him up. Said he would see if he could rehab him. Best I could do."

I take out my phone, and pull up the pictures to show to Hank.

"Is this him?"

"Yes, that's Lights."

"Sorry, he shipped to slaughter." I didn't see a reason to hide the truth. I knew it would hurt Hank, but it is what it is.

"What do you mean?" Hank just stares at the picture.

"That's him, waiting to be loaded on a kill truck, heading to Canada." Hank keeps staring at the photo, avoiding my eyes.

"Why is this picture on your phone?" He still hasn't looked up.

"I took the picture, before I drove the load to Canada." I want to be honest. Tears well in his eyes.

"What the hell do you mean? You took him to slaughter?" Hank is now looking directly at me.

"It's a long story. Something I'll never get over. But it happened, and I drove your horse up there, along with plenty of others."

Hank looks bewildered, lost.

"I really hoped Jake would do something with him. Lights was good to me. Christ, what have I done?" Hank starts to cry. "What the hell are we doing here?"

"Hank. It's a tough reality. I don't know what to say. This place tests the best of us, and we do bad things."

"I used to have a good string of horses, win decent races, be respected. Now it's come down to this, selling horses to slaughter, for every last penny." Hank is distraught. Perhaps I shouldn't have bothered him about his horse; it won't bring him back.

"I'm sorry." I try to console him, but eventually I just leave his barn, Hairy following me. We head to the track kitchen.

"Usual, Pete?"

"Thanks." Alice busies herself with my sandwich, and adds a couple of sausages on the grill. Hairy is wagging his tail expectantly. As much as this track sucks you down, there are places that are just good. One of those places is the kitchen, and that's because of Alice.

"Here you go, and a treat for Hairy." She hands me my sandwich and the two extra sausages. I go to sit at one of the tables to eat, Hairy chomps down his sausages.

My phone vibrates, it's a text message from Sarah. "Can you meet in Harrisburg Friday, 2pm? I know you have a runner, but hope this works."

I type back, "Sure, just give me the address, see you there."

CHAPTER 22

PETE, THURSDAY

THE NEWS THIS MORNING STUNS ME. HANK FREDERICKS hung himself in his tack room.

Hank had been a trainer at Missionville for more than thirty years, and before training, he'd ridden races. He was a fixture here, and was well-liked. For the last four or five years, his stable had shrunk; most of us assumed he was living off his old successes. He leaves behind two horses, and no family.

The police arrive at the track shortly after I arrived. I replay our conversation yesterday in my mind, over and over again. Obviously I shouldn't have shown him the Harbor Lights photo, for confirmation. But obvious only reveals itself in hindsight.

When I get to the track on my first horse, Pink Slippers, the mood is dark.

"Hey, Pete."

"Jess. Shocking."

"No way to deal with it. Hank was part of the family."

"So sad." We fall silent. The usual buzz of the track had fizzled. I jog back to the wire. The filly trains nicely, and is ready for tomorrow. The rest of the morning is more of the same. The energy of the backside is completely deflated. One of our own has taken his life. A few horsemen speculate why it happened. The backside wisdom suggests Hank had just fallen on bad times and couldn't carry on.

Adam, a freelance exercise rider who rides Hank's two horses, is now taking care of them. He even rode one of them today. As I finish up in the barn, a policeman stops by.

"Are you Pete Wright?" Shit, I was hoping my conversation with Hank wasn't going to be directly tied to his death. Although I knew it was.

"Yes. That's me."

"Can we talk?"

"Sure, come into my tack room. It'll be quiet."

"Thanks." We walk into the tack room, Hairy wakes up from his snoring. The policeman hands me a note: "Pete Wright will understand."

Christ! I killed Hank. He killed himself because of our conversation, and the police know.

"Can you tell us anything about this note?" The policeman wants my comment, but I just keep staring at the note. What the hell have I done? Hank was just a quiet, good guy. I pushed him with the Harbor Lights issue, now he's dead. Jesus, this isn't what I was expecting.

"Mr. Wright. Can you explain this note?" The policeman has a job to do, I have to snap out of it.

"Sure. We had a chat yesterday, after training," I begin. "We talked about the problems with training a small string of horses. How we deal with horses once they're done racing. One of Hank's horses went to slaughter. I have a picture of him on my phone. I showed it to Hank."

"Can I see the picture?"

I hand my phone over. "Here you go."

I feel terrible. I pushed Hank to do this, it was so unnecessary.

"You think this is why he wrote the note?"

"Yes. I confronted him about the horse. Christ, I can't believe I killed him."

"It's OK, Mr. Wright. You're not part of any investigation. Just putting all the facts together." That doesn't make me feel any better. I had a conversation with Hank, he's now dead, and his note confirms why he's dead. The policeman leaves my barn.

I text Amanda, "Can we meet tonight? A trainer hung himself this morning. I need to talk."

Amanda replies almost immediately, "Shit! Yes. Heard something on the radio on my way to work. Jessup's when I'm done, 6? x"

I type quickly, "Thanks, see you then. x"

I head to the kitchen with Hairy.

"Usual, Pete? Terrible about Hank." Hank was a close friend of Alice's.

Of course he was, he'd been here forever. So has Alice.

"Yes, so sorry Alice. You guys were close. Just awful."

"He was having a hard time. I just didn't know it was this bad. He was a good guy, Pete. This place sucked him dry I guess."

"Yes, just a very bad thing. So sorry, Alice." She's almost in tears. I imagine she's cried plenty this morning. Her face is red raw. She hands me my sandwich, and a treat for Hairy, who wags his appreciation. We go to sit down.

I get to Jessup's five minutes early.

"Hey, Charlie."

"Pete. Shocking news." Charlie would know all about it from the lunch crowd.

"Yeah. I was only talking to him yesterday. Today he's gone." Charlie hands me my bottle of Budweiser.

"He used to come in here regularly 'til about ten years ago. Only seen him once or twice this past year." Charlie has been at Jessup's for a very long time.

"Yes. I guess age slowed him down a little. Only had a couple of horses in the end. He used to have a barn full."

"Leading trainer, way back when." Charlie knows his customers, even those who no longer come regularly. "What brings you in tonight, you're usually at the track?"

"Meeting Amanda. Just needed to get away from the track tonight. Runner tomorrow, too."

"I like her. She's a keeper."

"I hope I get a chance to keep her. She's good for me." Right on cue, Amanda walks through the door and comes up to the bar.

"Usual?" Charlie inquires.

"Please, Charlie. Thanks." She gives me a kiss on my cheek.

"Can you grab a booth? I'll bring your drink over." Amanda goes to the corner of the bar, the same table I was at when Amanda rescued me a little over a week ago. It seems like a lifetime ago now.

"How was your day?" I ask Amanda when I get to the table.

"Probably better than yours. Did you know the guy?"

"Yes, everyone on the backside knew Hank. One of the good old guys."

"I'd seen him a few times too, but never really chatted with him much." Amanda's retirement project means that she has probably chatted with most of the trainers at Missionville at one time or another.

"He was the trainer of Harbor Lights." Amanda looks a little puzzled, but then gets it.

"Damn."

"I talked to him yesterday, showed him the picture of his horse."

"Christ! The suicide is connected, I guess?"

"He left a note. It simply said 'Pete Wright will understand.'" Amanda turns pale. I continue, "The whole thing's just awful. If I hadn't confronted him, he'd be alive today."

"You're right," Amanda begins. "But you can't beat yourself up about it. You don't know what other things Hank was dealing with."

"Maybe, but I do know that my conversation with him led him directly to taking his own life. Even without the note, I knew it; the note is just a haunting reminder."

"I'm really sorry. This must be very upsetting. What can I do for you?"

"I don't know. Yesterday morning I was on top of the world. I was really excited about some of the things we discussed at Sarah's. The first action I take with my new found enthusiasm ends with a man killing himself."

"I understand. But for the sake of Hank, we need to keep doing this. Fight for the horses. If he did kill himself because of your conversation, imagine how guilty he must have felt for letting his horse go to Canada. For his sake, you need to keep pushing." Amanda's smart. She knows how to handle situations and turn a very bad incident into a motivating force.

"I guess that's one way to deal with it." I'm still not enthusiastic, but what she said makes sense.

"I also want to stay the night at your place tonight, if that's OK with you?" she asks. I was not expecting that comment.

"That would be great."

"Perfect. I booked us a table at Zucchini's. You ready? It's on me this time." Wow, she really knows how to make things better.

Dinner at Zucchini's is delicious. We talk politics and religion, two potentially taboo topics but always good conversation fodder when you know someone. Thankfully Amanda is a Democrat. Not that it would have really mattered to me, but it's good that we share some similar values. I also invite Amanda to the races tomorrow. She's never been to a live race, which I find a little strange given how many times she's visited the backside at Missionville.

Throughout the evening I can feel the chemistry between us. The connection we have is something I've never felt before. I really couldn't wait to get back to the house. We've stayed up late before, we've fooled around a little, but I was hoping that tonight would be our night.

We are hardly through my front door when we literally rip each other's clothes off. We never make it upstairs.

CHAPTER 23

PETE, FRIDAY

I WAKE UP AT FIVE, AS USUAL. I SET MY ALARM ON MY PHONE, but most mornings I'm awake before it goes off. Before getting up I just lie there, listening to Amanda. Just knowing she's there, in a peaceful slumber, is thrilling. But I need to get up, today is going to be a long day. I have a two o'clock meeting in Harrisburg with Sarah. And Pink Slippers is in the sixth race tonight. I roll out of bed.

"Hey, morning," Amanda mumbles, her eyes still shut.

"Sorry, thought you were asleep."

"What time is it?"

"A little after five. You can stay in bed if you like. Just let yourself out later?"

"No, I'll head out now." Amanda sits up in bed, her naked body a beautiful vision to behold. She catches me staring at her.

"Last night was wonderful," Amanda sighs.

"Yes, amazing," I agree. She is still naked, just sitting up in bed. I'm aroused, but I need to get to the barn.

"Will it be OK for me to stay again tonight, after the races?"

"That would be great."

I busy myself getting ready for the barn. Amanda rises from the bed, still naked, and walks slowly to the bathroom. She has no inhibitions. She's beautiful naked, and she knows it.

"What time are we meeting at the races?" Amanda hollers from the bathroom.

"Say quarter to seven, if that works for you? The filly races at about eight o'clock. Meet in Pokers, the bar right by the paddock. You'll find it easily enough."

"Sounds good." Amanda walks back into the bedroom and starts to slowly get dressed. "Good luck with your meeting this afternoon with Sarah and the investigator guy. That should be very interesting."

"Yes, I'm curious to see what happens. If nothing else, I should learn some things."

I unfortunately have to get to the barn. I don't want to go, but I'm pretty religious about being punctual when it comes to feeding my horses. Horses do like their routine. I walk over to Amanda, who is still getting dressed. I give her a kiss, she puts her arms around me, and we squeeze each other tightly.

"I've got to run. Can you just make sure the door's locked when you leave?"

"Sure. See you later." Amanda watches me as I leave. Hairy is waiting for me at the bottom of the stairs. He leaps into my car and we head out to the track.

The horses are fed right on time, six o'clock. Now that we are through the worst of the winter, and spring is coming along, I don't need to worry that the horses' water buckets might freeze. It makes the mornings a little easier. I have three to train, and I want to leave the barn in good time to get home, take Hairy for a nice walk somewhere, and then head to Harrisburg.

I decide to train my two geldings before the break this morning, and then take Thunder Clouds to the track right after the break. The track can be a little better after the break sometimes, especially at this time of year, as the warmer weather and sun helps keep the dirt surface more consistent.

I'm still struggling with how to handle Ray; he'll want to see all three of these horses in their next races pretty soon. He's already talked about a couple of horses he wants to claim. I can't claim anything until I have a stall open, which means I have to lose one of these horses, or worst case, sell one of them. Neither of the options are appealing. But keeping Ray somewhat happy means I can stick around here, to hopefully do some good.

The mood at Missionville is still very somber. As I go back and forth to the track, typical morning greetings are replaced by short acknowledgments. Conversations focus solely on Hank, and what happened yesterday.

At break time Larry, the state vet, stops by the barn, to check on Pink Slippers. We go through the usual routine, and she passes. It's a pretty useless task, being the state vet around here. If Larry did scratch a horse, John, the racing secretary, would go nuts. So basically Larry does his job well by not doing it at all. Sadly, a few more horses breakdown in the races, because filling the races is the goal of the track – the fuller the field, the higher the betting handle. The betting handle is the fuel that feeds the beast, the cash that partially keeps the racetrack going. Of course, the slot money helps a lot too. Anyway, Larry approves Pink Slippers for tonight and confirms her Lasix requirement. Alfie will be waiting for him this afternoon, as usual.

I ride Thunder Clouds out to the track, getting to the gap a couple of minutes before it re-opens. I circle around a little; there are a few of us looking to get on the fresh dirt surface. Adam is here, aboard one of the two horses of Hank's. Well, I guess they're not Hank's anymore.

"Adam, very sorry about what happened," I offer.

"Thanks. I can't believe it. I threw up."

"Oh no, did you find him?"

"Yes, it was awful. He was just hanging, all limp like. The police catch up with you?" Christ, of course, Adam would have seen the note.

"Yes, they came by my barn later in the morning. I guess you saw the note."

"I did. I thought it was really weird. I knew he liked you, but I didn't know you two were close."

"We weren't. We just had a conversation a couple of days ago. It must have pushed him over the edge. I feel terrible about it."

"Can you tell me what it was about, or is it hush-hush? I won't share." Adam has always seemed like a reasonable guy. I don't like secrets, and there seems no harm in telling him.

"Sure. The horse you guys used to have, Harbor Lights?"

"Lights, yes. He was a cool dude, had him for a while, Hank loved him. Sad he broke down."

"Well, he went to slaughter. Don't ask me how I know, but I do. I wanted to check in with Hank because I had a picture of the horse, and wanted to confirm its identity." Adam just stares at me. "You know Hank sold him, right?" We are both on the track now and start jogging back to the wire.

"Yes, to Jake. He said Jake was going to try to rehab him." Adam looks like he is still struggling to process the idea that the horse went to slaughter. "Damn, I really liked that horse. He had a very easy way about him. He also won us a lot of money over the two years we had him."

"Well, anyway, that conversation put Hank over the edge, I guess."

"I imagine it would. He had a lot of pride, being a horseman all his life. He's taught me a lot over the couple of years I've galloped for him. He only had a few horses, but he knew his stuff, and he loved the life, being surrounded by horses. He really loved them."

"I believe you, for sure. I could tell based on his reaction when I showed him the photo of the horse. He was shocked, but I also think he felt over-whelmed with guilt. Like he'd really let down a friend in a big way."

"Thanks for letting me know. It helps explain things a little."

"What's going to happen with his horses now?"

"No idea. I'm going to look after them for a while. It'll give me a chance to see if I like the training side of the business. But things are very up in the air right now. They're both his own horses, so whoever is in his will will have to start making decisions. He had three barn cats too, so I need to keep them fed."

"If you need any help, please let me know. Training is a tough business, it's good to have friends."

"Thanks. I might take you up on that." Adam rides away. I turn Thunder Clouds to the right and we do our routine mile-and-a-half gallop. The old horse is feeling really good in the sunshine. After pulling him up, I bring him back to the gap.

"Good luck tonight, Pete." Jess smiles.

"Thanks, Jess. I'm excited to see how she does."

"She'll win for you tonight. The race really looks good for her." Jess is a pretty good handicapper, and she is right, the race does look like it should suit my filly very well.

"Let's hope so." I walk back to the barn and into Thunder Clouds's stall. I strip his tack and hand him off to Alfie. An hour later I leave the barn and head to the track kitchen for my sandwich and Hairy's treat.

"Hey, Alice. How're you doing?" I don't usually ask, but yesterday's suicide is personal for her. Hank would be in the kitchen most afternoons, just hanging out. These were two people who probably loved each other, without ever expressing their feelings.

"I'm OK. Or maybe I'm not. I always enjoyed Hank's visits. Yesterday afternoon this place felt empty without him. Today, our special is one of his favorites."

"I imagine it'll be very tough for a while. Has Shawn mentioned any kind of memorial service?" I assume that Shawn will be doing something, and Alice would be one of the first to know.

"I haven't heard anything yet, but Shawn's not been in here since it happened."

"Hopefully there'll be something, he was well-liked. One of the good guys. I'll get your special for today." Alice smiles a little, but I can see that her eyes are still pretty red. She cuts me a healthy serving of lasagna pie, and puts a couple of sausages on the grill for Hairy.

Ten minutes later, I'd eaten my food and leave with Hairy to go and find a place for a nice long walk. I want to clear my head, ahead of my trip to Harrisburg.

Sarah and I arrange to meet just before two in Harrisburg, to chat for a few minutes before our meeting. I was going to let Sarah lead the meeting; I would add any necessary perspective. I'd looked up Steve Timmins online, to get as much background information as I could find. He's worked for the Pennsylvania Racing Commission for about ten years. He's closed a few cases from what I could tell, and seems to be pretty effective at his job. He's a Pennsylvania guy, and had gone to Penn State for his undergraduate studies, like me. His focus was criminal justice. All good stuff.

When I swing into the parking lot of the building where we were to meet, Sarah is already here, waiting for me beside her car. I park next to her.

"Hey, Sarah."

"Pete, glad you could squeeze this in. I know today isn't ideal for you."

"No worries, I don't need to be at the track until around seven, so I've plenty of time."

"I was sorry to hear about Hank Fredericks. Amanda told me it might have been related to Harbor Lights shipping."

"I showed him the picture of his horse. It's very sad, everyone at the track is shaken by it."

"I'm sure. He just seemed like a nice guy. I remember him when I first started out. He had plenty of winners back then." We talk for a couple more minutes, and discuss our plan for the meeting, then head to Timmins's office.

"Thanks for agreeing to meet with us," Sarah says to Timmins, when we're sitting across the table from him.

"You're welcome. I don't get many calls from Missionville. I spend most of my time at the other tracks in Pennsylvania, for whatever reasons. It would be good to get out there sometime." Seems an odd thing to say, wanting a reason to be at Missionville. But I just listen.

"We'll try to keep this short. Pete has a runner tonight, so we'll need to get back," Sarah explains.

"Fire away."

"We think there are a few things going on at the track that need investigating. First, Marcus Longman, who has a reputation as a battery jockey, we think he's plugging horses in. Specifically horses owned by Harry Mitchell and trained by Mike Franks."

"Do you have any evidence of this?" Steve asks us.

"Pete's in the same barn. He watched Longman plug one of his horses in during a workout, which is typical for a rider to do, ahead of a race."

"Pete, is this true?"

"Sure. It was very obvious, the way the horse worked. Then I saw him drop something when he was galloping out. Unfortunately I don't have the physical evidence."

"OK, but what's the connection with the track owner and his trainer?"

"Longman rides all their horses. He works them all too. Just seems obvious," Sarah responds.

"I need evidence. A battery with his fingerprints. A battery found in his car. Or video evidence of him plugging one in." This seems obvious. "I can make a note, it might be worth my while to head your way and poke around a little. What else do you have?"

"We think Franks and Mitchell are cheating with their vet James Norwood. Pete has witnessed Norwood going into the stall of horses that are running the same night, with a syringe."

"Interesting."

"Yes, and Pete says that security is never near the barn, likely influenced by the track owner. Basically Norwood seems pretty cavalier about doing this stuff."

"I can explore that." Timmins takes notes. "I assume we don't know what the drug is they're using?"

"No, but they win races at a high rate, and sometimes with real long shots. Something's up," I add.

"OK, this is very intriguing. Better if I know the drug. What we need is a syringe that was used. We could then test it. Don't suppose you have one of those?"

"We don't, not yet. I'll see what I can do."

"OK, very good. Anything else?"

"We think the clockers are in on some stuff too. Faking workout times." Frankly, this wouldn't be too unusual, and probably happens at a lot of tracks, but maybe it's all connected at Missionville.

"OK, a tougher one. But I can look into that too. So clockers, drugs on race day, and battery issues, right?" Timmins summarizes.

"Yes, that's about it," Sarah concludes.

"Good. Let me give all this some thought, and get back to you. It would seem that all issues point directly back to the track owner, Harry Mitchell, right?"

"Pretty much, yes," I agree.

"OK, good. I'll do more background work on him too. I don't know that much about him, but can shake some trees to see what I can find. Sarah, can you call me again, let's say in about a week? We can follow up then."

"That's great, Steve. Thanks."

"Shocking news about the trainer who hung himself," Timmins says to both of us.

"Yes, a very sad incident," I respond. I don't know if Timmins knows the details as to why Hank hung himself, I'm not that interested in sharing if he doesn't ask.

"I hear he was a leading trainer back in his day. Sad that things seem to have gotten so bad for him, he chose to do that."

"He was. The whole backside has been rocked by it. He was a popular guy."

"Well, very tragic indeed." Timmins gets up. We shake his hand and leave.

In the parking lot, Sarah turns to me, "I think that worked out well. I've known Steve a little over the years. He's very thorough."

"Yes, decent conversation. Can you text me after you guys chat next week? We should then plan to get together again."

"Sounds good. Good luck tonight. I hear you're bringing a guest."

"Thanks. Hopefully the filly runs well, and Amanda enjoys herself. I'm not sure it's really her thing though."

"She may surprise you, she has an edge to her." Sarah smiles, I think I knew that already, or I was learning.

"It's early days, but I do enjoy her company."

"I hope it works out for you guys. She's top drawer, you're quite lucky!"

"I know, for sure." I climb into my car, and head back to Missionville.

I arrive at the races a little before a quarter to seven. I want to be at Pokers before Amanda gets here.

"Budweiser, Pete?"

"Thanks, Mary, and a glass of sauvignon blanc, or whatever white wine you have."

"You have a guest, hopefully she'll get her picture taken." Mary is referring to the tradition of getting our photo taken after a horse wins a race.

"She? Could be a he," I counter.

"Not likely, you ordered her a wine. I'm guessing she's a she." And right on cue, Amanda walks in.

"Wow, she's gorgeous." Mary lowers her voice to remain out of ear shot of Amanda.

"I know right, crazy world." Amanda and I retreat to a table. Amanda looks lovely, in a tight blouse that really highlights her figure, and a short skirt and stockings. She is turning heads at Pokers.

"You look sensational tonight."

"Thanks. I feel good, and when I feel good I like to dress up. I've not overdone it have I?"

"No way."

"Good. I'll look forward to later when you undress me." Christ, I'm getting aroused again. I guess this is one good way of getting distracted from the pre-race nerves I usually suffer from. "How was your meeting in Harrisburg? Sarah called me, she sounded enthusiastic."

"It was a good meeting. The guy seems to be pretty capable. As we were discussing the situation with him, one thing became very clear: Harry Mitchell is central to all the bad stuff."

"The track owner?"

"Yes." We chat for a few more minutes about the meeting.

We leave our drinks on the table to watch the horses for the fourth race in the paddock. There are only six runners, all low-level claimers, all have raced at the track god knows how many times, with little recent success. Emma Sparks has a ride in the race. She smiles at me as she rides by. I give Amanda a running commentary the whole time, trying to provide the necessary context to what she is basically witnessing for the first time. She is standing next to me, very close to me.

"Which horse do you like?" I ask.

"The grey horse, the jockey with the pink silks."

"Number 3, that's Square Cubed. He's 10-1. Do you want to bet?"

"Sure. Five dollars to win."

"OK, I'll go and place the bet, meet you back at the table." I head off to the betting windows. It feels so good hanging out with Amanda. My nerves are good, and I feel a sense of confidence that I haven't had for a long time. When I return to the table, Amanda is waiting for me. The horses are loading in the gate.

"They're in the gate," the track announcer states, "and they're off!"

We watch the six furlong race on the TV screen. Square Cubed goes straight to the lead. Amanda grips my arm, excitedly. The horse is three lengths in front at the head of the stretch, but another horse is starting to close the gap. Amanda wills him on, as if she's on board the horse. He holds on by half a length.

"Wow, that's cool. Fifty dollars for me!" I hand Amanda her betting ticket.

"Well done. You've got to love beginner's luck."

"Maybe I know something," Amanda teases.

For the next race we do the same. We go to the paddock, I provide a running commentary, which includes identifying Longman for Amanda, who is riding the favorite in this race. Amanda picks a different horse to bet and it wins. She is on a roll, and seems to be thoroughly enjoying herself.

Now it's time for Pink Slippers. Despite the fun we are having, my nerves start to overtake me, as they always do before a race. No matter how many times I've run horses, how long I've been training, I always wonder if I've got it right. Maybe that's a good thing; it would be a shame to get too complacent.

We walk into the paddock and wait by the number five stall where we will saddle the filly. Alfie leads her into the paddock, along with the other six runners. She looks a picture of health. She's the second choice in the betting. The favorite is a filly that has just won her last start, so she is moving up a condition, but she had won quite well. The handicapper noted that there might be more improvement. I study my filly as she walks around the paddock. She does look great.

The valets file out of the jocks' room with their saddles and number cloths. Alfie brings the filly into the stall, and we saddle her. She's a very easy filly in the paddock. There is a bit of a clatter in the next stall, as one of the fillies rears up, and then falls to the side of the stall. Slippers hardly notices. She has a bit of class. Once saddled, Alfie takes her for a few more spins around the paddock as Emma Sparks arrives, along with the other jockeys.

"Emma, this is a friend of mine, Amanda."

"Hey, very nice to meet you. I think I've seen you on the backside." They shake hands.

"Yes, on Saturdays. It's nice to meet you. Good luck!"

"Thanks, I'm excited for this race. It looks good for us."

"What do you think?" I ask Emma, wanting to know what her plan is for the race.

"I'm hoping we do what we should have done last time – get her covered up, then let her roll down the lane. Make sense?"

"I think so. It's your call. The favorite is a closer too, so keep an eye on her."

"Of course, but I think I have more kick." It's nice to hear Emma confident.

"Riders up!" comes the call from the paddock judge. I help Emma aboard Slippers and Alfie leads them out to the track, and hands them off to Jake.

"This is all pretty exciting." Amanda takes it all in.

"Yes, now if she does what I hope she does, we should be OK." My nerves are rattling, but I don't want Amanda to notice. I decide not to bet tonight.

"Ready for another wine?" I want to get that bottle of Budweiser.

"Sure, I'll see you in Pokers." Amanda waits outside as I go to the bar.

"Here's your Budweiser, Pete. A wine too?" Mary knows I always have a new beer, whenever I saddle a runner.

"Yes, thanks."

"She looks like she's enjoying herself. I hope you can handle her." Mary smiles.

"I hope so too. Thanks." I pay for the drinks and head to our table. Amanda is waiting for me.

"They're in the gate," the cue from the track announcer. "And they're off!"

We turn our attention to the TV screen. Slippers breaks well again, but this time Emma is able to restrain her a little, and get in behind two front runners, who are running very fast on the lead. This set up is much better for our filly.

"She's doing a good job, just where we want her." I try to provide some insight to my guest, but I also just want to watch and concentrate. They head around the turn and the two front runners start to weaken.

"Just as scripted. C'mon Slippers." Emma starts to put the filly into overdrive, and swoops by the leaders easily, rolling into a three-length lead.

"C'mon girl, keep rocking." At the eighth pole, she has a commanding lead, the only horse making a move on her is the favorite, but she's left it too late. Slippers wins quite easily.

"That's fantastic Pete, well done!" Amanda gives me a big hug. I'm elated, experiencing that euphoric feeling I only get after winning a horse race. I'm on top of the world, and on top of that, the filly was pretty convincing.

"C'mon, Amanda. We've got to get our picture taken." She follows me out to the track. Emma is riding the filly back to the winner's circle. Alfie is leading the pair, all smiles.

"Great stuff, Emma. Great ride." I give the filly a pat on the neck.

"Thanks! You've done a great job with this filly. I was pretty confident tonight. Thanks for sticking by me."

"It's great for all of us." We all head into the winner's circle to get our photo taken. This is one picture I'm going to keep; I order an extra copy for Amanda. Alfie is smiling proudly. I wonder if he's had a little bet. He then takes the filly to the test barn, where all winners, and an additional runner from each race, are sent to be drug-tested. They will be there for about an hour, then Alfie will bring her back to our barn and take care of her. We go back to Pokers.

"Phew, a relief. That was a big win for us, a needed win too."

"It was amazing. And I won again betting!" Amanda shows me her ticket. She'd placed a hundred dollars on her to win.

"Crikey, I'm glad I didn't know you had a bet before the race."

"It's Zucchini money. Dinner on me again next time."

"Sounds great."

I pull out my phone, and text Ray, "Nice race tonight. She won easily. Will call you in the morning, once I know how she is." Thirty seconds later my phone vibrates with Ray's reply, "I saw. She did well, just like she should have done last time too." Ray couldn't just be happy. He still had to put in a dig about the last race.

"You ready to leave?" I ask Amanda.

"Yep. Let's get back to your place." Amanda places her hand, which is under the table, on my crotch and gently squeezes. She's just staring into my eyes.

We can't get back to the house fast enough. And when we do get back, it is incredible. Amanda walks through the door, turns around and instructs me to take off her clothes, slowly. I do as I'm told, starting with her jacket, and then her blouse. All the time, I can't take my eyes off her. I slowly undo her skirt, which falls to the floor. She has on a pair of red panties and bra, a pair of stockings, and a garter belt. I unhook the bra, and her breasts pop out, beautiful and perky. I slide my hands down her back to remove her panties, slowly. I then kneel down to remove each of her stockings. All the time, Amanda just stands there, like a statue. She's now completely naked, her lovely strawberry blonde hair flowing over her shoulders.

The evening is just getting started.

CHAPTER 24

AMANDA, SATURDAY

THINGS HAVE MOVED VERY FAST WITH PETE OVER THE LAST few days. But what the heck, I know it when I'm with someone I like, and it's been a very very long time since I've had that feeling. Life's short, Pete and I have chemistry, and he seems to really like me too.

Pete is getting dressed; it's early. I just stare at him, admiring his physique. Not overly big, not bulky, but strong and lean.

"You want to come to the track with me, leave your car here, or go separately?" Pete asks. I sit up in bed, letting the sheets fall.

"We should go separately. I don't want Jake to see us together, in case he starts wondering why you want to continue shipping horses for them."

"Christ, good point, I hadn't thought of that. I guess we should act low key at the track."

"Yes, for now anyway. But not low key off the track." I don't want Pete to get the wrong idea. I get out of bed, and go to the bathroom. I can feel Pete's eyes on my naked body.

"OK, I'm heading out. Need to stop by Dunkin Donuts on the way. See you at the track."

"See you later, Pete." I take my time getting ready. I don't need to be at the track for another half an hour.

At the rail, I watch the morning training with my cup of coffee. It is a beautiful, crisp morning. Great to be alive. I overhear some of the conversations among the horsemen, discussing Hank's suicide. They speculate why he did it. Most conversations point to the plight of someone who was once somebody, who saw his life reduced to a two-horse string and no clients. The suicide note doesn't seem to be common knowledge. I guess that's a good thing.

Pete comes up to the track riding Thunder Clouds. He stands him in.

"Congratulations, Pete," says one of the onlookers.

"Thanks, Jose. It was a relief."

"You had that filly in great shape. Outclassed my girl." Sounds like Jose had a runner in the race.

"Thanks, she's been training well lately. I might move her up next time."

"You should, Pete, unless you're selling her." Pete walks off, glancing and smiling at me before moving into a jog. I keep my eyes on him for the entire time he's on the track. He exchanges words with the girl who works on the gap as he leaves and heads to his barn.

I chat with a couple of horsemen during the hour or so that I'm at the track. One trainer asks me to stop by his barn, he has a horse he wants me to advertise. I'd moved a couple of horses for him before, I'm glad that he keeps coming back to me. For these guys, it's easier just to sell to Jake and collect two hundred dollars. But doing the easy thing is not the right thing, and I'm happy I'm making a little more headway with some of these guys.

I leave the track to tour the barns.

As I walk to the second barn I want to visit, I spy Shawn, who comes over to me.

"Hey, Amanda. Good to see you again."

"Shawn, terrible about that trainer. I'm guessing you knew him."

"Yes, of course. I've known Hank for a lot of years. It's all very sad. I'm trying to deal with some issues for him, making funeral arrangements." It hadn't really occurred to me how important a role Shawn plays for the backside community.

"If there's anything I can do to help, please let me know." I don't think I can do much, but it's the right thing to say.

"Thanks. There'll be a memorial service for him on Friday, 1 p.m. in the rec room. Can you tell Pete? I need to see him about it." I guess Shawn knows Pete and I are connected, or at least that we are friends. No harm there, as long as Jake doesn't find out.

"Sounds good. Call me if you need anything." I walk off to my second barn to check on a horse that is advertised on the site. She's been on the site for six weeks now. No one has shown much interest. I want to talk to the connections a little more about her, to see if they can keep her around for much longer. Fillies are harder to move, unless they go into a breeding program, and that's not something I push for horses I work with. The third barn is to see the trainer I had chatted to at the track. I take the required pictures and video of his horse, write down some details, and then head to Pete's barn.

Coming into his barn is different now. I'm no longer wondering if Pete is going to ask me out. As I enter, Pete is in his tack room, chatting on his phone. When he sees me, he hangs up.

"Hey, you." In the privacy of his tack room he comes over to me and kisses me softly on my cheek.

"Good to see you. Good morning?"

"Yes, great morning. Have a doughnut." Pete hands me the doughnut box, with one or two doughnuts left.

"I think I'll pass," I smile. "Thunder Clouds looked good out there today."

"Yes, he's really training well. His ankle is good. I think I might have to find a race for him soon. Can't hold Ray off for much longer."

"I guess. How's your filly?"

"She looked good this morning. A little tired, but Alfie said she cooled out great last night. She ate all her feed, so she's doing well."

"Any word on Spicy Lemon?"

"Jorge came over for a doughnut. He said the horse is doing well. They have a race picked out for him. I forget when he said, but I'll let Sarah know."

"Thanks. Plans later?"

"I was hoping we would hang out."

"Great, me too. I need to do some stuff at my house. How about I swing by your place at seven?" I ask.

"Perfect. I'll book a table at Zucchini's."

I was curious about Harry Mitchell, and wondered if I could find anything about him online. After I finish adding the new horse to my website, I google the track owner. I knew Harry had purchased the track in the mid-1990s so maybe there are some stories about the purchase.

I find two reports of the purchase from the local paper, the *Missionville Times*. I click on the first link, and get a "page not found" error. I click on the second link and run into the same problem. Because they're old internet stories, the website must have moved. I note in my pad to call the *Times* on Monday to see if they have an archive of their stories.

I look at some of the other links from the first couple of pages of results. Harry has a LinkedIn page, which he's hardly updated. It does give a little of his background. He owns a chain of pharmacies, Right Relief, one of which is in Missionville. I think I knew that, but it's good to get it confirmed. Another link is to a news story about an award one of his pharmacies received, about ten years ago. There is also a story about how Harry got started, taking over a pharmacy that his parents ran. He'd been pretty successful to convert that into a local chain, buying out individual drugstores and making them part of the Right Relief brand. Seems like he's a real entrepreneur. I don't get the connection between the pharmacy business and the purchase of the racetrack. Maybe those stories in the local paper will reveal something.

I wonder what Pete knows of Harry. We haven't really discussed him. I undress and get into my shower to get ready. As hot as I can stand it, I shower for a good while. It just makes me feel great afterwards, and I want to be at my best when I get to Pete's. I also plan to stay the night again, I think we're just great together. I've not felt like this about a guy for, well forever. Usually I get bored and disappointed very quickly. Not with Pete. With Pete I feel liberated, challenged, and vital. I get dressed, add a little make-up, and head out.

I arrive at Pete's a little late and we head straight out to Zuchinni's.

When we arrive the host recognizes us. She takes us to a quiet table in the corner of the restaurant. We order drinks.

"Pete, what do you know about Harry Mitchell?"

"Not as much as I should. I know he's owned the racetrack for a good while, before the slots came in, I think. He's in the pharmacy business in some sort of way. He has horses here, and in New York. I know he's a dick."

"Yes, sounds about right." The waiter asks for our order. I ask for the seafood pizza, Pete orders a linguini dish. We also get a bottle of red wine. I continue, "I googled him this afternoon, didn't come up with much more. Do you know anyone who was around at the time he purchased the track?"

"I'm sure I can find a couple of people. It was about twenty years ago." Pete thinks. "Alfie for sure."

"It would be interesting to learn what the thinking was, back then, during the purchase. Were people surprised by it? I really want to understand why

Harry made the purchase. It just seems odd to me. Do you know if he had horses before he bought the track?"

"Honestly, I don't. But I get what you're trying to understand. I'll see what I can find out next week."

"Nice. While we're on the subject of Harry, do you know how his New York horse is?"

"Dancer's Foil? Needs a couple of months off, should be back at the races in early August. Harry will be upset he's missing the Derby. The horse that beat him in the Wood Memorial is the current favorite for the big race."

"Wow, bummer for him, but he's a dick, so I don't care."

"Yes, for sure."

"Oh, before I forget, Shawn wants to talk to you about a memorial service for Hank. Says it's planned for Friday."

"OK, great. I'll catch up with him tomorrow or Monday." We enjoy another wonderful meal at Zucchini's, followed by a long and beautiful night at Pete's.

CHAPTER 25

PETE, FRIDAY

SHAWN HAS ORGANIZED A MEMORIAL SERVICE FOR HANK Fredericks. I imagine it will be well-attended. Shawn asked me to say a few words. I was a little surprised by the request, but also a little humbled. I've thought long and hard about what I want to say, but still haven't figured it out.

I have a busy morning ahead of me, all four of my horses are training. I have a race picked out for Thunder Clouds for next Thursday, so Longman is working him after the break. I've decided not to have James look at his old ankle. We'll race him without the additional vet work. I worry that the ankle can't handle many more injections into the joint. He's training well, so leaving it alone makes sense, for now anyway.

To start the morning, I get my filly ready, and take her up to the track and stand her in.

"Morning, Pete."

"Hey, Jess."

"See you at the service later?"

"Yes, I'll be speaking too."

"That's good. Hank was a wonderful old man. Very sad."

"Yes, tough to have to take your own life." I jog off.

My filly has really come out of her winning race nicely, and the two days she's trained, she's seemed to have improved from where she was, going into her race. Sometimes a win can really pick up a horse. Today she trains great again. I might have to run her back pretty soon.

After getting her and both my geldings out to the track before the break, I head back to the barn at break time to find Longman waiting for me.

"Hey, Pete, all good?"

"Sure. The old guy will be ready in about five minutes."

"No rush. Usual pre-race work?" Normally, for a workout before a race, I like to go a half-mile in about 48 seconds. It's a pretty swift workout, designed to tighten them up for the race.

"Yes, that would be good, half in 48. The guy's been training well, so I'm hoping he gets the half-mile easily."

"Sounds good. I'll be right back." Longman wanders down the shedrow to Mike's side of the barn. He's worked Thunder Clouds two more times since the battery incident. Each time he worked him he did exactly what I wanted him to do. I imagine he'll do the same today. I just don't know what he'll do on race night, but I can worry about that next week.

Five minutes later Alfie has Thunder Clouds in the shedrow. I leg up Longman. Alfie hands the pair off to Jake, who is going to take them to the track, as usual, for the workout. I follow a few paces behind. A number of horses are already circling by the gap, waiting for the track to open. Adam is on one of the horses.

"Hey, see you later at the memorial?" Adam asks.

"Yep. Shawn asked me to say some words."

"Yeah, me too. Hard to think what's best to say. I'm keeping it short."

"Yes, me too. Hope a few others have some kind words."

The track opens, and everyone moves on quickly, wanting to get the best of the freshly harrowed surface.

"Thunder Clouds, half-mile, Jess."

"OK, Pete."

Thunder Clouds works perfectly under Longman, just as I thought he would. They go a half-mile in a little over 48 seconds, with the last quarter coming in at exactly 24 seconds. They gallop out an extra eighth of a mile in 12 seconds. For all his demons, Longman has a great clock. I'm happy.

As Jake goes to pick them up, I text Ray, "Thunder Clouds, 48 and change, galloped out nicely. Should be all set for next Thursday, if we get in."

I wait at the gap for them to return. Longman has a big smile across his face.

"You have this horse in great shape."

"Thanks, Marcus. Nice work. Spot on."

"Good. Look forward to next week." They leave the track and head to the barn. About an hour later, the horse is back in his stall, all cooled out. Alfie had just finished hosing his ankle. I'm bummed that Longman is going to ride him next week. I don't trust him, but my hands are tied. It's what Ray wants. I know I have the old guy in better shape than when I claimed him, so hopefully he will win anyway.

My phone vibrates with a call from Sarah.

"Sarah, news from Harrisburg?"

"Yes, just got off the phone with Steve. He's done some digging."

"And, any luck?"

"There're some suspicions surrounding Harry that date back to his early purchases of the drugstores he owns. Same suspicions when he bought the racetrack. Anyway, are you able to come over on Tuesday, after Amanda visits Owenscreek? Maybe we can all get together again and chat?"

"Yes, I can make that. Cool. Also, Spicy Lemon's in on Monday. Didn't know if you knew."

"Yes, saw that, thanks. Seems like an odd race for him, should be a tough spot, $20,000. We'll see what they do."

"Yes, kind of agree there. Anyway, Jorge says the horse has been doing well. Let's hope he has a safe run for you."

"Fingers crossed. Anyway, see you Tuesday, say around five again?"

"Perfect." I hang up. Interesting, I wonder what Timmins has uncovered. All in good time I guess. Jake comes over to see me. We go into my tack room.

"Pete, you OK for next weekend, take a shipment?"

"A week tomorrow?"

"Yes."

"Sure."

"OK, same time. Tom'll be expecting you."

"Great, thanks."

When Jake leaves my tack room, I text Amanda, "Things are happening. I've a shipment for Tom to take next weekend. x"

She responds almost immediately. "Very good, we can chat about it with Sarah on Tuesday. Good luck at the service, see you later x"

I have a couple of hours to kill before the memorial service for Hank, so instead of heading to the kitchen I take Hairy for a walk at one of our favorite spots. It's a trail about four miles from the track that leads up a pretty steep hill. It's semi-wooded, pleasant, and quite exhilarating – good for clearing the head.

I also thought it would be a good way to really think about what to say at the service. I've never spoken at anyone's memorial, and Hank and I weren't that close. But was anybody really close to Hank, other than Alice? He didn't have any family that I'm aware of. His whole life seemed to have been centered on the Missionville racetrack. He was a jockey for a little while, he set up training in the late 1970s, and was a leading trainer in the 1980s. He had a barn full of horses for a while, then his numbers started to fall off, and his clients started to move on to newer and younger trainers. Times moved on, but Hank really didn't. He was the sort of guy that everyone would have a good word about, but not many really knew him well. He spent most afternoons in the track kitchen, so Alice had become his true good friend.

All this was going through my mind as I try to conjure the right words for my speech. What really bugged me was that Hank's star had fallen so low that he had to sell one of his horses to Jake. He knew what its fate might be, and he was so riddled with guilt when it was confirmed, he ended his own life. There's a message there, but how could I use it without ruining Hank's good reputation? Perhaps it's just something I should avoid entirely. Frankly, I've sold horses to Jake. I knew the risks. I wouldn't do it again, but that doesn't make me any better than Hank – no way.

The walk with Hairy really didn't serve its purpose; by the time I return to the track, I'm still clueless as to what I'm going to say. Almost one o'clock, I leave Hairy in my car and head to the rec room, just adjacent to the kitchen. The place is packed. Hank has brought everybody together. Whatever you think about the backside at racetracks, the community will stick together when it faces adversity, or loses one of its own, as is the case with Hank's death. I seek out Shawn, who is chatting with Adam and a couple of others.

"Hey, Pete," Shawn acknowledges me as I move toward the group.

"Shawn, great crowd!"

"Yes, Hank's been here longer than most. We'll be starting soon. I'll say a few words. Adam will follow, then you, and then we'll open it up to everyone who wants to come forward and speak. I'll close with a prayer." It sounds like a simple and straightforward plan.

"Sounds good. I'll mingle." I move away into the crowd. I spot Alice in the corner on her own.

"Hey, Alice. You OK?"

"No. But it's good to see so many turn out. Good people."

"Yes, half the backside must be here."

"Hank will be proud." Alice looks like she's about to cry.

"Are you going to say something when Shawn opens it up for anyone to speak?"

"I'd like to, but no. He was too special to me, I don't think others would understand." I understand.

"Well I hope you can enjoy the service, like Hank would."

"Thanks." I move on and go to a seat near the back. Shawn goes to the front of the room, and the gathering starts to quiet and sit down.

Shawn's words are beautiful, as you would expect from someone who's had to do this for backstretch workers too many times. He knows how to choose his words, and he knows how to make them very personal to the individual. It turns out that Shawn rode horses for Hank back in the days when Shawn also freelanced as an exercise rider. He shares some light-hearted moments that really revealed some of Hank's personality. During his speech, I glance over to Alice, she is in a flood of tears.

Adam speaks about the respect he had for Hank as a horseman from the old school. How Hank insisted on doing things a certain way, like there is only ever one way to do things when training horses. Adam also talks about how Hank had served as a father figure to him, since his own family is in California and he rarely makes the trip west. Adam does a very good job.

Now it's my turn. I'm still not sure what to say.

"I, like many of you here, knew Hank, just because I'm here. I've been here for fifteen years. Hank had been here much longer. He'd been a part of this community at Missionville for more than thirty years. A jockey, and then a leading trainer.

"It's very sad to acknowledge that his racing stable had dwindled from a barn full of winning horses, to a stable of just two. The same person, with more wisdom and less horses. It's sad to speculate why Hank ultimately took his life. Some will wonder if his business had gotten so bad, that he could think of no other way out. Others might speculate that there was another issue, which we were completely unaware of, perhaps he suffered from depression. *I believe Hank took his life because Missionville had sucked that life right out of him.*"

I pause. Complete silence.

It is what I believed, it's a sentiment Alice has shared with me. I decide to leave my remarks there, and sit down. Shawn looks a little puzzled, but gets up.

"Thanks, Adam and Pete. If others would like to share their stories about Hank, please come forward." Thankfully others do. It would have been a shame for Hank if the remarks were concluded with my message. Backstretch workers who worked for Hank over the years, or just knew Hank as an ever present member of this community, come forward to offer their stories and thoughts. Then Shawn concludes the service with a prayer. It's all over in forty minutes. I depart before I get wrapped up in any small talk.

CHAPTER 26

PETE, MONDAY

AT BREAK TIME ON THE TRACK, JAMES STOPS BY MY SHEDROW.

"All good, Pete?"

"Yes James. I'm entering Thunder Clouds for Thursday, usual pre-race, if he gets in?"

"Sounds good Pete, Bute and Banamine. I guess you didn't want to do any additional vet work?" James is referring to injecting his old ankle with some steroid.

"The ankle's responding well for now. I think we'll run him as he is. Thanks." James walks down to Mike's part of the barn. I've already trained the old horse this morning. He's come out of his final workout nicely. All's looking good for his race, aside from the troubling Longman issue.

With only my filly left to train for the morning, I take my time to tack her up. Sometimes it's better to arrive at the track about ten minutes after the break since the rush to get on the fresh surface is over, it's much quieter. This works well for a filly. We walk up to the track, and pass by a few who are already exiting after their training sessions. I turn her in at the gap.

"Last one, Pete?" Jess asks. She had been preoccupied for most of the time I was at the track before the break.

"Yes, early day hopefully. It'll be nice to get out of here and take Hairy for his walk."

"Enjoy it. I thought your words the other day were a little odd." I had wondered if anyone would pick up on that.

"Yes, sorry. Maybe they were a little out of place. I hope I didn't offend anyone."

"No, I thought they were interesting. You really think this place brought Hank down. Too much for him?"

"I think that some of us get institutionalized. We couldn't survive outside of here. Hank was probably one of those people. He couldn't let go, he saw his star fall, and keep falling. Very sad. Maybe if he had retired ten years ago, it would've been a different story. But what would he do if he wasn't training horses? We all need a purpose in life, I think." I'm rambling, but I was still trying to sort out, in my own mind, what happened to Hank. Some of my struggle is driven by an overwhelming sense of guilt.

"Maybe. It's all very sad."

"It is." With that, I walk away, and jog off to the wire. I wait at the wire for a while and watch a few horses train, while turning over and over again in my mind what had happened to Hank. No matter how I look at it, I can't help but focus on the part that I played in his death. I am thankful that it still hasn't become common knowledge. Eventually I turn my filly to the right, and we gallop a mile and a half.

I return to the barn and put the filly in her stall. Alfie is waiting to take her from me.

"Hey, Boss. Jorge came looking for you."

"OK, thanks." Strange, he has Spicy Lemon in tonight, but I wasn't expecting any race-day updates. I wander over to his section of Mike's barn, at the far end from where my four stalls are.

"Hey, Jorge."

"Senor Pete. I have something for you." Jorge carefully pulls out an object from his coat pocket, lightly wrapped in a swath of cotton. He hands it to me. I can't tell what it is.

"For you. You can test it. From Spicy Lemon this morning," Jorge says in a hushed and quick tone. I put the object in my pocket.

"Thanks," I reply, not sure what I'm thanking him for yet.

"Si, senor. Test it." I walk back to my tack room. I open the cotton wrapping carefully, and there it is, a syringe. Christ! Jorge had got a syringe, I assume used by James, to inject Spicy Lemon this morning. This could be huge.

I text Amanda, "I might have the smoking gun re: Harry. More later x" While pretty vague and silly, I wanted to tell someone something.

Then I realize I need to tell Sarah too. I text, "I think we have our smoking gun. I have a syringe that was used on Spicy Lemon this morning. Will bring over to you tomorrow."

I can't believe what Jorge has pulled off. He had no way of knowing that we were in Harrisburg the other day, and that we were working on a plan to discover what Harry is up to. But he did say he would help me, when we talked about his horse shipping to slaughter. But why would he help us? It can only mean he'll lose his job and likely get deported. But then the why isn't too important right now. I need to preserve the syringe and figure out what we can do with it next. Sarah would know best.

I spend the next hour finishing up with my horses. Jorge's actions have distracted me from Hank's demise. When I'm done, I walk over to the track kitchen with Hairy. Alice puts a couple of sausages on the grill for Hairy, as she prepares my usual sandwich. I buy my *Daily Racing Form*, and head to a table to study it. I want to see what kind of race Spicy Lemon is running in tonight.

It is a conditioned race, for horses that haven't won for six months; the claiming price is $20,000. This is a big step up for a horse that has recently been running, and getting beaten, at the $10,000 claiming level. The handicapper has him listed at 12-1, the fifth choice in a field of seven. A couple of other horses in the race have competed at a higher claiming level, and came close. They appear to be much stronger, on paper, than Spicy Lemon. Anyway, we shall see tonight how the old horse runs. Clearly Sarah can't claim him back for this price.

I finish my sandwich and head to the racing secretary's office to see the draw for Thursday night's races. Thunder Clouds's race is the fifth of the night. He's in the three post in a six-horse field, Longman aboard. I text Ray the details.

I leave to take Hairy for his walk. I'll be back by six o'clock to watch the night's racing. Amanda and I have discussed her joining me during the evenings at the track, but we decided that we shouldn't be seen together too often. It's nice to know, though, that she will be waiting for me at home, after the races are over.

Spicy Lemon is in the third race. I'm not interested in too much else this evening, so I'll keep my night short, and catch up with the other races on the internet when I get home to Amanda. I arrive twenty minutes before the first race.

"Budweiser, Pete?"

"Thanks, Mary." She gives me my bottle of Budweiser and I sit at the bar, reviewing the *Form*. The first race is another maiden race, which is typical. But these are two-year-olds, they're only racing four furlongs. Two-year-old races only begin running in mid-April. They are usually short fields – like most of the races here nowadays – as there are not many two-year-olds around here ready to run. Anyway, the races can be entertaining, as the young runners experience racing for the first time. I go to the paddock to look at the five runners.

They all look small, a couple act up in their new surroundings. Emma has a ride on number four, Princess Pennsylvania. She is a small, wiry filly. I hope Emma has a good neck strap that she can ride off and keep her center of balance. They walk past me before heading out to the track.

"Good luck, Emma."

"Thanks, Pete." She smiles, perhaps a little nervously.

The race itself is quite uneventful, a relief for all. A first time starter from Jim Johnson's barn wins by three lengths. Princess Pennsylvania and Emma come in second, having led the field for most of the race.

The second race is a $5,000 claimer for horses that have not won in six months. The contrast of horses in this race to the first race is considerable. These guys don't have much scope for improvement, but what they have is a lot of experience, which means they walk around the paddock with their heads hung low, going through the motions they have been through many times before. The winner of the race is a ship-in horse from a local training center. The guy who trains the horse hasn't had a winner in over a year. He'll be celebrating tonight, I suppose.

I return to the paddock for the third race, the $20,000 claimer. Jorge leads Spicy Lemon around. The horse looks good in his coat, he's a bright red chestnut gelding, with three white socks. Jorge has him sparkling. Longman is by the saddling stall, in conversation with Mike. I assume they are talking tactics. Jorge then brings his horse over and waits for the call from the paddock judge; then it comes, "Riders Up!"

Longman looks confident aboard Spicy Lemon while they circle the paddock for the final time. They are 10-1 on the board, so the betting public doesn't exactly share that sentiment. Once out of the paddock, Jorge hands his horse and Longman off to Jake, who takes them to the start. I return to Pokers, order a Budweiser, and stay to watch the race on one of the TV screens by the bar.

Longman rides hard for the first part of the race, pushing Spicy Lemon into a three length lead. As they round the turn, two horses start to make a move on him to narrow the margin. When they straighten up in the stretch, Spicy Lemon draws away from his foes and wins rather convincingly. It all looks like a routine win for the track owner and the leading trainer. The horse pays $21.50 to a $2 win bet. I go outside to the rail to watch the horses come back after the race. Jorge glances at me as he leads Spicy Lemon into the winner's circle. He isn't smiling.

CHAPTER 27

JORGE, MONDAY

(TRANSLATED FROM SPANISH)

I KNOW THAT ONE DAY HE WOULD SLIP UP. I COULDN'T HAVE hoped it would be with Spicy Lemon, but sometimes that's how it works. The vet came into my stall, gave my horse a race-day shot, and then as he was putting the syringe into his jacket pocket his phone vibrated. He pulled out his phone, and the syringe fell out from his jacket. He walked out of the stall and didn't realize his mistake. My heart was pounding, but I wanted to do it. I scooped up the syringe with some straw underneath it and carried it out, like I carry out loose droppings. I then wrapped the syringe in cotton and placed it in a bag. I look for Pete, but he was out on a horse. When he comes back I give it to him.

Spicy win tonight. I knew he would. I didn't bet, I didn't feel good about the whole thing. We see what happens next.

CHAPTER 28

AMANDA, TUESDAY

PETE IS GETTING READY WHEN I WAKE THIS MORNING. It had been another wonderful evening, after Pete returned from the track. I'm getting used to enjoying replaying the night's activity in my mind, while watching Pete get dressed.

I turn my phone on to a message.

"Amanda Peters, it's Chad Collins of the *Missionville Times*. Sorry to take so long to return your call about the stories we ran on the racetrack purchase. You can reach me at the paper any day in the afternoons. I'm usually here until around eight." I had called the paper a little over a week ago. I make a mental note to call back after the auction today.

Today is going to be another busy Tuesday. Before I can look forward to our meeting at Sarah's this afternoon, I have some work issues to deal with that have been troubling me. The consulting firm we hired is due to submit a proposal to me this morning; I have a strong feeling that they will recommend closing our branch in Pottstown. I get dressed and leave for work.

Ten o'clock and the consultants' report is on my desk. I have an hour to digest it before heading to the auction. It's a reasonably brief document, full of facts and figures about the performances of each of our branches and the declining foot traffic we are experiencing.

The proposal outlines two choices: to reinvent what a branch experience should be for the bank, or reduce our number of branches. As I suspected, the report recommends the latter, starting with Pottstown. I already knew that the Pottstown branch was our weakest performer. Pottstown has the highest concentration of banks in one town of all the towns that we occupy. My sense is that while closing Pottstown might help relieve our issues in the short term, it doesn't address any longer-term issues. Which branch would then be next, as we slowly decline?

I was more interested in the first choice, reinventing ourselves.

The plan proposes a follow-up meeting in a month, to discuss the findings. In that month, I need to work on a solution that sustains all our branches, and more importantly, the people who have worked for us loyally over the years. It's an interesting challenge.

Time to change and drive over to Owenscreek for the horse auction. Oftentimes I'll be at the horse auction, immersed in my experience there, and voila! I solve a business problem I'm facing at the bank. It happens the other way around too. I might be focused on a banking issue, when I suddenly realize something about the horse industry that hadn't made sense to me before.

Now that it's spring, more and more people come out to the auction to look for their summer project. This is a better time for the horses that are at the sale.

When I arrive, I see a few new faces walking through the back of the barn looking at the collection of horses. Sometimes I'll engage these new purchasers in conversation, especially if they're showing interest in any of the Thoroughbreds. I find six Thoroughbreds at the back of the barn today, thankfully none are already in Tom's kill pen. A couple of teenagers are looking at the Thoroughbreds, I approach them.

"Looking to buy a Thoroughbred?" I inquire of the two young ladies.

"Are they yours?" the red-headed girl responds.

"No, not mine. I just like to keep an eye out for the racehorses."

"Oh, OK. We're both looking for a horse each. A project for when we get out of school."

"Great. Well, hopefully you take a couple of these guys. They're always willing and athletic."

"Yes, we've ridden ex-racehorses before. We want to try to do some retraining, to sell on at the end of the summer," the blonde girl adds.

"Sounds very worthwhile. I hope it works out for you, and of course, the horses." I start moving into the first corral that had three of the Thoroughbreds.

"What are you doing?" asks the red-head.

"I try to identify each of the racehorses, before the sale. Check their tattoos, take pictures."

"Neat, why?" asks the blonde.

"I like to keep on top of where the Thoroughbreds are going, who they are and who buys them."

The red-head frowns, "And if we don't buy them?"

"It depends. Some other private buyers or rescues maybe, but most likely one of the two kill buyers."

"Yes, we kind of knew that. So hopefully we can save a couple from that fate. And then have some fun and make them more useful," the blonde replies.

"I hope you do. The horses will appreciate it." The girls move on to look around at some other horses. I start my task of documenting lip tattoos and taking pictures.

I count 76 horses going through the sale today. The two girls did buy a Thoroughbred each, which is great. Of the remaining four Thoroughbreds, Tom picked up two, Fred took one, and the fourth went to a dealer. Not a good fate for any of those four. I also notice that prices are creeping up. A horse that might have sold for $300 two months ago is now selling for about $450. This is part of the seasonality of the sale, and it thankfully cuts into the margins of the kill buyers.

As I leave the sale I call Chad Collins of the *Missionville Times*. He picks up on the first ring.

"Chad, this is Amanda Peters."

"Amanda, good to catch you."

"I appreciate you calling me back yesterday. Do you have those stories I was referring to in my voicemail?"

"About the purchase of the Missionville racetrack, yes I can get you copies. But I can do better."

"Oh, yeah, what's that?"

"My mother, Margaret, wrote those stories. She always keeps great notes, so she might have additional background."

"Chad that would be great." Wow, that's not what I was expecting.

"Yes, small town newspaper, we've kept it in the family, as it were."

"Can I talk with your mother about the stories, and her notes?" It's probably a bit of a longshot that she's got a good enough memory for this particular story, but you never know.

"She sometimes comes to the office, still helps out a little. I can set it up for you guys to meet here if you like. We only publish three days a week now, so does either Sunday, Wednesday or Friday work for you?" Those are the days before each publishing day.

"Can I get back to you on that?"

"Sure, either way, you'll need to swing by and pick up the copies of the stories."

"Great. I'll call you tomorrow, if that's OK?"

"Sounds good." Chad hangs up. What a stroke of luck that the writer of the stories is still around.

I arrive at Sarah's a little after three o'clock. I smell the coffee brewing as I enter her kitchen.

"Hey, Sarah. Good to see you."

"Amanda, glad you're here. I suppose you heard that Spicy won last night?"

"Yes, Pete told me."

"Crazy, he should never have been able to win that race. Pete says he has a syringe? That's fantastic news."

"Yes, he brought it back to his house. Spicy's groom, Jorge, gave it to him. Pete was pretty stunned by it all."

"Very good. I haven't alerted Timmins yet, I want to see it for myself. You and Pete living together now?" Sarah changes the conversation.

"I've been staying at his place for a few days."

"And? Tell me more. We can talk racetracks, drugs, and horses when Pete gets here."

"What do you want to know?"

"C'mon Amanda, my life is dull. Spice it up for me a little," Sarah smiles.

"He's great. Great to be around, great in bed. Very tender, yet strong. Thoughtful, but knows when to assert himself. Should I be falling in love with this guy? I think I am."

"Wow, that's quick." Sarah hands me a cup of coffee.

"I know, but what the heck. Sometimes you meet the right guy, you get that feeling and you have to run with it."

"Well, I'm very happy for you. You're my best friend, one of my only friends actually. It feels good to me you're doing so well. How's work?"

"That's a bit of a problem right now. I need to figure out a plan for the branches we have, or we'll start closing them, one by one. The consulting firm we had in, left me a report. It's pretty grim."

"I know if anyone can handle a tough situation at work, it's you." Our conversations continue as we finish our coffees and head out to the barn to bring Sarah's horses in and feed them. She's now filled Spicy Lemon's old stall with a two-year-old she has just started training. My guess is he won't see the races until the back end of the year. Sarah is never in a rush with her horses.

A little later, we are back in Sarah's kitchen when Pete arrives.

"Hey, guys," Pete says as he walks through the door. He has a package in his hand, and places it on the kitchen table. "The syringe, used on Spicy Lemon yesterday morning."

"That's amazing Pete. Are we sure it is the same one that was used yesterday on Spicy?" Sarah asks Pete.

"I'm sure James has been injecting some race-day runners. Jorge had no idea I was looking for something like this, so I can't imagine he faked this. Jorge also seems determined to help us, for whatever reasons."

"OK, good. I'll call Timmins in the morning, and let him know what we have. I imagine we can get it tested somewhere and discover the drug they're using. I also assume we can take any fingerprints from the syringe and run them against the track licenses."

I hadn't thought of that. ID'ing the drug is one thing, but tying the syringe directly to James would be very cool. Sarah continues, "Of course, there's nothing we can do about this win, assuming they are not testing for the drug they are using, but if we can determine the drug, they can start testing for it, and then catch them."

"That makes sense, I'll leave it all with you. Your horse ran a crazy good race last night, drawing away from the field like he did. It must have either been the drug, or Longman buzzing him."

"Or maybe both?" I say to Pete and Sarah.

"Sure, why not? What did Timmins have to say about Harry?" Pete asks Sarah.

"Basically, there are suspicions over how he's acquired the capital to make the purchases he has made. He started with one pharmacy, which his parents ran before him, Right Relief, back in Missionville. He then went on a spree of drugstore purchases to build out his chain of pharmacies, which now stands at twelve, all in this area of Pennsylvania. Then he switched and purchased the racetrack."

"So he bought a lot of stuff," Pete ponders.

"But his businesses weren't making the kind of money needed to generate the capital for the purchases, and they were cash purchases, no debt." I was listening to all this, very interested. He must have had a means to make a lot of money off the books. He was using that money to expand his business empire.

Sarah continues, "Then the racetrack purchase just didn't fit into the same type of business he was operating in, obviously, so it raised another red flag."

"Interesting. I checked with a few people on the backside who might remember the purchase. Alfie, my hotwalker, remembers it well. He said there was a lot of relief at the time, many of them thought the track was about to go under."

"Makes sense. The track, at the time, didn't have the casino money, and was a losing proposition, which made the purchase all the more curious," Sarah explains to us.

"Alfie also said that he didn't think Harry had any racehorses in those early days. So he wasn't purchasing because he was already a fan of the sport, a player?"

"This is all good. I followed up with the *Missionville Times* about the two stories that are no longer available online. Turns out the person who wrote them keeps great notes, and she's still around. I need to set up a time to see her, and see what else she may have uncovered?"

"That'll be good. So basically, he made money, off the books, which enabled him to expand his pharmacy businesses, then he purchased a racetrack. What does a racetrack allow him to do?" Sarah questions.

"Launder money?" I suggest.

"What do you mean?" asks Pete.

"Well, let's say Harry is still making money off the books. He needs to 'clean' that money, so it's on the books. A racetrack allows him to do that in multiple ways, either through the casino, which I know wasn't in operation at the time of the purchase, or the horse racing side. He has horses at Missionville with Mike, how many?"

"He usually has about fifteen at any time, I think," Pete replies.

"How does he pay his bills?"

"Cash mostly I think."

"Bingo! He pays his bills in cash. But his betting wins and his purse wins are legitimate, IRS approved." I'm enjoying explaining something to the others. They know horse racing like I know money and banking. "There are plenty of other ways he can convert cash into legitimate receipts, and he probably doesn't lose too much money doing it all, especially with his cheating. The drugs, the use of Longman, the clockers, and whatever else." As I tie it all together, the others pay close attention.

"So we have a theory, reason, and motive. I'll relay all this to Timmins, along with the syringe. See what he has for next steps." Sarah now busies herself around the kitchen, preparing our dinner. Wine is also being poured, Sarah even has a few bottles of Budweiser in the fridge for Pete. "Are you guys staying the night?"

"Yes, I think so, right?" I ask Pete.

"Why not, we can right the wrongs of the world and enjoy doing it." Pete takes a swig from his Budweiser. "Sarah, I have a trip scheduled on Saturday for Tom, taking horses up to Canada."

"Oh good. You up for it?"

"I guess."

"I think all you need to do, for us, is take pictures of each of the EID documents, so we can see who is signing them. Especially those of the Thoroughbreds."

"Sounds easy enough."

"Yes, should be. What route do you take, this side of the border?" Sarah asks.

"I go up 81 mostly."

"OK, I figured that. We need to find a friendly farm along the route, for another time. I'll make some inquiries. I'm thinking we could all meet at the farm, unload the horses, and do some more thorough identifying. You'd be up for a brief stopover Pete, when we sort this out?"

"Sure, Sarah. If I'm to continue driving, it needs to be worthwhile."

"Very good. Dinner's almost ready. Amanda, can you top up the drinks?" I do. We chat about Hank's demise and his memorial. Sarah seems to agree with Pete, Hank had become institutionalized by the racetrack, and couldn't survive doing anything else. Sadly, he couldn't survive any longer at the racetrack either.

A lot of wine is consumed, although I have to admit, Pete is still quite cautious with his own drinking. We retire to bed the other side of midnight, and Pete and I waste no time undressing and enjoying each other.

CHAPTER 29

PETE, THURSDAY

THE OLD HORSE IS IN THE FIFTH RACE TONIGHT, a $15,000 claim-er. It's only a six-horse field, but it's a pretty good group of horses at this level. Thunder Clouds is the fourth choice at 7-1 on the morning line. As is usual with my runners, I had Alfie walk him for half an hour, first thing. He then hosed his bad ankle, and returned him to his stall. The rest of the day will be about relaxing for the old guy and waiting. I had my three other horses to train this morning, and they all go well.

Throughout the morning fellow horsemen wish me luck tonight. It's not because everyone likes me, but because they have a fondness for an old campaigner like Thunder Clouds. In his youth, he was a real runner – he's still respected for that. He's obviously slowed with age, but mostly because of the ankle I've been working on. Still, a war horse is a war horse, and they are all respected. Fingers crossed I can do the old horse justice tonight.

At break time Larry, the state vet, stops by to see Thunder Clouds. Five minutes later he leaves; the horse is racing. There's no way Larry is going to scratch him out of a six-horse field anyway, but the old horse jogged up pretty sound.

I was finishing up my morning chores in the tack room, where Hairy was blissfully snoring away, when my phone vibrates with a call from Sarah.

"Hey, do you have a few minutes or are you busy?"

"No, fire away. Just finishing up at the barn."

"I just got off the phone with Timmins. He wants us to meet him again."

"Great, when?"

"Can you make it early next week, Monday?"

"Sure. Same time?"

"I'll check with Timmins and let you know. We can take the syringe over to him. He was obviously very interested when I mentioned it, tying it to Spicy's win."

"Good. He mention anything else?"

"Turns out that Harry also owns a compound pharmacy. I'm not entirely sure what that is, although I assume they make drugs." Interesting, so he has a means to make his own synthetic drugs.

"Maybe the drugs he's giving the horses, he makes himself?" I try to connect more dots.

"Seems to fit the picture we're developing of Harry," Sarah replies.

"Yes it does."

"OK, will text you about Harrisburg."

"Sounds good." I hang up. This is getting more and more interesting.

As I walk over to the track kitchen, with Hairy, Sarah texts me, "We're on for Monday, 2 p.m. See you outside the building 1:50?"

I reply, "Perfect, see you Monday."

I order my usual sandwich, Alice places a couple of sausages on the grill for Hairy.

"Good luck tonight, Pete. See you've got the old campaigner in."

"Thanks, I'm hopeful he'll run well."

"I'm sure you've got him ready as can be."

"I hope so. You doing OK?"

"I'm OK. I've got to be. I miss Hank, but I've got to keep going." She hands me my sandwich and the two extra sausages. Hairy is waiting expectantly for me to pass his food down, he isn't disappointed, as he wags his tail like crazy.

"Thanks, Alice. See you tomorrow."

As the day goes on, I get progressively more nervous. My nerves are bad enough before an ordinary race, but I have real misgivings that Longman is aboard my horse tonight, but I can't do anything about it. This is what Ray wants, and I had to do the best I can to nurse the horse into this race. His ankle is an additional issue that has me concerned. I decided not to put more steroids into the joint, but I don't know if that's the right decision.

I just want the horse to run a decent race, and come back in good shape. I've grown quite fond of the old guy. I wait in the saddling stall for number three as Alfie leads him around. He looks good, his brown coat is gleaming. He's a good two inches taller than the others.

The valets file out of the jocks' room. Alfie brings the old horse over to be saddled. Thunder Clouds has done this so many times. He just stands there with his ears pricked.

"Good luck, Pete," John, the valet, offers.

"Thanks." John disappears back to the jocks' room as the six jockeys enter the paddock. Longman walks over to me as Alfie takes Thunder Clouds out to turn a few more circles.

"Good luck, Marcus." I didn't see much point in offering any instructions, nor asking Longman what his plan is.

"Thanks, Pete. No worries. I'll make it two for two for you." Longman is referring to back-to-back winners after the filly won the other day.

"Riders up!" comes the call from the paddock judge. I put Longman up on the horse. I don't really have anything to say, but my stomach is in knots. Alfie leads the pair over to the track, Jake picks them up and takes them to the starting gate. I head back to Pokers.

"Here you go, Pete." Mary opens a bottle of Budweiser and hands it to me.

"Thanks, Mary."

"Good luck." I take a few quick swigs of the beer.

"Thanks. I need it."

"You'll be fine, maybe a second win for you."

"I just hope he runs safe." I take another couple of swigs of my beer. I wander over to a corner of Pokers so I could be on my own. I just stare at the TV monitor.

"They're in the gate," the track announcer says, "and they're off!"

Thunder Clouds breaks nicely from the gate. He should, he's done it nearly a hundred times. He lies fourth in the field of six heading down the backside. Longman is just sitting on him, motionless. As they round the turn he's still in fourth, edging just slightly closer to the leaders. I'm just hoping he can keep it going, maybe place, and be safe. I will him on.

Around the turn, at about the quarter pole, I notice it. His tail swishes slightly, and his stride clearly lengthens. The commentator reacts, "And Thunder Clouds is now in a full drive as he sweeps three-wide coming into the straight. Thunder Clouds, who hasn't won a race in over a year, has pulled three lengths clear of the field which has fallen away. It's all Thunder Clouds, five lengths to the good."

I don't know what to do. A couple of people come over to me to congratulate me. A high-five here, a slap on my back there. I need to get out of Pokers and see my horse. I know exactly what Longman did. I go outside, more congratulations are offered as I walk down to the rail, by the winner's circle. Alfie is leading the horse. Thunder Clouds looks completely stressed out, bug-eyed, veins bulging out of his head and neck, blowing harder than a freight train. I glance at Longman, who has a grin on his face that says to me, "See, it's up to me, and I decided to win the race." I give the horse a pat, try to chill him out a little. Alfie doesn't have his usual grin after a win. He knows.

"Easy game, Pete." Longman says to me, walking into the winner's circle. "Two for two, you're looking good."

I don't know what to say. I don't want to repeat my performance after the first battery episode. We take the win photo, then I text Ray, "Thunder Clouds did it. Won easily."

I then text Amanda, "The old guy won, they screwed us. x"

Ray texts me back, "Good job Pete. Job well done." I imagine he bet in Vegas.

Amanda texts me back, "Very sorry. x"

I go back to Pokers.

"Nice win, Pete. Budweiser's on me."

"Thanks, Mary. I just need to think." Mary looks at me, probably puzzled by my response, but leaves me alone. I go to a quiet table in the corner. I'd let them plug the old horse in. I knew they were going to do it. I did nothing about it. I've never seen a horse come back after a race and look so freaked out. Damn.

CHAPTER 30

AMANDA, FRIDAY

I ARRIVE AT THE MISSIONVILLE TIMES OFFICE, JUST OFF THE main street in Missionville, at six. I have a meeting scheduled with Margaret Collins, Chad's mother. As I enter the office I'm greeted by a number of posters and pictures on the wall of the reception area. They showcase awards and front pages of major stories that the paper has published over the years. It's an impressive display. The front covers from the 70s, 80s and 90s document some of the major events that have occurred in our town, including Missionville's victory in the Little League World Series in 1973 and the closing of the mining plant in 1987.

"Hi. I'm Amanda Peters, I'm here to see Margaret Collins," I say to a young man behind the desk.

"Amanda, right on time. I'm Chad, we spoke on the phone." Chad shakes my hand. "I'll just go and get my mother." I sit down and continue to admire the wall displays. The paper must have been a substantial enterprise back in the day. I only know it as a free paper that I sometimes pick up from the gas station.

An older lady comes into the reception area.

"Hello, Amanda, I'm Margaret, won't you follow me. I've got about twenty minutes, I need to help Chad get tomorrow's paper proofed." I follow her and we retreat to an office behind the reception area. The office includes more wall displays highlighting the storied past of Missionville. One cover story, in particular, catches my attention, "Mining company cited for pollution and corruption."

"That's an impressive display of news stories you have," I comment, as I return my gaze to the mining story.

"Yes, that story took me six months of research and investigation. We ended up exposing some really nasty issues, corruption and deliberate pollution. It led to the mine closing six months later. Unfortunately it also meant a big loss of local jobs. There was a time when we were an important media organization. We did real investigative news stories. I ran this newspaper with my husband for more than thirty years. Sadly he's passed."

"I really didn't know much about your newspaper," I confess, even though I'm impressed.

"Yes, sadly we've seen our business dwindle in recent years. We had a daily circulation of more than fifty thousand. Now we publish three days a week, and only have a ten thousand circulation. We're now a free paper, as you know. We don't have a substantial online presence. People really don't read newspapers like they used to."

"It's a tough business to be in. I'm in banking and we're struggling too."

"Yes, I know. You run the Susquehanna Bank system." Interesting, she's done some background research on me.

"Yes, and our business is getting eaten by big banks and online banking, probably similar to your experiences."

"Makes sense. Anyway, it's very nice to meet you. I remember writing those stories about the racetrack purchase. I remember them well. And I remember Harry Mitchell." The tone of her voice suggests she doesn't have particularly fond memories.

"When I first heard about the purchase I was excited. I knew Mitchell's parents. They'd run the Right Relief pharmacy here in town for a lot of years. Nice people, who always supported the community. Harry took over their business, and it seemed like he had been very successful, buying up a dozen or so pharmacies in other towns." This was all making sense, based on what I already knew. "I'd planned to write a story about Harry, a local entrepreneur, who's done very well. Given the economic climate at the time, it was supposed to have been a feel-good story, kind of bucking the local trend, what with the mine closing, and everything else. But to write that story, I needed to interview Harry, and I needed answers to a couple of key questions."

"Fascinating," I interrupt.

"When I sat down with Harry I immediately knew he was not the person I'd hoped he would be. You can just tell, you know. He wasn't like his family at all. He was also very evasive when I started asking specific questions, and they were simple questions like, 'How were you able to expand your pharmacy business?' and 'Why have you decided to expand your business interests into horse racing?' There was nothing I could find at the time to suggest that Harry had any previous interest in the racetrack here at Missionville. I don't think he'd even attended the races. The purchase didn't make a lot of sense. And he couldn't answer either of those questions convincingly. It was almost like he was unprepared."

"Did you keep pushing?"

"I did, and Harry got pretty upset with me, but his vague answers just weren't good enough. Anyway, he ended the interview early, and the articles I wrote were basically fluff pieces, nothing like what I wanted to write."

"Do you have any thoughts about how he's been successful, and why he bought the track?" Margaret was clearly a smart reporter in her day. If she was capable of closing down the mining plant with all her work and research, surely she had a good hunch about Harry.

"I do. I think the guy's a crook. He makes large sums of cash, through some kind of dodgy business. He used that cash to buy out local pharmacies, then decided he needed a business he could use to launder money." Bingo! We think the same way. "I even wrote something to that effect in my notes. But I decided not to pursue it for a story. Frankly, no one at the racetrack was interested in me exposing Harry. They were just excited someone wanted to bail them out. At the time, the purchase made no sense at all. The racetrack had kept reducing its purses because their betting handle was in a free fall. Horsemen were leaving and going to other racetracks where they had a better chance of making money. Of course Harry got lucky, the slots turned his money laundering enterprise into a place where he could generate real money. But at the time of the purchase, slots weren't even a consideration." Margaret was recalling the time as if it were yesterday.

"This is all really good."

"There's a story there, probably still worth pursuing."

"It's why I contacted you. Something's not right with the racetrack, and what's going on over there. Everything you've told me backs up what I've been learning."

"Good, I'm glad to help. I was sad to learn about Hank Fredericks."

"Yes, it was shocking. Did you know him?"

"Sure. We used to cover horse racing in the eighties. Hank was a leading trainer. He was always worth a good quote. I really liked him. Of course we lost touch when we stopped covering racing, shortly after Harry purchased the track. It's a shame, I always enjoyed going to the races. What happened to Hank? The radio just reported a death at the track and gave his name."

"Suicide. He hung himself in his tack room."

"Oh no! That's not the Hank I knew. He was happy-go-lucky, and very successful. Things must have gotten really bad for him."

"He was down to a two-horse stable, and no clients. Things were grim." I didn't want to add the part about him selling a horse for slaughter.

"Sad. Well, I need to get back with Chad and get tomorrow's paper finalized. If you guys have something on Harry, maybe we could work together. I still like the investigative work, even though the paper no longer does that kind of reporting. I also have connections at larger newspapers like the *New York Times*. Might be helpful."

"Great. I'll be in touch. You have been very helpful." I get up to leave. Margaret looks right at me, "Harry's no good. I wish you luck, please let me help if you need anything."

"I will."

I get to Pete's a little before seven o'clock. Hairy is waiting for me, his tail wagging his glee as I open the door to let him out. Pete has had a tough day at the barn today. He'd texted me about Thunder Clouds, who hasn't come out of his race very well. His ankle is now very large. Pete also has a long weekend ahead of him, shipping horses to Canada for Tom.

I want to make tonight special for him.

I've planned a lovely dinner. I haven't done much cooking over the years, the result of being mostly single. But I do enjoy cooking when I have the chance. Pete always enjoys a good meal. I also bought a couple of nice bottles of wine, and some of Pete's beer. Pete is planning to be home by eight o'clock. He wants to spend some time at the races, but isn't going to stay to the end.

With the food in the oven, I go upstairs to take a nice long, hot, shower. It's the best way to restart a day, to feel fresh and ready for a new beginning. I was planning to make sure that Pete really wants me tonight, not that I've had to try very hard before. But sometimes it feels so good to know that someone really desires you. That's what I want.

And that's what I got. When Pete arrived, I had the dinner on the table, with a bottle of Budweiser opened for him, and my glass of wine poured. I was sitting, naked, at the kitchen table. We enjoyed the evening.

CHAPTER 31

PETE, SATURDAY

THIS TIME I DIDN'T WAKE UNTIL MY ALARM WENT OFF. Amanda's insatiable appetite for sex is something I haven't experienced before. When I got home last night she was waiting for me, naked. She made me eat my dinner, slowly, and engage in normal conversation, just as if she were fully dressed. The dynamic was crazy. Once the meal was over, she casually cleared the table, put everything in the dishwasher, and then laid on the table. I can still see the look in her eyes when she said I could do anything I liked with her. It was an amazing night.

Amanda appears to be in a deep slumber. I creep out of bed.

"What time is it?" Guess she wasn't asleep.

"Just after five. Go back to sleep."

"Why? I want to watch you get ready."

"Last night was wonderful," I sigh, leaning over to kiss her.

"Yes, I think we're great together. I wanted last night to be special, for you." She gets out of bed, still naked, and walks slowly to the bathroom.

"What time are you heading to Tom's?" Amanda raises her voice from the bathroom.

"I said I'd be there at eleven. I'll try to get there a little earlier again, I think."

"I'll miss you tonight." I'd be staying over in Quebec, before driving back tomorrow.

"Yes, I'll miss you too!" Although some extra sleep might be a good thing

I suppose. "I'm heading to the track, I'll see you over there a little later."

"See you later."

I arrive at the barn at six o'clock as usual. My four horses are waiting to be fed, their heads hang over their stall webbings. As I prepare their breakfasts in the feed room, I can hear them getting a little restless, which is always a good sign. A couple of minutes later they are busy eating their food. Nothing will distract them now for the next few minutes. I pull off each of the horses' leg wraps, leaving Thunder Clouds's to last.

Yesterday I poulticed his two front legs. His ankle on the right front leg is very sore and swollen after his last race. I'm really not sure what we can do for the old guy, but I'll need to wait a few days before making any decisions. I'm sure that Longman buzzing him made him run harder on his legs than he could handle. Now I'm left to pick up the pieces.

I start mucking stalls as I wait for Alfie to arrive at seven. He is punctual as usual.

"Alfie, can you cover again for me tomorrow? I'll ask Jorge too."

"Sure, boss. For the day, right?" Alfie is referring to my brief disappearance the last time I took a day off.

"Yes, this time only for Sunday. Can you take care of Thunder Clouds first thing, hose off his poultice and walk him?" I'm now referring to this morning's work.

"Sure, boss. Do you want me to hose that ankle afterwards for fifteen minutes?"

"That'll be great." I go to the tack room to get the tack for my filly. I only have three to ride this morning; I want to try to leave early, so I can get Hairy walked before I head over to Tom's place.

Ten minutes later I'm on the racetrack.

"How's the old man, Pete?"

"He's OK, Jess. Some aches and pains after the race." There's no need to say too much about his condition.

"He ran an amazing race for you. Like a three-year-old again."

"He did, thanks." People are genuinely happy to see the old guy run so well. No one seems to be suspicious that he won so easily.

"You're on a roll. Maybe she can help keep your win streak going." Jess is referring to the filly I'm on. She is still training well after her win and seems to be improving.

"Fingers crossed!" I walk off. Amanda is on the rail. I smile in her direction and then trot back to the wire. The few days after a win, everyone who sees me for the first time congratulates me. It makes me feel good, even though I know in this case we cheated, and the horse might have been ruined as a result. Although Longman planned it, Ray must have been in on it. My choice was either to go with it, or lose all my horses. Hanging around here for the next couple of months might prove worthwhile, so keeping the horses is important.

The filly trains nicely again. So do my other two geldings. Before I leave the barn, I find Jorge and ask if he can help out tomorrow while I'll be out.

"No problem, I help. Everything else good?" Jorge probably wants to know what I've done with the syringe.

"Yes. Will give you an update soon. OK?"

"Very good, I can help." We are on the same page. Jorge is one of the real good guys around here, for sure.

I return to my shedrow, where Amanda is waiting.

"Hey, Pete."

"Amanda." We walk into my tack room, Hairy stops snoring and looks up at us, then he lays his head back down. I kiss Amanda passionately.

"It's great to see you," Amanda says.

"You too. Are you OK to look after Hairy, stay in the house?"

"No problem. I'm going to go home, get some work done, then I'll be over."

"Awesome. I'll text you tonight when I get settled into a motel."

"Take care of yourself. Can't wait to see you tomorrow."

"You too." Amanda leaves. I clean a bit of tack, and then head out. I skip the kitchen, and instead take Hairy for a nice long walk.

I get to Tom's at about a quarter to eleven. Like last time, there are many horses, in many small paddocks, all huddled around, munching on large, round bales of hay. It's just a depressing sight when you understand the reality of the situation.

I don't see Tom when I arrive, so I head to the house and knock.

"Yes, come in." It's Tom. "Pete, good to see you, a little early again. I need another ten minutes to get all the paperwork in order for you."

"No worries, I'll hang out outside." Good, I'd hoped to be able to take a look at the load before we herded them into the stock trailer. The set-up is the same as last time. The truck and trailer are backed up against the large barn. The horses are loose in the barn, thirty of them.

I take out my phone and pull up the camera. I switch it to video and record the complete scene. Then I switch back to the still camera to take pictures of the horses that look like Thoroughbreds. There are six of them. The whole time, I try to be very discreet. If Tom, or anyone else who might be here, sees me taking pictures, I'll be in big trouble. They don't. My phone is back in my pocket and I'm idly watching the horses when Tom comes out of his house.

"Here's the paperwork for this load. Same as last time. This paperwork is for the border." Tom hands me some papers, "and this paperwork is for Quebec." Tom hands me a stack of EIDs, needed for the slaughterhouse. "Put them all in the cab, so you know where they are, then we'll load this lot." Tom glances over to the forlorn horses. Ten minutes later I pull out of Tom's driveway, a ten-hour trip in front of me.

The long drive means that I have to pull over at a gas station a little over halfway, while still in New York State. It's a quick stop, and a good time for me to take pictures of each of the EID forms. This is all I need to do for this trip, other than deliver these horses to their death. I photograph each document carefully. I need to make sure that the signatures are readable. Of the thirty forms, eight are signed by Jake Jenkins. Six of those eight signed forms are for Thoroughbreds.

Two hours later, I come to the border crossing into Canada. I pull up to the security booth and hand over the necessary paperwork. The border official gets out of his booth and wanders up and down the trailer, peering inside. The horses are crammed together, so there's no chance that he's doing a visual inspection. He counts the number of horses, and matches that number to the papers. He puts a seal on the back of the truck. The seal number is placed on the paperwork for the slaughterhouse. The truck is to remain sealed until I arrive at the plant. He lets me through; the whole thing takes less than thirty minutes.

I arrive at the slaughterhouse, in the village of Massueville in Quebec, at 9:45 p.m. I go over to the office to hand in the paperwork. I'm instructed to unload at corral four. The guy in the office comes out with me to help me unload my stock. I back the trailer close to the corral. The guy breaks the seal on the back of the trailer, and we drop the ramp. The horses spill out into what is nothing more than a large round pen. There are plenty of squeals and bucks from a few of the horses. A few look like they have already accepted their fate. They will all be slaughtered on Monday. I'm at the slaughterhouse for less than thirty minutes. I head back towards Montreal and stop at the first motel on my route. After checking in I text Amanda.

"Long day. Horses delivered. EIDs documented. Jake signed 8. Checked in to motel x"

Amanda messages back almost immediately, "Sleep well. Hairy is chilled. Can't wait to see you tomorrow. X"

CHAPTER 32

PETE, MONDAY

I ARRIVE OUTSIDE THE OFFICE IN HARRISBURG AT 1:45 P.M., as planned. Sarah is waiting for me as I step out of my car.

"How was your Canada trip?"

"Exhausting and stressful, but I got it done." I take out my phone, and pull up the photo gallery and hand it to Sarah.

"If you swipe backwards, you'll see all the EID forms. You'll see a number of signatures are Jake Jenkins's. That's the pony guy." Sarah studies the images for a few moments.

"Great job. This may be very useful." Sarah continues, "So today we have the syringe for Timmins and we'll get an update from him regarding what he's learned about Harry."

"We should also tell him about Amanda's conversation with the reporter at *Missionville Times*. I'm guessing what she said will match a lot of what Timmins has learned. He needs to know she kept notes for the stories that she wrote of the racetrack purchase."

"Yes, agreed."

"I'd also like to show him Thunder Clouds's race, if we have time. I want him to see what it looks like when a jockey plugs one in."

"How's your horse?" Sarah really can't stand Longman.

"Unfortunately his ankle is bad. Tomorrow I plan to get James to take a closer look." Which I guess is a little ironic, since we're here today in part to implicate James in a conspiracy to defraud.

We walk into the building and up to Timmins's office. Timmins welcomes us.

Once in his office, Sarah places a package on his desk.

"The syringe I mentioned on the phone last week," Sarah explains.

"Very good. Remind me how you acquired it?"

"A groom of Mike's, Jorge, gave it to me, shortly after James Norwood injected Spicy Lemon, a runner of Mike and Harry's, who raced that night and won," I answer.

"And how was this groom aware you were looking for such a thing?" Timmins asks. "Seems a little coincidental." He is right.

"It's a bit of a coincidence. But we've had other conversations about some of the goings on in their barn. Jorge seems to be frustrated by it all. He obviously knew this was a problem, and took action when he could." I explain it the best way I can.

"I see. Very good. I can get the syringe tested at our lab. We'll try to identify the drug, and see if there are usable fingerprints. It might take two to three weeks if we find something, shorter if we don't. I've already requested that we save some of Spicy Lemon's blood and urine from that race, so we can test it later when we know the drug."

"Makes sense. Should be helpful right?" I ask Timmins.

"Very. But we cannot directly tie the syringe to that horse, for that race, obviously. What we could do is, if we identify the drug, we could then test for it in the future, to catch them. We might also be able to verify if Spicy Lemon was also, in fact, drugged for that race. It might be more complicated than that, I'll have to really think things through."

"What's the complication?" Sarah asks. I'm curious too.

"Ideally we'd like to just catch them in the act, after a race. But if we have a fingerprint of Norwood, we might need to go after him, and because of that, he would obviously no longer be drugging the horses on race day. Kind of a catch-22. But maybe we don't have to do that. I just need to figure things out." This is more complicated than I thought.

"Either way, this is very good. Jorge has done us a huge favor," Timmins continues. And he has. I need to make sure he knows how important this might be.

"So I did some digging on Harry," Timmins changes track. "It seems that his business dealings have alerted the feds in the past. I have a friend at the local FBI office here in Harrisburg who was looking into some of his purchases." I'm listening.

"He took over his family business, the Right Relief pharmacy in Missionville. It had been successful for a number of years, but was a small-time pharmacy. Soon after Harry took control, he was able to purchase a similar drugstore in a neighboring town. It was a cash purchase. He then repeated the same for a number of other pharmacies in the area. All cash purchases. But there was no understanding as to where the cash was coming from. Harry then bought the racetrack, much of which was financed by cash. He also owns a compound pharmacy. Unfortunately my friend at the FBI wasn't able to really pin anything on Harry, mostly because he's under-resourced, not because he doesn't think Harry had done anything wrong."

"This matches a lot of what we've learned from a reporter at the *Missionville Times*. You might want to contact them. Margaret Collins kept notes for the stories she wrote about the racetrack purchase. She had suspicions," I tell Timmins.

"I'll call them, thanks." He makes a note.

"The guy generates a lot of cash through his business interests, and needs to bury that cash somewhere, so the feds don't get a hold of him?" I ask the question while making a statement.

"It seems to be something like that. And the compound pharmacy could be used to make illegal drugs, as well as legal prescriptions. That's where the racetrack connection could help us, and the feds, solve the case."

"How do you mean?" Sarah asks.

"If we can identify a fingerprint on that syringe and tie it to the vet, we might be able to get the vet to turn on Harry, and establish the source of the drug. If it turns out to be the compound pharmacy that Harry runs, that could lead to his other businesses." It makes sense, and Timmins sounds pretty enthusiastic about it.

"This sounds promising," Sarah observes. "What are the next steps?"

"There's not much to do until we get the lab report on the syringe. That's the crucial piece of evidence that could make or break the case we're building. As soon as I hear something I'll call you. In the meantime I'll contact the *Missionville Times*." Timmins is closing our meeting, but I had something else I want to discuss.

"Do you have a TV monitor where we can watch a race from Missionville?" I inquire.

"Sure, we can go into the conference room and set things up. Which race do you want to show me?"

"The fifth race last Thursday night, the one I won with Thunder Clouds. I want to watch the race with you so I can show you how it looks when a horse gets plugged in." I want Timmins to know that Longman is happily running the show as far as races are concerned, plugging in horses when he chooses to do so.

"OK, any chance you have the battery he used?" asks Timmins.

"Sadly, no. I know this is only conjecture on my part, but I thought you should see."

"Follow me, we'll set it up." We move to the conference room; five minutes, later the race is ready to be shown.

"OK, before we run the tape, just watch Longman and my horse carefully. Longman is very relaxed on him down the backside, not making any kind of move, which is good. Midway around the far turn you will see my horse's tail pick up, swish a couple of times, then the horse accelerates, basically running at a perceptibly faster pace, all the way past the wire." Timmins and Sarah are listening to me carefully. I ask Timmins to play the race. It's more obvious to me in hindsight, and I hope my explanation before showing the race makes it obvious to Timmins.

"Wow, I heard about Longman, but since I never use him, I've paid little attention. Something definitely happened around the quarter pole," Sarah says to both of us.

"It does seem so," Timmins adds. "Still not sure what I can do without the physical evidence, but I'm a believer." That is good enough for me, for now. A few minutes later we are back in the parking lot.

"A very good meeting, Sarah."

"Things seem to be coming together. Thanks to Jorge."

"Yes, and he said that Spicy Lemon is doing well after his win last time. Although I'm sure all that is very frustrating for you."

"As long as he's doing well, I'm happy for now. It's when he stops doing well that I'll worry. Thanks for keeping an eye on him for me."

"No problem. Better be heading back." We part.

I sit in my car for a minute and text Amanda, "Great meeting with Timmins. If the syringe comes up trumps we could do some real good here x"

I begin the drive back to Missionville.

It has been an interesting few weeks, and this meeting only reinforces that

Harry is central to all that is wrong with Missionville. It also seems that we have a chance to blow up his broader business activities, something the feds have been unable to do. It wouldn't surprise me if his cash business is drug-related. It makes sense given his drugstore background, and the fact that he also owns a compound pharmacy. I wonder what other drugs he produces, and for which markets?

We were lucky that Jorge got the syringe, there's no escaping that. Sometimes, hard work needs a little luck to move things forward. Jorge knew what he was doing, and seems to want to help fix things. I wonder if he knows more. I need to have a longer conversation with him.

The slaughter issue is something else entirely. While it's important for us to continue to pursue that angle, based on the fraud in the system – how could Jake possibly know the drug regimen of the eight horses for which he signed those EIDs? – the issue wouldn't be of any interest to the Pennsylvania Racing Commission, which is why Sarah and I chose not to address it with Timmins. We want to keep him focused on issues he can address with some level of passion. The enthusiasm he displayed during our meeting suggests we made the right decision. Sadly, the slaughter problem is just too toxic for any racing body to address head on.

While I know my training career is nearly over, I feel liberated that I can try to help do something more important. And then there's Amanda. Life is really good. She'll be waiting for me when I get home.

CHAPTER 33

AMANDA, SATURDAY

FIRST SATURDAY IN MAY

SINCE I RECEIVED THE CONSULTANTS' REPORT I HAVE BEEN spending more and more time trying to develop a plan that will sustain all the branches at the bank. Why not? Either I succeed at that, or realize that the Susquehanna Bank will eventually fold into another bank and disappear.

But today is my day at the track, so my focus is back on the racehorses. Then Pete and I are going to head to Jessup's and watch the Kentucky Derby. With Harry's horse on the shelf, the horse that just beat him, Northern Peaks, is the favorite for the big race. Pete tells me he's been training well in the lead up, and had a dazzling workout earlier this week.

Pete is getting ready to head out to the barn. It's crazy how things are working out between us. He's like a new guy, with his energy and enthusiasm for going after Harry. He knows the consequences of his actions will end his career, but he's determined to help. I really like that. He isn't worried about the future, just the here and now, and how wrong that here and now is. He's also a terrific lover, and I love the mornings after, when I just watch Pete get ready for work. Pete has suggested I should move in permanently. I've spent one night at my house since we got back together. Things are right between us, so what the hell?

"I'll see you at the track," Pete says to me, as he leaves the bedroom.

"See you soon." I roll out of bed. I'm awake now, so I might as well get ready. A good long hot shower makes for a great start to the day. I don't have a plan for the racetrack this morning. I'll just grab a coffee, head up to the track and watch for an hour. I am curious about Jorge, I want to find an excuse to meet him.

I arrive at the track at around seven. It's getting much lighter in the mornings now. The dark and cold winter months are behind us, we're running headlong into summer.

I grab a coffee from the kitchen. Alice is busying herself setting things up for the day. We exchange our usual short greetings. Hank's suicide has definitely been very hard on her, even now I can tell she has lost a piece of herself. We've never been close, but after doing the same thing every Saturday for a couple of years, you pick up on these things.

I walk up to the racetrack. The mood is very upbeat. While we are a long way from Churchill Downs in terms of the type of racing we have here at Missionville, the horsemen still enjoy the big races. The Kentucky Derby is the biggest, as far as I could tell, and it seems that today everyone has an opinion. And that opinion appears to be evenly divided between those who think that Northern Peaks will win easily, and that his final workout was similar to Barbaro's before his Derby win, and those who think that Northern Peaks will be defeated, because his final workout was too fast.

An hour or so later, I leave the track and wander from barn to barn. I spot Shawn, who is doing much the same thing as me, making himself visible to the backstretch community.

"Hey, Amanda. Who's your pick?"

"Not my expertise really. I'll go for the favorite. You?"

"He's been looking good coming up to the race. I have some dates for the banking program to run by you. How do the final three Saturdays in June look?"

"I'm sure they're good. If you don't hear back from me in the next 24 hours, assume I'm in."

"OK, very good. It was a success last time, as you know. I love these programs that broaden the lives of our community."

"You do great work." Missionville is a much better place thanks to Shawn.

We go our separate ways. I admit, I really enjoy teaching the banking program. It's pretty basic stuff, but I know it makes a material difference to those who attend. The bank gets a few new accounts too.

Finally, I head to Pete's barn, which is now always my last stop on my

Saturday mornings. Pete is in Thunder Clouds's stall, wrapping his legs.

"Hey, Pete. How's the old guy?"

"Not good, unfortunately. I had James take a look, and he just thinks we need to put some steroids in the ankle, and run him back soon, on the drop. The old me might have gone that route. Not now."

"I like that."

"Our options for him are limited. Anyway, no need to worry about it today. How's your morning been?"

"All good, lots of chatter about the Derby. Not much else." I look down the shedrow, in case I spot Jorge, although I wouldn't really know if I spotted him. "Jorge, is he around? I'd like to meet him."

"Do you think that's wise? For now anyway?" Pete is right of course. We all need to remain low profile. But I am really interested in who this guy is. Without him, we wouldn't be as likely to be able to nail Harry.

"You're right, can't help being curious though."

"I am right. I've got about a half hour's work left here. Want to meet back at my house for lunch? I'll grab something for both of us on my way home."

"Sounds good."

We get to Jessup's at a little after four. I know it's not too smart to be seen together in public, but we don't do it too often. And today is Derby day, and we want to enjoy the festivities of the occasion. Pete assured me Jessup's would be hopping and when we arrive it is already packed.

"Budweiser and wine?" Charlie asks.

"Thanks!" we respond in unison.

"Made your picks?"

"Just watching, but ready to enjoy the race. You?" Pete asks Charlie.

"Northern Peaks. Just looked terrific in that final prep." Charlie gives us our drinks.

"You might be right, but 3-1 in a twenty horse field, seems like slim odds," Pete observes.

"We shall see." We move away from the bar as Charlie starts getting drinks for another customer. Pete seems to know half the people at Jessup's, and directs me over to a table that includes three others.

"Hey, Jorge," Pete greets one of the three, who is apparently Jorge.

"Senor Pete, good to see you. You know Javier and Martha." They all nod to each other.

"Jorge, this is my friend Amanda. Amanda, this is Jorge." I want to be discreet, but Pete makes it clear to me that this is the Jorge I want to meet.

"Jorge, nice to meet you. You look familiar?"

"Si, Ms. Peters. You taught the banking class. We all attended." Javier and Martha smile as Jorge makes the connection.

"Sure, I recognize you, all of you. Nice to see you again."

"It was a great program. We all bank with Susquehanna now. Gracias. You join us?" Very cool, this is what life should be about. Doing little things, helping people. Pete and I pull up chairs to hang out with the group. The next hour passes quickly as we chat about who we like for the Derby, and more.

Jorge seems like a genuinely decent guy, as do his friends. All three of them are so easy going. They'd all been at Missionville for a little more than two years. They're from the same home state in Mexico, just trying to do the best for their families. They all work for Mike and use their Susquehanna Bank accounts to send money home to their families every two weeks. Pete is generous ordering the drinks for the group and some nachos. As Pete said, it's the least he could do after Jorge bailed him out when he disappeared for a few days.

Post time for the Derby is approaching, the horses are now in the paddock. Charlie has turned up the volume on the TV screens, and turned off the jukebox. Chatter amongst groups dies down now. Everyone is focused on the TV.

Northern Peaks looks exceptional in the paddock, which most people in Jessup's note. He is a steady 3-1 on the board. Winning the Wood Memorial makes a horse a leading contender for the Derby, along with the winners of the Florida Derby, the Arkansas Derby and the Santa Anita Derby. But the way the horse has trained since the Wood Memorial makes him a standout. The Florida Derby winner, Holy Way, and the Santa Anita Derby winner, Frog's March, are both listed at 6-1. The rest of the field are 8-1 or higher.

Pete goes to the bar for another round of drinks. Everyone is listening to the TV commentary, some responding to the comments. There's no doubt that many in the crowd at Jessup's think Northern Peaks will be a convincing winner today. His final workout is replayed on the TV screen, and the commentator acknowledges that no horse since Barbaro in 2006 has worked as impressively during his final workout. Even I know how Barbaro was able to destroy his Kentucky Derby field, before being tragically hurt in the Preakness.

The horses are loading in the gate. This is my first time watching the Derby among horse racing people, and the atmosphere is incredible. I don't have a pick, but I'm guessing I'm rooting for the favorite. I know it's the horse that Pete likes.

Twenty horses break from the gate and charge down the straight for the first time. Northern Peaks is sitting in third place, two horses wide, as they enter the first turn. It looks like a promising position, and the commentator says so. He then rattles off the names of the other seventeen runners, which I thought was an incredible feat. By the time he finishes, the horses are moving onto the backside. Northern Peaks holds his position, he is just on the outside of Holy Way. A longshot is in front of them both. They raced the first half-mile in 46 seconds, which is apparently quite quick when they have to go a mile and a quarter.

As they move into the far turn, the front runner starts to weaken. The rider on Northern Peaks lets him run up to the lead. A few at Jessup's start urging him on vocally, one or two think they've moved too soon. I just keep staring at the screen. The horse appears to be getting stronger and stronger, and there doesn't seem to be much behind him ready to take on the challenge. As they hit the homestretch, Northern Peaks is four lengths in front, and then draws off to a six-length lead.

The commentator is almost shouting now, "And it's all Northern Peaks, in a sublime performance," as the colt crosses the wire, all alone. It's an incredible performance to witness, if only from a TV screen.

Pete leans into me, "Durkin said the same thing when Barbaro crossed the wire in front." I don't know who Durkin is, but Pete seems impressed with the commentator's choice of words.

CHAPTER 34

PETE, MONDAY

(THREE WEEKS LATER)

MY STABLE IS NOW DOWN TO THREE HORSES, SINCE ONE OF THE geldings I trained for Ray has been claimed from us. Ray has his eye on a couple of new horses to claim, so it won't be long until I'll be back up to four horses. Thunder Clouds has taken a while to recover from his last race. But he is sound now, or at least 'racing sound.' Ray is keen to run him again; thankfully Longman hasn't been around to see what's going on with the horse. I assume he's not so keen to ride him back. That fits the same pattern of a year ago: ride once and win, and then let others toil with the horse for a while. Frankly, Thunder Clouds needs to be retired. Sarah has offered a spot for him on her farm. I've just got to convince Ray.

The filly won another race for us last week. My numbers are looking good lately. But I've completely lost the passion for the game at this level. I'm still focused on only sticking around long enough to see if we can do something about Harry. And the slaughter situation. These two issues are related, but the slaughter situation reaches much further than just Harry.

I've talked with Jake about doing another run for Tom to Canada. He doesn't appear to suspect anything, just told me that he'd sort something out soon. Soon couldn't come quickly enough. I want to get this last run done, with whatever plan Sarah has concocted for it.

Amanda and I have spent each of the last few Tuesday nights over at Sarah's. Amanda and I are now a serious couple, and I'm loving it. Sarah and

Amanda appear to be becoming closer friends. Our nights spent at Sarah's would inevitably focus on Harry, his goings on, and the slaughter situation. We did come up with a theory why Harry's horses go directly to Tom's kill pen, rather than be available for bid at the auction. Harry doesn't want to be exposed for sending his horses to slaughter. That would be bad press. He is also likely worried about the drugs his horses have taken; he doesn't want that to be exposed either. We guessed he doesn't want any loose ends, best to get rid of the horses and know they went to slaughter.

We are all eagerly waiting to hear back from Timmins. He had said two to three weeks, so for the last week, especially, we figured we might hear from him. Timmins had also said that it would be longer if they discover something. I'm guessing they have some kind of verification process in place once a drug is identified. Whatever the reasons for the three weeks we are at now, we are getting more and more anxious, and curious.

My morning routine has pretty much remained the same, though it's shorter with three horses. But that's good, as we head into summer. It gets up into the 90's pretty early in the day now. I try to get my three horses trained and done before the track break. And having done that again for this morning, I'm just finishing up in the barn for the day. I wander over to see Jorge. He still has Spicy Lemon, and I'm sure they're getting close to another race for him.

He is wrapping Spicy Lemon's legs when I find him.

"Hey, Jorge. How's the old horse?"

"Good. He ready to run again. Maybe Friday."

"Thanks. I'll let Sarah know." Jorge and I have hung out a little more since watching the Derby together. We haven't directly discussed the syringe he gave me yet, and I know Jorge wants to know what we are doing with it, but I want to wait to hear back from Timmins first. Soon enough, I hope.

The horse that won the Derby, Northern Peaks, went on to win the Preakness too, the second leg of the Triple Crown. Frankly, not many people wanted to take him on in that race. He was the 1-5 favorite in a six-horse field. He won by ten lengths. A few of the commentators alluded to the fact that Northern Peaks is clearly the standout of the division; the only time he's really been challenged was by Harry's horse, Dancer's Foil. Apparently there is hope that Dancer's Foil might make a return in early August, at Saratoga.

I finish up my morning's work and head over to the track kitchen with Hairy. Time for my sandwich and his treat. Hairy devours his feast in two chomps. As I finish up, my phone vibrates with a text from Amanda, "Consultants' meeting with board went well. Green light to start reorganizing the branches! X"

I text back, "Great work. We should celebrate at Zucchini's tonight? X" I no longer go to the races each night. I guess part of me is letting go of Missionville. Soon enough I'll be gone for good. Tonight we will celebrate.

Amanda replies, "I'll book a table for seven. See you when you get home. X"

Amanda has worked really hard to convince the bank owners that it makes sense to keep all their branches open, but change the role of the branch for the bank. Rather than have branches dedicated only for transactional experiences with a teller, she has the vision that the branch can serve more as a community hotspot, with Wi-Fi and other amenities. It is a pretty compelling plan. She shared a draft with me, and I was even able to add some insight, which surprised me more than Amanda. Anyway, we will celebrate tonight at our favorite restaurant.

As I leave the track I see Jake outside our barn with his truck and trailer. I watch for a little while from my car. Five minutes later, two of Mike's horses are led out onto the trailer. I can't tell if they are Harry's, but I do know that they are likely beginning a journey that would soon end their lives. The joy I feel for Amanda evaporates. This is the reality of Missionville for a number of our athletes. Jake seems pretty ambivalent about the whole thing. Just another way for him to make money. He is a good horseman though, that can't be questioned. But he seems to separate things out quite easily, and has no qualms making a quick dollar as he sends a horse down the proverbial road. I guess if it wasn't Jake, someone else on the backside would be doing it. Money ensures the system works, or something like that. I drive out of the stable gate and head to a favorite walking spot for me and Hairy.

I arrive home after feeding – Alfie wanted the afternoon off – at a little before six o'clock. Amanda is already here; I can hear the shower running as Hairy and I walk through the door. Amanda loves her showers, and when she's out of the shower she looks and smells so wonderful. It's tempting to go upstairs now, and wait for her in the bedroom, but then we wouldn't make our dinner date. We've done that before. We'd planned a whole night out, and then gotten totally distracted; the next morning we were starving. Today I wait downstairs, and watch the news on TV. Ten minutes later, she comes down to join me.

"Hey, Pete, good day?"

"It was better after learning about your success."

"I'm psyched. Champagne tonight when we get back?"

"Nice idea?" But we don't have any champagne.

"I bought a bottle on my way home. It's chilling in the fridge." God, she's great.

"I love you." I do, and anyone who thinks to buy champagne deserves to be loved anyway.

"You too." Amanda comes over and gives me a deep, passionate kiss. She smells lovely.

"OK, let me run upstairs and get changed and freshen up." I'm getting aroused, but I want to get to Zucchini's.

We have a wonderful evening. Great food, great company, and a wonderful night, including champagne in bed.

CHAPTER 35

PETE, FRIDAY

I HAVE TO GO TO THE RACES TONIGHT. RAY HAS A HORSE picked out to claim in the second race, Rupert Bear. He's a gelding who's lost a bit of his old form. His trainer has dropped him down from a $20,000 claimer to a $10,000 claimer. It's an obvious claim, given some of his past form, and it wouldn't surprise me if a few others go in for him. Spicy Lemon is also running tonight, in the third race, so I'll stay for that too.

My first horse to the track this morning is my filly. She has come out of her second win for me very well, just like her last race. She's definitely making me look good! I stand her in at the gap.

"Gorgeous morning, Pete."

"Yes, just a beautiful time of year, until it gets too hot after the break!"

"You're right. Your filly looks great after your second win."

"She's doing well." I walk her off then jog her back to the wire.

I stand at the wire for a while and just enjoy watching some of the training scene. Adam gallops by, smiling in my direction. He is on one of Hank's ex-horses. He recently took his trainer's test and is the trainer of record for those two horses; he also claimed one recently to make his a stable of three too. Adam's a nice guy, I hope this place doesn't just beat him down. A couple of breezers charge down the lane, head-and-head. They look like two-year-olds, still learning their trade. I will miss training at the track when I leave.

I turn my filly to the right and move her off into a gentle gallop. She goes very nicely for the mile and a half, and then walks home off a loose rein. It's just how you want a filly.

Thunder Clouds trains all right, but his stride has become a bit more of a shuffle. He used to be a nice long-striding horse, but he's had to compromise to keep himself comfortable. If I did run him back, it would have to be in a very cheap race, and I know someone would take a chance on him. I might as well be signing his death sentence. The longer I can hold Ray off, the longer I'll be able to stay on the racetrack. It would be a deal-breaker for Ray and me if he insists on running the old horse again.

My other gelding goes well, and I finish training again before the break, and the heat. At break time I walk down the shedrow to catch up with Jorge.

"Spicy Lemon ready for tonight?"

"Si Pete. No James, he runs, no win." Jorge knows how things work. Harry's smart. He doesn't try to win every race. That would be too obvious. It seems he likes to pick his wins, and I'm guessing he then bets on them in Vegas, just as Ray would.

"Good luck tonight." I return to my shedrow. My phone vibrates, it's Sarah.

"Pete?"

"Yes?" Immediately my adrenaline kicks in.

"Timmins called, the test came back positive for Dermorphin, frog juice. Norwood's print was also identified." Exactly what we wanted to hear.

"Crazy. Wow." That's all I can muster.

"Timmins wants us to meet him early next week. Does Monday work for you, same time? Will see if Amanda can get off too."

"Yes, whenever you schedule the meeting, I'll be there."

"Great, this is great!" Sarah hangs up.

I text Amanda quickly, "Call me after you hear from Sarah. X"

She does, minutes later, "Pete, this is amazing."

"I know. Can you make the meeting, whenever it is?"

"I will, for sure."

"Great. I've a long day here, I'll be at the races until after the third, but let's have dinner afterwards?"

"Sounds good. Can't wait to see you." Amanda hangs up.

Jake comes over to my shedrow.

"Pete, you OK for next Saturday?" Jake asks, referring to another trip to Canada.

"Sure, Jake. That would be good. Same time?"

"Yes, just be at Tom's around eleven in the morning. Same drill."

"Will do, thanks."

You wait for what seems like an eternity for something to happen, then it all happens at once.

I text Sarah, "Shipping for Tom next Saturday."

She replies almost immediately, "What a day! I'll set something up."

I get to Pokers before the first race, it has been a while since I've been to the races. Mary has noticed.

"Budweiser, Pete?"

"Thanks, Mary."

"We miss you."

"Thanks."

"You buying tonight?" Mary knows I don't have a runner, and quite frankly I don't care whether she knows.

"Sure, maybe," I smile.

"Good luck." Mary attends to another customer. I go off to a table. The first race is a maiden race, as usual. It is a cheap claiming event, and the runners are a pitiful group of horses based on their previous form. I wander out to the paddock to see them. Their appearance is no more inspiring than their past performances. Emma Sparks has a mount; she smiles at me as she rides by. She's now won twice for me on my filly; Ray is starting to realize the wisdom of keeping her on his horses.

The first race is as advertised. It was very slow with the field well-strung out at the end. Emma's horse won, which is the only good thing about the entire event.

I go back to Pokers. I want to read through the form of the second race one more time before heading to the paddock. Rupert Bear is the 2-1 morning line favorite, and while he hasn't won a race for six months, he's never run in a race this cheap in his career. His last two defeats were third place finishes for $20,000, so he was still quite competitive at that level. The drop to $10,000 is significant. I just need to see him in the paddock, make sure he's not limping around there. I go outside. I notice a few more horsemen than usual outside the paddock looking in. It's a sure sign that I'm not the only one looking at the horse. There are no other horses in the race worth a claim. Rupert Bear, a small bay gelding, looks fine, or at least there is nothing I could observe that makes me think I shouldn't put in a claim for Ray. I walk over to the racing secretary's office and fill out the appropriate paperwork.

Rupert Bear is first out of the gate, and goes straight to the lead. Down the backside he looks very comfortable racing in fast fractions. He comes around the turn on his own in front, the race looks very easy for him. But then in the homestretch he literally stops. Four horses are able to run by him as his jockey nurses him across the line.

Shit! Something's happened to him. No doubt that's why they dropped him.

It turns out that two other trainers put in claim slips for the horse, and we lost the shake.

I text Ray, "Rupert Bear broke down, we lost the shake." It's a brutally honest assessment of the race and our good fortune. Sadly the horse's outcome will be very uncertain. He has a new owner who just paid $10,000 for him. He is now being vanned off the track.

I return to Pokers and over to Mary for a second Budweiser.

"Get lucky, Pete?" Is she referring to losing the shake? Who knows?

"It's a quiet night for me." I return to my table. I want to take a quick look at Spicy Lemon's race before heading back out. He is the 3-1 choice, and that's mostly because of his last win. If you toss that race out, he would be about 6 or 7-1. There are a few horses in the race that are better than him. I take a couple of swigs of my beer and then head out to watch him in the paddock.

Jorge is leading him around, he has already been saddled. The horse looks well, his red coat gleaming. I nod at Jorge as he goes by. Longman is in the paddock talking to Mike. They both look very relaxed. It's an eight-horse field, which is quite a good field size for Missionville. The days of twelve-horse fields are long gone.

The paddock judge calls, "Riders Up!" and Longman jumps aboard his mount and Jorge leads them out, and hands them off to Jake.

I go over to Jorge to hang out for the race.

"Good luck, Jorge."

"Gracias. No win tonight, you see."

"No juice?" I reference James not drugging him. I want to make sure he hadn't stopped by later in the morning.

"Si, no juice."

"We tested the syringe." I keep my voice very low. Jorge doesn't flinch.

"Bueno, Pete. Gracias." That's all he says. We watch the race in silence. Spicy Lemon finishes sixth, beating only two horses.

I arrive at home a little before eight o'clock. Amanda is waiting for me, with Hairy, who is snoring on the couch.

"I've booked a table at Zucchini's for eight thirty." Amanda hands me a glass of champagne, "A quick refreshment for you as you get ready." She then gives me a long slow kiss. How did I get so lucky?

"Great, I'll be right back down, ready to leave." I head upstairs. Staying in does seem like a better idea to me, but it's a night to celebrate.

This is our second visit to the restaurant this week. A lot of our conversation focuses on the drug that was discovered in the syringe. I'd heard of it before. There had been cases down in Louisiana and areas nearby a few years ago, but I hadn't heard of any cases up in Pennsylvania. Amanda explains some of the properties of the drug to me; she has a chemistry degree and did a little research this afternoon after hearing the news. The drug has tremendous pain killing properties, which is no surprise, but also stimulates a euphoric effect in the animal. The consequences of the combination sounds crazy, and very dangerous.

It is quite late when we leave the restaurant, but Amanda insists on having a nightcap somewhere. We end up at Jessup's.

"Usual?"

"Thanks, Charlie, but do you have any champagne?" Amanda wants to continue our celebrations. I doubt that it's likely though, not at Jessup's. Even if Charlie does have champagne, I imagine it won't be the best.

"Sure, Amanda. Let me go out back and fetch a bottle." Amanda buys the champagne, and we take two glasses and find a table.

Jessup's is hopping with its usual Friday night crowd of racetrackers. The jukebox is at full volume. The all-you-can-eat buffet is still available. Half the jockey colony is here enjoying themselves, glad that their week is over. Longman is surrounded by his usual posse of hangers on, which includes his valet, John. I was a little worried that Jake might be here, but fortunately he isn't. It has been a long time since I've been to Jessup's for a proper Friday night out, and it might be forever until I do it again, so I'll enjoy it tonight.

CHAPTER 36

AMANDA, MONDAY

EVEN THOUGH IT'S MONDAY, I ARRANGED TO TAKE THE afternoon off from the bank to ride down to Harrisburg with Pete for our two o'clock appointment. To keep everything going at the bank – it's a busy time for me with my reorganization plan – I'm going into the office very early. Pete is getting ready to head to the track as I roll out of bed.

"Hey, honey." I kiss him on my way to the bathroom.

"Hey. You look lovely." I can sense Pete staring at me as I move away from him.

"I'll meet you around twelve then, at the bank?" I holler from the bathroom. We've planned for Pete to pick me up, grab a quick lunch, and then drive to the meeting.

"Look forward to it. See you later," Pete shouts on his way down the stairs. I can hear Hairy barking his excitement for the day.

I am really looking forward to meeting Timmins. I am curious to see what he has planned for the next steps. Surely we have enough to do something about Harry. The drug they found is really nasty. Not only are horses at risk of catastrophic breakdown as they run through their pain in a kind of euphoric haze, but also riders' lives are at risk. All for some extra money. Human greed is what separates us from other animals. It's not something we should be proud of. I turn on the shower, make sure it is very hot, and step inside.

I get to the bank at seven. It's very quiet. I have arrived early like this several times now that I am living with Pete. I can get an hour's work in without any disturbances, which is great thinking and planning time. Ideal for plotting the restructuring of our branch network. I have a meeting scheduled for each of the branch managers to attend on Friday, and I want to figure out what I want to accomplish for the meeting.

The first thing I need to do is to dispel any of the rumors that a branch is closing, that will be the easy part. Phyllis, who runs the Pottstown branch, has had a really tough time of late over there keeping the morale up.

Then I want to design a brainstorming session to get everyone to imagine the new version of a bank branch. I've already come up with my own detailed proposal, but I want the managers to come up with their own ideas, and see if we can marry it all together.

The morning passes quickly. Pete arrives right at twelve o'clock. He comes into my office, sandwiches in hand.

"Hey, you brought lunch! Good morning at the track?"

"Not bad for me, which is good for a Monday morning. Unfortunately the horse ambulance had to come out to take one of Jim Johnson's horses. He's had some tough luck lately with breakdowns."

"Bummer, I hate to hear that."

"Yeah, it's not good. The dirt track was pretty hard after all the rain we had yesterday. He was breezing horses." We continue chatting as we eat our lunch. Twenty minutes later we head out.

The drive to Harrisburg is very pretty along the Susquehanna River. Pete drives as I gaze out at the river, imagining the boat traffic during the days when this area was an industrial powerhouse. From time to time, Pete places his right hand on my knee and gives it a gentle squeeze.

As we enter the parking lot, I see Sarah waiting for us by her car. Pete pulls his car up next to hers.

"Hey, Sarah. Good to see you," I greet her.

"Good to see you guys. This meeting should be very interesting. If you guys like, I'll ask the questions, then you follow up with anything I might have missed?" This plan seems straightforward to me.

"I guess the main thing we want to learn is what the next steps are?" Pete says to both of us.

"Exactly. We want to make sure Timmins has a plan, which I'm sure he does based off our previous meetings," Sarah agrees.

We walk into the building and up to Timmins's office. He comes out to greet us, "Come on through."

"Steve, this is Amanda. She hasn't been able to get to our previous meetings, but thankfully skipped work this afternoon."

"Nice to meet you, Amanda." Timmins leans across his desk to shake my hand firmly.

"OK, so you all really delivered, as you know. The drug in the syringe was identified as Dermorphin, which is also known as 'frog juice.' We needed to do a split sample test, to make sure we'd got it right, hence the delay in letting you know. But it's Dermorphin for sure."

"Is this a common drug? I mean, common for an illegal drug?" Sarah asks.

"We haven't seen it in Pennsylvania, so we were surprised. There were a spate of positives for the drug down in Louisiana, Arkansas and New Mexico, a few years ago. It was very hard to test for back then, but we now have more sensitive testing procedures." Interesting, but I knew all this. I googled the *New York Times* article from 2012 that covers the issue in some detail.

"Why is it called frog juice?" Pete asks.

"The original drug is some kind of excretion from a type of frog in South America." A vague, but accurate response from Timmins. Maybe chemistry, or biology for that matter, isn't his thing. He continues, "But this is a synthetic version of the drug. This drug does not come from a frog, but from a compound made by a chemist."

"So what you're saying, Steve, is that this drug could be made locally, at a compound pharmacy?" I ask Timmins. I want confirmation on my hunch.

"Precisely." We are all thinking the same thing: Harry owns a compound pharmacy. Steve continues, "So we're working on the theory that Harry is making the drug at his compound pharmacy. But we need to make that connection through the vet, James Norwood. We need Norwood to tell us where he gets the drug." Makes sense. We have Norwood's fingerprint, so I assume we can use that to make the connection.

Steve adds, "There were two sets of fingerprints on the syringe. We ran the fingerprints against the track IDs. They are from the vet, James Norwood, and a groom for Mike Franks, Jorge Salazar."

"Jorge Salazar is the groom who gave us the syringe," Pete responds.

"I figured that, but I needed to confirm. OK, so this is how we are going to proceed." We are all listening intently. "We'll start testing for Dermorphin at the track, along with the other drugs we test for. We'll wait, and hope Norwood and Harry continue with their business, and we can catch them. The sooner the better. When we do, we'll go after Norwood, to get him to turn on Harry." Excellent! I had worried that Timmins and his team would settle for getting the positive and ban Norwood and Harry for a while. That would be the standard procedure. But they'd be back, find another drug, and continue their business as usual. This way, we have a better chance of nailing Harry for good.

Timmins continues, "We were able to save some urine and blood from Spicy Lemon's win, the day the syringe was discovered. We'll also run that against our new test, to try to tie it to the horse."

"I like it," Sarah says.

"Yes, this is very good," I echo Sarah's sentiment.

"Very good. The new test will be in place beginning next Monday's races." Timmins rises, indicating that the meeting is over.

As we walk out, Timmins adds, "Pete, I'm not ignoring the battery issue. It's important, and likely connected. But for now, we need to get this drug issue sorted, and get to the bottom of Harry's business practices. I talked to the reporter at the *Missionville Times*. She's going to fax me her notes for the stories she wrote, and we'll probably end up meeting. The FBI guy is also involved in what we're doing. We're going to get Harry, we just need to be smart so it sticks." I really like this guy.

Pete adds, "There's another interesting thing we need to consider. Harry doesn't drug every horse he races. He picks and chooses which ones. Spicy Lemon was drugged, he won easily. Last week he wasn't drugged, he ran a dull race. I'm thinking Harry is doing this deliberately, and betting in Vegas."

"Interesting. I'll keep that in mind."

We are back in the parking lot a half hour after we arrived.

"Great meeting, guys," says Sarah. We agree. "See you at my place tomorrow?"

"We'll be there."

CHAPTER 37

AMANDA, TUESDAY

I PULL UP TO SARAH'S PLACE AT AROUND 3:30 P.M. The auction at Owenscreek was very busy today; 103 horses were sold. Seven of them were Thoroughbreds as far as I could tell. I took photos of the lip tattoos of six of them. It was a busy day for the kill buyers: Tom and Fred bought 63 horses between them, snagging all the Thoroughbreds. There were also two Thoroughbreds already in Tom's kill pen before the sale; Harry's horses most likely.

The prices the kill buyers are paying remains quite high for this time of year. I guess the two slaughterhouses they are buying for have strong demand for their horse meat in Europe. I'm exhausted when I leave the auction – both physically and mentally drained. I'm looking forward to hanging out at Sarah's, hearing her plan for Pete's trip this weekend, and drinking wine together. The coffee is brewing when I enter her kitchen.

"Ugh, long day at the auction."

"Coffee's nearly ready. We'll hit the wine soon enough." Sarah reads my mind. I guess that's what close friends do.

"Sounds perfect." We chat for a while over coffee, rehashing our meeting yesterday with Timmins. Sarah is clearly excited by all the recent developments. As a trainer, who runs her own horses at the track, she has a lot at stake. Spicy Lemon is also on her mind, especially after the dull race he ran the other night.

"I just hope we nail Harry before Spicy disappears."

"I'm sure we can. I know Pete's keeping an eye on Spicy too. Jorge takes care of him. He's a good guy."

"I'm sure he is, but if Harry wants him shipped out, there's nothing Jorge or Pete can do." She has a point. We finish our coffee and head to the barn.

A while later, the three of us are sitting around the kitchen table. A chicken is roasting in the oven.

"So I've been thinking through a plan for your trip this weekend, Pete," Sarah begins. "You take 81 in New York State, right?"

"Yes, mostly."

"Good! I have a friend with a farm, about two miles off the highway. I'll text you the address."

"OK."

"This side of the border the truck isn't sealed, so we can offload the horses without anyone being the wiser." Makes sense. "My friend has an enclosed paddock area you can drive the truck directly into, it shouldn't be a problem. Amanda and I will meet you there."

Sarah continues, "We'll unload the horses, just drop the ramp of the trailer. We'll video the horses coming off the trailer. We'll also record the trailer, its license plate, and so forth. We'll video each of the horses, and the lip tattoos of any of the Thoroughbreds. Basically we'll document anything and everything. Then we'll load the horses back up, and you'll be on your way."

"And that's it? We'll just get a bunch of video. Is that enough to close things down?" Pete asks the obvious question.

"That's the beginning. We'll also need you to photograph all the documents, the EID forms of each of the horses, the VS10-13 form, and the International Health Certificates. You can do that at a gas station stop, right, like you did before with the EID forms?"

"Yes, easy enough."

"Unfortunately these horses will be slaughtered, there's nothing we can do about that. But if there are Thoroughbreds on the truck, and we can show that they had received drugs at some point, we can then expose the fraud in the system and potentially get things closed down. Basically there are three more steps for us, after you return.

"We'll make requests with both the CFIA, Canada's version of the USDA, and the USDA for the VS10-13 and EID forms for this shipment. They have to provide them to us. These forms will prove that those horses were slaughtered. We need to then get documents from the vets that attended to the Thoroughbreds to show that the EID forms are fraudulent and that the horses were not viable for slaughter. Timmins could get those records for us. Then we contact the *New York Times*, or a similar organization, to help us blow it all up."

"This sounds pretty reasonable. Our friend at the *Missionville Times* could connect us with the *New York Times*. Do you want to ask her if she wants to come along with us on Saturday and observe?" I know the slaughter issue is not just about Harry, but it might be useful to have her come along if she's willing.

"Can you ask her? It might make sense."

"No problem."

"I've thought it all through, I think this is our best option. We'll need to be patient as we wait for the documents from the CFIA or USDA, but we'll get them eventually." We agree, as Sarah then busies herself preparing the chicken feast.

CHAPTER 38

PETE, SATURDAY

"YOU READY FOR TODAY?" AMANDA ASKS AS SHE STRETCHES in bed. I'm already up.

"Excited to get it all done."

"Me too. Excited, and a little nervous in case something goes wrong."

"I think we'll be fine, as long as the set-up on the farm is good. We just can't afford to lose or injure any of the horses." Sarah has texted me the address where to meet. It's a small farm just north of Syracuse, in Pulaski, New York.

"I know we'll be fine, I just want to get it done, and set the wheels in motion." Amanda gets out of bed, naked, and strolls over to the bathroom. She continues, "I'll see you at the track. I may snooze for a little longer."

"Sounds good." I head downstairs. Hairy is waiting for me at the bottom. He starts jumping up and down and lets out a couple of excited barks. The day has begun.

I could get used to running a three-horse stable. I want to leave the track soon after the break, so I can get Hairy walked and be at Tom's by eleven. With only three horses to train, that's easily doable. Just in case, I plan to be on my first horse just as the track opens, to get a head start. I put in their feeds, the horses immediately begin munching down on their breakfasts.

I take off their bandages. The filly's legs are nice and tight, she's really doing well both physically and mentally. My other gelding has a little heat in his left leg, just above the ankle. I've been keeping an eye on it, but I don't think it's anything too serious. He should be racing again sometime next week I hope. Emma worked him two days ago, and he breezed OK. Thunder Clouds's ankle is still large, and has quite a bit of heat in it. Alfie is now hosing it twice a day, once in the mornings, and then he comes back at feed time and does the same. I really don't know if it makes much of a difference, but we have to try. Ray wants him to run back soon; I won't run him as he is now for sure.

I grab the filly's tack and am getting her ready when Alfie arrives.

"Hey, boss."

"Alfie, morning. Can you cover for me again tomorrow?"

"No problem, boss." I got really lucky when Alfie came to work for me when I started out training. I don't know too many more loyal people on the backside.

"Thanks. I'll ask Jorge if he can get the stalls again."

"Sounds good, boss. Watching the Belmont?"

"No, I'll probably miss it. A shame, that horse could make a bit of history today."

"Let's hope so." Alfie pulls out my filly and gives her a turn around the shedrow then puts me up. We head out to the track. In all the excitement of our plans for today, and the meeting with Timmins earlier in the week, I haven't paid too much attention to the Belmont Stakes. But Northern Peaks has a shot to be our next Triple Crown winner. I don't think there's too much in the race that can stop him.

I enter the track, I am the first one out here for a change.

"Morning, Pete, early for you?"

"Yes, Jess. Busy day, trying to get finished early."

"You watching the Belmont?"

"I'll try. Hopefully we'll have a Triple Crown winner."

"Has to be, after American Pharoah did it, Northern Peaks should be able to do it." Jess is comparing Northern Peaks to our most recent Triple Crown winner, the oddly spelled Baffert trainee.

"Fingers crossed." I walk my filly away and jog her to the wire. Being first on the track in the morning is a cool experience, it's just not something I do too often. The dirt surface is in good condition, and I have the whole track to myself, for a minute or two anyway. The track seems very large when you are the only one out here. When it's busy it can almost get claustrophobic.

As I stand my filly in at the wire, a string of horses from Jim Johnson's barn emerges from the gap. They are followed by a couple of Mike Franks's horses, and Jake is ponying a Franks horse in behind them. The peacefulness of the track is about to be interrupted. But being a Saturday, it will be a slower day out here. A lot of the jockey colony will be recovering from last night's revelries at Jessup's.

I turn my filly to the right, and she gallops off nicely. I plan to let her gallop on for the last half-mile of our mile-and-a-half gallop today. She'll have tomorrow off – I won't be here – and I want to get a little wind into her lungs. She might be running again soon. So as I gallop by the wire after going the first mile, I let my reins slip out just a little as I squeeze my legs. She extends her stride and moves into a half-speed gallop. I shift her closer to the inside rail. She moves very nicely around the turn and on to the half-mile pole. I then let her ease back. It is a very nice move, she is blowing a little bit as I walk her back to the gap.

"You're looking good out there, Pete." Jess, always has a kind word.

"Thanks, not bad for an old man." I smile and walk back to the barn. I hand the filly off to Alfie and get Thunder Clouds ready.

I've started putting front wraps on him when he gallops. Just another little extra thing to hopefully protect that ankle, although I'm not sure it makes too much of a difference.

A few minutes later we are walking to the track. I see Amanda on the rail, chatting to John Swank. She's helped John place one of his horses. There are plenty of horsemen on the rail, relaxing and watching training. One or two of the jockeys are out here too, trying to find some extra business no doubt.

I overhear the general chatter, and it's all Belmont talk. Can Northern Peaks go into the history books today? It's odd how few horses have won the Triple Crown. Granted, the Kentucky Derby is a bit of a lottery, but if the best horse wins the Derby, you'd think it could go on and easily sweep the series. But year after year, between the end of the 1970s and 2015, no horse had been able to do it. American Pharoah made it look easy in 2015. Northern Peaks is 3-1 on, to do it today. I'm sure Jessup's will be packed. I hope I'll be somewhere north of Pulaski, New York, when the race goes off.

I walk by Amanda and smile, then jog Thunder Clouds back to the wire. He shuffles his way over there. We stand in for another minute or two, then he shuffles around the racetrack in our gallop. I feel sorry for the old guy. He was a very good horse in his youth. But once that ankle started to bother him, he was on a slippery slope, all the way down to where he's at now. And along the way, he gets riders like Longman who know he can run faster if he's really pushed to do it – to hell with the consequence. Drugs or battery, the connections win, the horse loses.

I bring Thunder Clouds back to the gap, stand him in for a while, and then head to my barn. My other gelding trains fine, I was easily able to make the break with him, and I am done nice and early. I wander over to see Jorge. I want to see if he can help Alfie tomorrow. He's in Spicy Lemon's stall, getting him ready to train.

"Hey, Jorge, any chance you can help me tomorrow?"

"Sorry, Pete. I work this weekend."

"OK, no problem. How's Spicy?"

"He's OK. Back leg a little sore again after race. I work on it."

"Thanks, see you Monday."

"Si."

As I was walking back to my shedrow I pass Jennifer. She'll probably help me out if she can. I know she needs all the cash she can get to support her family.

"Hey, Jennifer, any chance you can help me tomorrow, are you working?"

"I'm not working, Pete. What do you need?"

"Could you get my stalls, come in around seven thirty? I'm heading out for the weekend."

"You off to New York for the Belmont, to see a Triple Crown winner?"

"Nothing like that, just going away for the night."

"OK, no problem. I'll always help you when I'm free." Jennifer's a good-hearted person. I think she's someone who's let life just slip by a little. She has a young daughter and a mother she takes care of. They are her world.

"That's great. I really appreciate it. I'll give you some cash on Monday. I'll tell Alfie you'll be here at seven thirty."

"Sounds good. Enjoy your weekend."

I text Amanda, "I'll be heading out in fifteen minutes. If I don't see you, see you in Pulaski, 5pm X"

A couple of minutes later, Amanda texts back, "See you later. Hanging out with Shawn, discussing banking program, to start next Saturday. X"

I arrive at Tom's a little before eleven. I don't need to grab any pictures this time, so there wasn't any rush to get here too early. I did want to see the horses before they are loaded onto the truck, to make sure there are Thoroughbreds in the group. I head directly to the barn. The truck and trailer are already in place. Tom is waiting for me.

"On time, Pete. Here's all your paperwork." Tom hands me two piles, one for the border crossing, one for the slaughterhouse. After chatting about our plan on Tuesday, I'm a little more familiar with the different sets of paperwork and the overall process. I put the documents in the cab. We then go around to lower the ramp of the trailer and begin herding the horses inside. I count seven horses that look like they might be Thoroughbreds. That is important since the other horses won't be as easily identifiable when we do our video work.

With lots of squealing and bucking, the two of us manage to load the horses. For all the trips I've been on, I'm amazed the horses all unloaded unscathed. Let's hope this journey is the same. At 11:05 a.m. I'm on my way to Canada, via Pulaski, New York.

Once I had left Tom's place, I text Sarah, "On the way, Thoroughbreds on board." If there weren't any Thoroughbreds, we would have aborted our plan. I also look through the VS10-13 document I have for the shipment; it lists a number of Thoroughbreds.

I now have a six-hour drive ahead of me until I will meet Sarah, Amanda, and Margaret Collins at the farm in Pulaski.

I turn left off the highway, just north of Pulaski. I drive down a narrow road for about two miles, when the farm appears, just over a ridge. I turn into the driveway. I see Sarah's car and the three of them waiting for me. Just before the main area of the farm is a paddock on the right with its gate open. Sarah signals for me to drive into that paddock. Once I'm in the paddock, they shut the gate behind me. I turn off the truck and jump out.

Margaret has a video camera in hand, and begins recording the truck and trailer all the way around the outside, making sure to get the tags of the vehicle too. Once she finishes, we all stand there; we haven't discussed how we are going to do the next part, and we need to be pretty quick. I don't want to delay this journey any longer than I have to, in order to avoid any suspicion at the slaughterhouse.

"OK, this part could be dangerous. I suggest the three of you get out of the paddock while I drop the ramp. We're on the fence line, so you'll still get decent footage of the unloading, Margaret." No one argues.

"We need a couple of halters. I assume we have some?"

"Yes, I left them by the car. I'll fetch them," Sarah responds.

"Good, so I'll let them out, and we can see how they react as Margaret takes video. Once they settle a little, we'll go into the paddock and get the Thoroughbreds for closer inspection and video. Make sense?"

"Sounds good to me," Sarah says, while Margaret and Amanda nod. They all leave the paddock. I look to see if Margaret is ready with the camera, and then I drop the ramp. The horses start coming down the ramp, slowly at first, with their heads lowered and a lot of snorting. But once two or three of them are in the paddock the rest follow quickly, and start to spread around the small field. A couple of them are very lame, including one of the Thoroughbreds. I move around to keep from getting too close to any of the more inquisitive horses. It's a sad sight, just knowing that these mostly healthy animals are the unsuspecting victims of our throwaway society.

Sarah has collected the halters, and the three of them are poised to enter the paddock.

"Let's target one horse at a time. I think I know which are the seven Thoroughbreds. We'll start with the bay one over there," I instruct as I point to a corner of the paddock where a small bay gelding is starting to graze.

"Sarah, can I have a halter?" She passes me one of the two halters. I lead the four of us to the gelding. I look deeply into his eye; over the years I've found this trick is a good way to make sure that a horse doesn't move away from me. It works, and I easily slip the halter on. I stand by the horse as Margaret videotapes him more closely, making sure to get the USDA tag number that's placed on his rump. I flip his lip up so she can record the tattoo number. Amanda writes the number down as we all try to decipher it. Sometimes it's easy to read a lip tattoo, but most of the time it's not, especially for the older horses. You end up having to guess one or two of the numbers. Anyway, having the video footage should ensure that we get them right in the end.

We repeat this process for the six other Thoroughbreds. One of them looks a little familiar, but I can't really figure out why. None of them give us any real problems. While Thoroughbreds have a bad reputation, they are well broke and used to humans. A few of the other horses in the paddock appear to be much more nervous and potentially dangerous.

After twenty minutes, we finish. Our last task is to get the animals loaded back into the truck.

I had parked the trailer so the fence line of the paddock serves as one boundary. This should help us funnel the horses in and get them back loaded. But we need to do something about the other side of the trailer. Sarah has brought a lunge line with her, and we also have a couple of bull whips, to urge the horses forward.

Because Margaret isn't a horse person, she remains on video duty and stays out of the way and just documents the whole thing. Sarah and I each take a whip, and Amanda takes the lunge line which now has one end tied to the back of the trailer, the opposite side of the fence line. Sarah and I slowly gather the horses into a herd, and begin moving them towards Amanda and the trailer. We aren't in a hurry, we just need to get it right.

The horses at the front of the herd walk slowly toward the trailer, and begin moving up the ramp. All seems to be going well. In a few short moments, half the horses are either on the ramp or already in the trailer. Sarah and I continue to walk slowly forward. Then a grey horse, close to the back, darts forward and turns right, bringing three or four horses with it.

It all happens in a few short seconds. Amanda is knocked to the ground, and lies motionless.

I bolt over from my position, Sarah follows. Margaret keeps filming, but we've abandoned the horses by now.

"Christ, Amanda, are you OK?" I ask, I am shaking. I can see she is breathing, but she doesn't respond.

"I think she took a direct hit from the brown horse that was following the grey," Sarah says to me.

"Amanda, can you hear me?" I ask as I gently lean over.

She groans.

"Can you move your arms, your legs?" I haven't had any emergency training, but I've seen a few riders injured at the track; I've observed the drill enough times. Don't move them, let them move themselves. Make sure there are no back injuries, make sure their airways are clear. Amanda gently moves her arms, she groans again.

"Amanda, can you move your legs?" She is moving around a little more now.

"What happened?" Amanda asks, groggily.

"You were run over by a horse. You probably hit your head," Sarah responds quietly.

"The last thing I remember is writing down a lip tattoo number." Not surprising, memory is a funny thing in accidents like this.

"Can you sit up?" I ask. Some of the horses are starting to come close to us, curious about the goings on. Amanda gently raises herself up. I put my hand under her armpit to support her. She coughs a couple of times.

"Wow, I guess that's a little horse rustling for you," Amanda jokes, trying to make light of the situation.

"Just sit here for a minute, we're in no hurry," I reassure her. We are actually in a hurry, but you can't rush these things. And now we have the extra complication of loading this bunch with one less helper.

Five minutes later, Amanda is out of the paddock, sitting in Sarah's car. Sarah recruits some extra help from the farm, the friend of hers who owns the farm and a guy who works for her. Between us all, with me on the end of the lunge line this time, we manage to herd the horses back into the trailer, slowly.

The whole operation takes us seventy minutes, much longer than I'd hoped, but it is done. Fortunately Amanda looks like she's going to be fine, but will probably be a little concussed for a day or two. Twenty minutes after six, I am back on the road, on my way to the border crossing.

I arrive at the border at around seven thirty. I was a good hour and a half behind my usual crossing time. I hadn't thought about what time the slaughterhouse might stop taking horses. I assume if that is an issue, Tom would have let me know.

The crossing itself is very routine and done in twenty minutes. The guy reviews my paperwork, wanders around the trailer for about five minutes, peering in, and then puts a seal on the back of the truck so the horses can't be unloaded until I get to the slaughterhouse. He returns my paperwork with the appropriate stamps and seal number. Off I go.

Two and a half hours later, and one stop at a gas station to fill up and photograph all the forms, I drive into the slaughterhouse. I'm absolutely exhausted, but am grateful to see someone is still at the plant, in the office. I wander over with the paperwork.

"Shipment of thirty horses from Tom Baker," I declare as I place the paperwork on the desk.

"You're running late, eh," the guy behind the desk remarks.

"Traffic, and a long delay at the border crossing," I offer, which they can't really question.

"Corral twelve, back your truck up to its offload ramp. I'll come over and check the seal." I move the truck to the appropriate place, and wait for him. The horses once again exit the truck, no doubt glad to be free from their cramped quarters. In two days they will be slaughtered.

An hour later I check into a motel, ready to crash. I call Amanda.

"Hey, how are you?"

"Ugh, sore head. I have a really bad headache, but otherwise fine. Sarah's here with me, she's staying the night."

"That's good. Christ, we were lucky. It could have been much worse."

"Yes, I'll live. I'm drinking a lot of tea." It's so good to hear Amanda's voice. I'll be honest, I was frightened when I saw her lying on the ground. "How're things up there?"

"The border crossing was fine. Took all the pictures at a gas station. Arrived at the slaughterhouse a little late, obviously, but it wasn't a problem. I'm just shattered. Do you know who won the Belmont? I've not heard anything up here."

"Northern Peaks. He's your new Triple Crown winner. He won easily."

I'd missed it all. I reply, "Great stuff. OK, I'm planning on leaving here early in the morning, so I can get back and be with you. Hope to see you at lunchtime, will text you along the way."

"I love you, Pete. I'll see you tomorrow."

"I love you too."

CHAPTER 39

PETE, TUESDAY

I CREEP OUT OF BED. AMANDA HAS EXPERIENCED a persistent headache since Sunday morning, so I try not to disturb her. She took Monday and today off of work, which is unusual for her. Hopefully it will give her a little time to recover more fully. I know from my own experience that when you bash your head, you need to be careful for a few days.

I get dressed in the bathroom and then quietly sneak out. Twenty minutes later, I'm feeding my three horses at the track.

The buzz on the track yesterday was all about the new Triple Crown winner, Northern Peaks. Is he going to retire, or is he going to finish out his three-year-old campaign? Those who favor his retirement are emphatic that he has nothing left to prove, and his value as a stallion is now sky high. He should retire before something goes wrong. Those who prefer that he stays racing – me included – argue that he's only just turned three; he has plenty of scope to improve, and should be given a chance to prove how good he might be. He should be pointed for the Breeders' Cup Classic, in November, where he would face older horses. A decision on whether he will continue to race or retire will be made in the next couple of weeks.

Racing needs him.

Dancer's Foil, Harry's horse who only narrowly lost to Northern Peaks in the Wood Memorial, is now back in training, according to a report I read in the *Daily Racing Form*. Todd Brown, his trainer, has suggested that he might be pointed to the Travers Stakes in Saratoga, which is the marquee three-year-old race for the late summer. If that's the case, and if Northern Peaks doesn't retire, the two horses may face each other again. That would be an interesting contest.

I go to the tack room and get my tack for the filly. She's probably going to run again in the next week or ten days, so I'm planning to have Emma Sparks come over to breeze her tomorrow. Today, she'll do her normal routine gallop.

Alfie arrives at a little after seven. He pulls the filly out for me, and sends us on the way.

"Morning, Pete. Still buzzing about the Triple Crown?" Jess asks, at the track. We chatted for almost ten minutes yesterday. Jess reckons Northern Peaks was more impressive than American Pharoah when he won his Triple Crown. I'm not sure I agree. When I watched the Belmont online, the win wasn't as convincing to me as it should have been, given the weak caliber of his opposition. But a win's a win.

"Sure, I just hope they keep the horse in training. We need these athletes to compete, not retire."

"I know. The breeding guys make it hard, with all the money that's involved." Jess repeats the economic argument that just makes it too easy for the owners of the top horses to retire them. Sadly we struggle with a different economic argument when we need to retire our horses at Missionville.

"Shame none of that money spills down to our type of racing," I comment, and then head to the wire. My filly trains very nicely. She feels like she almost floats across the ground as she gallops.

When I come back to the barn, James is in my shedrow.

"Hey, James."

"Pete, all good? How's your old guy doing?"

"He's shuffling along. Nothing much different there." James has stopped by a few times since Thunder Clouds's last race, inquiring into his wellbeing. I think he assumes I'll want him to inject that ankle soon, and then run him on the drop. I've decided that I'm not doing that, but I don't see any reason to let anyone know yet.

"OK, let me know if you need anything." James won't flat out ask me if I want to do anything with the ankle, since it wouldn't be appropriate. James wanders into Mike's shedrow. I watch him. Sure enough he ducks into a stall with a syringe in hand, and then leaves the barn almost immediately. I take a closer look at which stall he'd entered. It is a horse that's racing for Mike and Harry tonight.

Thunder Clouds trains in his typically shuffley way again this morning. My other gelding gets through his training routine, just as he's done day in and day out since I've had him. No problems at all. I am all done training by the break time on the track, when Amanda calls me.

"Hey, you."

"Hey." She sounds very drowsy.

"You sound like you're still asleep."

"I just woke up, I haven't slept this long forever."

"I'm guessing that's a good thing. How's your head this morning?"

"Better than it was. Slight headache, I think, but I haven't been up and about yet, so I don't really know."

"Are you planning on going to the auction today, before Sarah's?"

"I think I'll skip it. Can you pick me up?"

"No problem. I'll drop Hairy off after we go for a walk, and then get you."

"Great, we can leave here about three. I'll let Margaret know." Margaret Collins is going to come with us to Sarah's. She's going to bring all the video that she took in upstate New York.

"Sounds good. Take it easy, I want you to get better quickly." Amanda's only been under the weather for a couple of days since the accident, but it is two days too many for me.

After I finish things up, I head over to the track kitchen with Hairy.

"Usual, Pete?"

"Thanks, Alice." She starts preparing my sandwich after putting a couple of sausages on the grill.

"Exciting to have another Triple Crown winner." I didn't stop by the kitchen yesterday, so we haven't had a chance to discuss racing's big story.

"Yes. So soon after American Pharoah too. I guess they'll start saying the Triple Crown's now too easy to win."

"I remember when Affirmed won it, the year after Seattle Slew. They said the same thing then, series is too easy."

"Yeah, and look what happened, no more winners until American Pharoah, more than 30 years later. A few came close, one or two should've won it I suppose."

"Spectacular Bid might be the best horse that never won the series." Alice knows her racing. Spectacular Bid came up short in the Belmont, and he's considered one of the very best Thoroughbreds of the 20th century.

"Real Quiet was close in 1998." He really should have won it. I was pretty young then, but I'll always remember that stretch duel with Victory Gallop.

"Yes, Silver Charm was another who went close, the year before." It's a fun conversation. And it's good to see Alice animated about something. She's struggled a lot over Hank's suicide, but time and a positive event can be a good healer. Alice hands me my sandwich and two extra sausages. I go to sit down; Hairy chomps down his treat as I contemplate my afternoon activities.

We pull into Sarah's driveway before four o'clock. Fortunately Amanda's headache is improving, although she's sensibly continuing to abstain from wine. Margaret was good company on the way over, telling us stories about the good old days when the *Missionville Times* had a wide circulation, and she undertook a number of investigative pieces. I'm impressed with her research and persistence when she almost single-handedly took on the local mining company. Margaret seems excited about our project, and has already put out feelers with a couple of contacts at the *New York Times* to see if they might be interested in the story. She thinks they will be.

Sarah is waiting for us in her kitchen, with a cake and a couple of balloons.

"Surprise!"

"Christ, Sarah, you remembered."

"June 15, your birthday, not quite the big 4-0 yet!"

"Thirty-nine."

I had no idea it was Amanda's birthday. I'm embarrassed, "Wow, I'm sorry, I didn't know."

"Don't worry, how could you have known? I didn't tell you."

"Fair enough, but I'd like to have bought you something."

"You've done enough for me, Pete. I wake up every morning thankful we're together." I didn't expect that. "You just need to remember June 15 for next year." Amanda smiles at me.

Sarah cuts the cake and passes around slices; we enjoy the little celebration. We then go to the barn, to help Sarah get her horses ready for the night. About an hour after we'd arrived, we were all back in the house, ready to watch the video.

Margaret takes over, "So I'll play the video, and stop it at specific points of interest. There's about an hour's worth of content to get through. It might take us a couple of hours."

"That sounds good. Let me fill the drinks up first," Sarah says.

"Water for me," Amanda requests, which is I guess how she will be celebrating her birthday – dry.

"I'll have wine if you have it." Margaret really fits in with this group. Sarah gets me a Budweiser.

"I ran all the tattoos," Sarah begins, as we all settle down, "and have the details of each of the Thoroughbreds, so we can match them all up as we go through the video."

"Nice," Amanda responds.

Margaret starts the video. The opening scene, around five minutes, is capturing the truck and trailer in detail. Then the scene cuts to me, lowering the ramp, and the horses moving into the paddock. You can easily pick out the one or two very lame ones, one of which was a Thoroughbred. You can see the nervousness of the horses. This whole experience would have been alien to their routine.

It takes about four minutes for all the horses to get off the trailer and into the paddock. The video cuts again.

The next segment is of the first Thoroughbred. Margaret slowly and carefully videoed the animal in detail, making sure to be able to match the USDA tag number to the horse and its lip tattoo number. We didn't want to take any chances that there could be any confusion.

"This is Gail Warning. Owned by Harry Mitchell and trained by Mike Franks." Bingo! The first horse we identify was one of Harry's. Margaret pauses the video as Sarah continues, "Harry had this horse for three starts. Claimed him back in February. The horse won one race for them. Was fifth in his last start, which was only two weeks ago. In all, he raced 34 times for seven different trainers. Made a little over $130,000 with five wins." It sounds so depressing.

Sarah nods to Margaret to continue. The video switches to the next horse. The segment begins like it did for the first horse, with detailed coverage of the entire horse, its tattoo and USDA number.

"This is Tymark." Shit! I knew I recognized this horse, but I couldn't figure it out. I had him as a two-year-old, a few years ago. He'd grown since. I raced him three times, and won one with him. He had made money for me. Sarah continues, "He was a five-year-old. Not raced for six months, so not sure where he had been lately. Somewhere off the track. He won four races in all from seventeen starts. Had a whole year off at one point."

"I had this guy for a little while. I knew there was something about him when we were there on Saturday. I just couldn't figure it out." I wait for their reaction.

"When did you have him?" asks Amanda. This really does bring it all home for me.

"When he was two. I raced him three times I think. He won once, and was then claimed from me in his next start."

"Yes, looks like you won for $15,000 with him, lost him for $10,000." That sounds about right. Sarah reads from the horse's past performance sheet. She must have already known I had the horse. She continues, "No worries, Pete. You wouldn't have known. This is just how the claiming game works. We know that." I'm still shocked to be confronted by reality like this. I drove the guy to his death. He made me money. I'd forgotten about him; had he forgotten about me?

Margaret plays the video, cutting to the next horse. We watch for a little while, this was one of the lame horses, you can see he was uncomfortable moving around.

"This is Rupert Bear," Sarah begins. "He was a four-year-old who raced twelve times. He was a pretty decent horse for a while, and earned $95,000 from four wins. He raced at Missionville last week, dropping down from claiming $20,000 to claiming $10,000. He was the heavy favorite, but looks like he almost pulled up going to the wire. He was claimed from that race. Now he's gone."

"I watched the race, I was at the track that night. He looked like he was going to win easily, was clear turning for home, and then stopped. Ray wanted to claim him. We lost the shake. There were multiple trainers trying to get the horse." It's shocking to see him on this video, to know I'd sent him on his final journey, when he looked so good in the paddock last week. I'd paid extra attention to him. He could so easily have been ours after the race instead.

Margaret restarts the video. The fourth horse we identify as a Thoroughbred is on the screen. Sarah gives a running commentary on who it was, and his racing history. This guy hadn't won a race. He'd started four times and had been beaten easily in each of his starts. He just wasn't cut out to be a racehorse. He's now horse meat.

The fifth horse is now up. Sarah cuts in, "This is the second horse which belonged to Harry Mitchell, Fiery Temper. A chestnut gelding. It looks like they bought this horse at the end of the Churchill Downs meet last year. He had some decent form at Churchill Downs for a couple of years, winning two allowance races for Lukas. He then ran in high-price claimers, his final race at Churchill was for $20,000. Two months later, he was running at Missionville for $10,000. He won two races for Harry, the last one a little over a month ago."

Margaret starts the tape again, and we go through two more horses and their details. The video then cuts to us reloading the horses onto the trailer. We watch, wait, and then see it: Amanda gets flattened.

"Ouch!" Sarah exclaims.

"Ouch is right. That horse really did mow me over. No wonder my head's been hurting."

"It could've been a lot worse. Thank goodness you're OK," I say. I'm not sure what we would have done if it had been more serious. Thankfully it wasn't. The video continues, and shows our second attempt at loading the horses. The video then cuts to me, driving the truck and trailer out of the paddock and down the driveway of the farm.

"So, while this is depressing, it's also very good. We have documented evidence regarding who these horses are. Once we get the information back from the CFIA or the USDA, we'll have evidence that they were slaughtered. In the meantime, we can write the story." Margaret is taking the lead on how best to use this information.

Margaret adds, "I did some digging with the *New York Times*. I'm sure they'll want this story. They've gone after the racing industry before with a lot less. They partnered with PETA to try to bring down a top trainer. That backfired because most of the evidence they had was circumstantial at best, and what they uncovered wasn't enough to do anything. We have so much more here. I'm making some inquiries."

"So for now, we should just leave everything in your hands, Margaret?" Amanda inquires.

"Yes, I can work with Sarah to put the story together. I may ask you more about Owenscreek, Amanda, and pay a visit. Once I'm done with the story, I'll run it by everyone. Does that work?"

"That works for me," I respond. Amanda and Sarah nod. I continue, "Oh, and on another issue, I watched James Norwood give a shot to a runner of Harry's. It's racing in the sixth tonight. We might want to watch it?" I wasn't sure if I should mention this tonight, but since the track should have started testing for Dermorphin this week, it makes sense to watch.

"Interesting. That race is in about a half-hour. Let's eat first, I've something that's been cooking in the oven." We all move to the kitchen, and enjoy a pot roast. Amanda decides to have a glass of wine, a positive step forward I hope. When we return to the living room, we watch Harry's horse win by four lengths at odds of 6-1. Longman is all smiles as he heads into the winner's circle.

CHAPTER 40

AMANDA, SATURDAY

PETE IS GETTING READY FOR THE BARN, GETTING DRESSED on the side of the bed. I rise up, stretch, and yawn.

I'm starting to feel much better. I went back to work on Wednesday, I need to keep pushing forward with my reorganization plan; too many days off would have put me too far behind. By Thursday evening, I was almost back to normal, we went out on a date to Zucchini's. Pete wanted to celebrate my birthday, which was sweet.

"Pete, come back to bed, you can be a little late today." I want him, I really want him. Last night was wonderful, but I want more. I guess I really do feel much better.

"I can't. I need to get going."

I move over to where Pete is sitting. I place my hand over his crotch, and kiss him. I'm tingling. Pete responds, I can feel his reaction. I have him. We connect like two people who are crazy in love with each other. I then fall back to sleep.

When I wake again, it's seven thirty. I'm going to be late to the track, but it doesn't bother me too much. I'm supposed to meet with Shawn at eleven o'clock, to run the first in our series of banking programs at noon, over lunch. I'll have plenty of time before then to do my usual work.

I arrive at the track an hour later and go to the kitchen to get a coffee. It's a busy place, during the break time. All kinds of horsemen are getting a quick snack, coffee, or whatever, to hold them over for the rest of the morning. Alice looks like she is enjoying the chaotic scene. I order a coffee, and wander up to the track slowly.

When I get there the tractors are still getting the surface ready for the onslaught after the break. It will be busy for about ten minutes, then things will get pretty quiet for the rest of the morning. Saturdays are usually the quietest training days.

The first horses to appear from the barn area are Jim Johnson's. The old man is following them on foot. He has a jockey with him. I nod to the pair as they approach the rail.

"Sounds like that horse found a nice home, Amanda," Johnson says to me. I'm surprised he wants to chat. While I think he's a decent guy, sometimes these old timers don't want to be too bothered by those of us who aren't really in the game.

"Yes, Mr. Johnson. I'm really happy he found a home so quickly."

"You do good work, young lady. I may have one or two more for you in the next couple of weeks. I have more horses coming in."

"Do you want me to stop by your barn today?"

"Not today. I'll sort a few things out this week. Stop by next Saturday."

"I will." He returns to his conversation with his jockey. It feels good to make inroads with such a big barn. I know he's had some bad luck with horses breaking down. Maybe he's realizing we can do a little more for these horses.

I hang out at the track for about forty-five minutes. There isn't much point in staying any longer, the activity on the track has completely died down. Pete hasn't been out here. I guess he got all his horses trained before the break, despite his delayed start to the morning.

I have two barn visits to make, a couple more horses to add to my website. It takes me a half-hour to get the horses videoed and photographed. I then head over to Pete's barn. On my way I hear an announcement for our lunch program.

"Blessings. This lunchtime attend our free banking session, back by popular demand. Lunch is included. Begins at noon, in the rec room." Shawn is a constant presence of the backside p.a. system, letting the community know of upcoming events for their entertainment, education, or spiritual needs.

Pete is in his tack room when I arrive.

"Hey, lovely to see you." He kisses me on the cheek.

"Good to see you. I hope I didn't upset your morning's work too much."

"No way, I love that you're feeling much better." I am, and needing Pete is proof of that.

"It might be rough for you for a few days." I'm only half-joking.

"Jake came to see me." Pete changes the subject.

"And?" I'm not sure what Jake could have wanted. I hope he doesn't suspect anything.

"He says Tom needs me again, next weekend." Oh. I hadn't really thought about Pete continuing to drive for Tom, but I guess it makes sense.

"Bummer. I suppose you need to do it. We don't want to raise suspicions until we blow the whistle on all this crap."

"That's what I thought, so I said 'great,' with a little enthusiasm." We chat for a little while longer, as Pete finishes up cleaning his tack. We then head over to the track kitchen with Hairy.

"Usual, Pete?"

"Thanks, Alice. And a coffee for Amanda." I'm planning on eating at my banking presentation. Alice looks a little puzzled to see us together, but she smiles. We've never really tried to make much conversation, but I imagine she's a good person. She seems to be the heart and soul of this place. I also notice she put a treat on for Hairy, two sausages.

Pete and I retreat to a table with Hairy. I'm excited to get to the banking program and see if many people attend. Shawn spots us and comes over to our table.

"Hey, guys." Shawn sits down.

"Shawn, we ready?" It's just before eleven. I know we need to plan a little, but we have another hour before the session is scheduled to begin.

"Yes, no hurry. I've heard from a few people who plan on attending. We'll just do the same as we did for the last program, if that's good with you?"

"Works for me. The bank is very enthusiastic about this program." It is, because I basically run the bank, so if I'm enthusiastic, the bank is.

"Well, it's a great service for the backside workers, especially the immigrant community." I knew the 'Homewire' service we designed is popular, and it was very easy to create. "I'll leave you guys to it. See you just before noon, Amanda." Shawn moves to another table, sits down and starts chatting to its occupants.

Pete and I hang out for a while longer before Pete leaves with Hairy to go on their daily walk. I go to wander the backside, to collect my thoughts for the banking presentation.

At a little before twelve, I return to the rec room, which is very crowded. That gets me totally jazzed. Everyone is sitting down, chatting away as they munch on their free lunch, which might be part of the draw. But when I start my presentation, everyone turns their full attention to me, and for forty-five minutes I have them completely focused. After I finish, I answer a few questions, and then ask them to complete sign-up sheets if they are interested in opening a bank account with Susquehanna. Thirty people sign up, a new record for one of my presentations.

After finishing up, Shawn comes to thank me. We go back to the kitchen and chill out over another coffee.

CHAPTER 41

PETE, SATURDAY

I HAVE ANOTHER LONG WEEKEND AHEAD OF ME. I NEED TO be at Tom's at eleven o'clock this morning for my trip to Canada. I really am not too happy to have to do this run, but I guess we need to keep up the pretense until we get the *New York Times*, or whichever media, to run the story. We have all the material for the story in place, except for the reports either from the USDA or CFIA, which would prove that those poor horses were slaughtered. The sooner that paperwork arrives, the better. I'm rehashing all this, again and again, as I get ready for the track. Amanda is fast asleep. She looks lovely as she sleeps: her strawberry blonde hair tousled over her face. I've become a little more successful lately at not disturbing her in the mornings. I guess that's a good thing. It's also very good that she seems to have fully recovered from her bout of headaches.

Hairy is waiting for me at the bottom of the stairs, wagging his tail and jumping up and down. He is about to bark his enthusiasm for the day as I open the door for him to run out. I slide out of the house and head to the track.

I only have two horses to train today. I ran the gelding earlier this week. He ran a decent race, finishing third. Ray isn't too happy with the result, but I'm not sure the horse could have run any better. Ray had also hoped he would get claimed, which he didn't. Our options for him are running low. Anyway, he has a few days off after the race, which makes this morning's routine straightforward. I'm also excited that the filly is in a race on Monday. She might be the favorite. She's going for three in a row for me.

When I arrive at the barn for the morning feeds, it's peaceful. But as soon as my horses see me, I hear a whinny, and a couple of bangs from one of them kicking at the walls. They are ready to eat. Fortunately, their breakfast meal is a straightforward scoop and a half of a mixture that's already made up by the feed company, so there's no time wasted between my arrival and their chomping down in their feed tubs.

Once fed, I remove their wraps and check their legs. The filly's legs are still ice cold, which is a great sign. Thunder Clouds's ankle is still large, but a lot of the heat has come out of it. Maybe Alfie's extra work, hosing the ankle twice a day, is paying off a little. He still shuffles around the racetrack during training though. My other gelding's front legs are covered in poultice. Alfie will wash that off when he gets here. I start mucking a stall as I wait for Alfie, who arrives right at seven o'clock.

"Hey, boss. You want me to hose that poultice off?" Alfie always knows what needs to be done. He always asks, he doesn't like to assume anything.

"Thanks. Can you cover for me again tomorrow? I'll get Jorge or Jennifer to help."

"No problem, boss. You see the news?"

"What?"

"Northern Peaks isn't retiring. They're pointing him for the Travers, and then the Classic. Was announced last night on ESPN." I've been sidetracked with Amanda and haven't really been keeping up with the latest racing developments; it doesn't surprise me that I missed this last night.

"That's great news. Racing needs this." It could make things interesting if Harry's horse continues to train well. He's scheduled for a workout today at Belmont Park.

"Yes, boss." Alfie walks over to the gelding's stall to get him ready to hose and walk. I head to the tack room to get my tack for the filly.

Ten minutes later I'm on the track, standing in at the gap.

"She looks good for Monday, Pete."

"Thanks, Jess, fingers crossed. Three in a row would be something!"

"You can do it. Emma loves her."

"Yes, they're a good pair. See the Triple Crown winner's racing again."

"Yes, good news. We can get excited for some big races in the fall." Jess does enjoy her racing. I walk my filly away, and then we go into a jog to the wire. I stay at the wire for a few minutes, there is no rush this morning.

Adam gallops by on one of his own horses, he smiles in my direction. I plan to stop by his barn later to see if he would get on my filly tomorrow. He's a good rider, and I prefer my filly does something the day before she races. I'll be in Canada.

A couple of breezers come by, neck and neck. The track is busy for a Saturday morning. After a little while longer, we turn to the right and do our routine gallop. She floats across the ground, as she has been doing lately. I walk her home off a loose rein. Alfie takes her from me when I get back to the barn. Thunder Clouds's turn is next.

Fifteen minutes later, I'm walking up to the track on the old guy. It's a beautiful morning at Missionville, just a light breeze to keep us from getting too overheated. When I get to the gap, I exchange a few more words with Jess. I catch sight of Amanda on the rail, chatting with Randy Marsh. Randy was the previous trainer of Thunder Clouds; a decent enough guy, I suppose, although we've never really had much to do with each other.

I smile at Amanda as I walk away, and then we move on into the old guy's shuffle. It's surprising how many racehorses adapt their stride pattern to their injuries, even some of the top horses can only shuffle around in their training in the mornings. I remember watching California Chrome during his Triple Crown run in 2014. He always looked uncomfortable when he first jogged off. Despite that he showed the racing world what a great race-horse he was. Anyway, Thunder Clouds isn't going to be showing the world anything anymore if I can help it. A couple more months of delays, and hopefully Ray will just give up on him.

An hour later, I'm nearly finished at my barn. I head over to find Adam, who is in his barn with his three horses.

"Hey, Adam. How's the training business treating you?"

"Pete. It's good, I just need to get that first win."

"I saw you had a second last week, not too bad."

"She ran well. I was really hoping she could get it done. Her ankle is starting to bother her, so she might not have too many good races left."

"Welcome to the world of training. Hey, can you do me a favor?"

"Sure, what do you need?"

"I'm away tomorrow, and my filly is in on Monday. Any chance you can get on her for me?"

"For you, Pete, sure."

"Awesome. Just gallop her a mile and a half, steady, from the wire. What time works for you?"

"Is just after the break OK?"

"Sounds good. Can you text me when you're done, let me know all's well?"

"No problem." Adam is genuinely a good guy. I hoped it wouldn't be a problem. He's also a good hand on a horse, so I know my filly will be well taken care of.

"Great. I'll let Alfie know. See you Monday."

"Have a good weekend. Cool about Northern Peaks, right?"

"Yes, very cool." I head back to my barn, I just need to square things up with Jorge or Jennifer. I see Jorge first, grooming one of his horses.

"Any chance you can help me out again tomorrow, Jorge?"

"Si, Pete, no problem."

"Great, seven thirty?"

"Si."

"My filly needs to train, can you get her ready for the first set after the break?"

"No problem."

"Thanks, Jorge. Spicy OK?"

"Si, OK. Running soon again I think. Everything OK with you?"

"Very good. You helped a lot. Soon, things will happen."

"Si, Pete. I help."

I return to my shedrow, where Amanda is hanging out with Thunder Clouds.

"Can't wait to get this guy over to Sarah's place." Amanda has arranged everything for his retirement. We just need Ray's consent. Of course Ray's looking for the easy win on the bottom, and the claim purse. That's the $15,000 dilemma.

"Fingers crossed," is my weak response. "You sticking around here for your banking program again, right?"

"Yes, I'm supposed to meet Shawn again around eleven."

"OK, I need to head out. I want to get Hairy walked and back to the house before I head over to Tom's."

"I'll walk out with you." Amanda, Hairy, and I leave the barn and head to my car. When we get there she gives me a deep, passionate kiss.

"Look after yourself. Call me when you get done?"

"Of course, I'll call you from the motel."

"I love you, Pete."

"Love you too." I open my car door. Hairy jumps in ahead of me. I can't wait for Sunday afternoon, to be back at the house with this trip behind me.

I arrive at Tom's place a little before eleven o'clock. Tom is by the barn, waiting for me. He looks anxious to get me going.

"Pete, the paperwork is in your cab. Let's get these guys loaded." Tom is wasting no time. We enter into the area where the horses are, loose. All we need to do is herd them in the direction of the trailer, and the funnel that Tom has designed to make sure the horses filter onto the ramp. Thirty horses are waiting for us. In the group are six huge work horses huddled in one corner.

"They're some big horses, Tom. Will they fit on the trailer OK?"

"It'll be a squeeze, more so than usual, but we should be able to get it done. We need to get thirty horses up there before Monday's slaughter." My guess is that this is part of Tom's contract with the slaughterhouse. Thirty horses to be delivered each week. We start moving the horses in the direction of the trailer. For the most part they are happy to cooperate.

"Where did the work horses come from?" I'm curious about them.

"A local farmer just went bankrupt. One of my dealers brought them in last night from the farm. There's no need to keep them here, they're fit and healthy already." These horses are a victim of the economy. The six join the larger gathering of horses as they all move to the trailer. About half the stock is now loaded. We continue to move them forward. I spot three or four Thoroughbreds in the group. I'll check the EID forms later, when I photograph them all, to see if they're from Jake.

The six work horses are last to load, and it gets pretty ugly. Both Tom and I have to use our bull whips and be pretty aggressive to squeeze them in. It's too crowded. Frankly, it's sickening, but I had to play along.

"It's a tight load, but you'll be fine. The weather's good, so you shouldn't have any problems."

Before I started shipping for Tom, I had googled, "horse slaughterhouse shipping," and similar keywords. I'd read some stories about traffic accidents involving slaughter-bound horses. It appears that a few of the accidents were caused by overcrowding the trucks and the driver losing control of the rig as a consequence. I'm not a very experienced truck driver. This load makes me nervous.

At eleven thirty, I pull out of Tom's driveway. The rig is heavier. I can feel it when I use the brakes and when I make turns. I just need to be much more deliberate with my driving.

Five and a half hours later, just before the border crossing into Canada, I stop to fill up with gas. I also photograph all the documents. Jake Jenkins signed off on four horses, presumably all Thoroughbreds. I study the other EID forms. I'm guessing Tom has all his dealers sign the forms. It would be too risky for him to do it, and expose himself to the potential for fraud. There are four names that account for twenty-five of the horses. The remaining five horses are signed by five different people, probably their previous owners. I'm learning way too much about a system I knew little about only three months ago.

At the border crossing everything goes smoothly. The CFIA guy does his usual walk around the truck, peering in to see if he can count the horses, and make sure they are all still standing. He then seals the back of the truck, stamps some paperwork and sends me on my way. I arrive at the slaughterhouse a little after nine thirty in the evening and head over to the office.

"Made good time today, eh." It's the same guy who was here the last time I delivered for Tom.

"Yeah, straight across the border this time, no traffic." I try to keep my story straight. The guy is looking through the paperwork.

"Tom always brings up good stock from Pennsylvania. One of our top buyers." I'm guessing he's trying to make small talk, which is not my thing at a slaughterhouse. I just want to get out of here.

"Yes, hopefully these horses are good for you." Ugh, to hear me say such crap.

"OK, corral eight, I'll meet you over there." I leave the office and maneuver the load to the off ramp at corral eight. The guy is waiting for me. He breaks the seal, and we drop the ramp to let the horses out. It's such a sad sight to see these horses move into their new temporary space. I head out of there, with a short thanks to the guy. I hope never to see him again.

An hour later I check into the motel. I'm staying at the same one I've been at for the last two trips. It isn't a great place, but it's adequate, and I know it. Once in the room, I call Amanda.

"Hey, Pete. Another long day for you," she notes since it's close to ten thirty. I am pretty tired.

"Yes, tough day. I hope I don't have to do this again. It's soul-destroying."

"I hope you don't have to either. I love you for doing it. I love you for everything."

"I love you too. OK, I'm going to crash. I'll get an early start tomorrow, and text you after I cross the border."

"Sounds good, night."

Before calling it a night, I log onto the internet. I'm interested in seeing if Harry's horse, Dancer's Foil, had his scheduled workout. I pull up the *Daily Racing Form* site. Two headlines catch my attention, "Northern Peaks to return to the races in August. Classic final target." And "Dancer's Foil impresses in Belmont workout."

I click on the first article and read the plan for the Triple Crown winner. His next start will be either the Jim Dandy at Saratoga, or the Haskell Invitational at Monmouth Park. They will use that race as a prep for the Travers Stakes. Then head either directly to the Breeders' Cup Classic, or take in one more race on the way to the Classic. It's a fairly standard plan for a top three-year-old.

I pull up the second story. Dancer's Foil worked a half-mile in forty-seven seconds flat. He did the workout easily, and his trainer is quoted as saying that he will work two more times at Belmont, and then once at Saratoga. If all goes well, he'll run him in the Jim Dandy Stakes at Saratoga, and then point to the Travers Stakes.

So there it is, the distinct possibility of a showdown in August. Harry must be getting pretty excited.

CHAPTER 42

PETE, MONDAY

IT TOOK ME LONGER TO GET BACK FROM CANADA YESTERDAY than I'd hoped. I only got home at six thirty in the evening. Amanda was waiting for me. We went to bed early. When I woke this morning, Amanda was already awake. She made everything seem unreal and wonderful, and allowed me to forget my trip north quickly. I arrive at the barn a little after six, late for the usual feed time.

I have a quiet morning ahead of me, with just Thunder Clouds going to the track. The filly is in the third race tonight. She's the favorite, even though we've stepped her up in the claiming ranks. She's running for $20,000 tonight. Adam texted me yesterday, shortly after he galloped her. He was enthusiastic about how she went. He's ridden a lot of horses, so that can only be a good sign. Her legs are ice cold again this morning.

Thunder Clouds trains with his typical shuffle. He's fine, and really we're only going through the motions. I've stopped looking in the condition book for a race for him. Sometimes Ray will find a race himself, and text me. I'd come up with an excuse either why the race isn't suitable, or how the horse isn't on top of his game. I know this impasse can't last forever, but it only needs to last until we're finished trying to nail Harry. Once that's done, I think Ray will quietly let the horse go. Ray and Harry are pretty tight.

As I'm working in the barn during the break, Sarah texts me to call her. She says it's important.

"Sarah?" I greet her as she picks up my call.

"They've got a positive. Remember the horse we watched win at my place? Came back positive for Dermorphin. They ran the split sample to confirm." I realize I'm shaking. This is what we need. "Timmins wants to meet, as soon as possible. I know your filly's in tonight. Can you get over there this afternoon, say two o'clock?"

"I can do that. What about Margaret?"

"I'll call her, and let you know. Amanda's busy with work."

"Yes, I figured that. She's under pressure to get things done with the bank reorganization."

"I'll message you about Margaret. See you down there just before two."

My day just got more interesting. I get Hairy and we head over to the track kitchen. Alfie is going to finish things up and wait for the state vet to visit, so there is no need for me to hang around.

"Usual, Pete?"

"Thanks, Alice. Good to see Northern Peaks is going to run again." Alice starts preparing my sandwich, she also places two sausages on the grill.

"Yes, it should make for more interesting racing in a month or two."

"Maybe he'll race against Harry's horse?" I'm curious to see what others think about the likelihood of that happening.

"Yes, Pete. I like that horse, don't care much for his owner."

"You and me both, Alice." She hands me my sandwich, and the two sausages. I go to a table and watch Hairy gulp down his meal before I've even started. We have time to go for a nice long walk before I need to head down to Harrisburg.

Sarah sends me a text, "Can you pick Margaret up, 1 at the Missionville Times office?"

"I'll be there."

The drive down to Harrisburg is uneventful. Margaret gives me a rundown of the story she is preparing regarding the horse slaughter situation. She is new to the issue, so she has done a ton of background research. As we drive, she tells me some of the things she's learned that even shock me. She also went to the Owenscreek auction last Tuesday with Amanda. She struggled with it. She talks excitedly about her conversations with the *New York Times*. They are going to let her write the story for them, as long as the documents come back from the USDA or CFIA, and verify the story.

We pull into the parking lot, where Sarah is waiting by her car.

"Hey, Sarah."

"Hi. Good trip down? I've no plan here, let's just see what Timmins has to say."

"Sounds good to me." I'm curious about the next move. I imagine James won't be a vet at Missionville for much longer, but I'm not sure how it will all go down.

We head upstairs to Timmins's office. He comes out to greet us and we follow him in.

"Steve, this is Margaret of the *Missionville Times*. I think you've spoken on the phone," I explain as I introduce them.

"Nice to meet you Margaret. Your notes were very interesting, to say the least."

"Thanks, I'm glad they could help after all these years."

"They did, they supported some background information we are working on. So we have the new positive, we identified the drug. We have the syringe you gave us, same drug, compound and so forth. We have James Norwood's fingerprint. Spicy Lemon's test also came back positive. We plan to 'interview' Norwood tomorrow."

"What do you mean, interview?" I ask Timmins.

"We're going to intercept Norwood, when he leaves the track tomorrow, after his morning rounds. I plan on coming up myself. We checked, Harry doesn't have any runners tonight or tomorrow, so there's no harm waiting until tomorrow lunchtime. Obviously we need to keep this quiet. Our goal is twofold, to make sure Norwood can no longer inject horses with this substance, and to get him to tell us where he gets the drug. If our hunch is correct, he will lead us to Harry's compound pharmacy. We then plan to go after the chemist, and keep pushing until we get to Harry."

"What specifically are you looking for?" Sarah asks Timmins.

"Aside from tying Harry directly to this case, we want to know what he's doing that generates large volumes of cash. Cash he's used to make his pharmacy purchases, and then the racetrack purchase. We're convinced he's now using the racetrack to launder his money." This all makes sense.

"Do you have any hunches?" Margaret presses Timmins.

"We assume it's all drug-related. We think he's supplying some kind of drug on the black market, most likely made at his compound pharmacy. That's our working theory. Obviously when we talk to the chemist, we should know a lot more." So Harry's no more than a drug dealer, exploiting the system.

Our meeting continues for about another twenty minutes as Timmins details some of the conversations he's had with his FBI colleague, who's been on Harry's case for a number of years now. As I listen to all this, I keep thinking how remarkable of Jorge to deliver the smoking gun to the authorities that they needed to bring down someone who's managed to evade them for years.

When we get back to Missionville, I head straight to the track. I have an hour to kill before the first race. If I go home, I'd only have enough time to turn around and come back. I had planned on calling Amanda to fill her in on the Timmins meeting, but she's been under more pressure at work lately. I figured we'd catch up tonight, after the races. I go to Pokers and order a drink.

"Good luck tonight, Pete. You're here early?"

"Thanks, Mary. Yes, I needed to be in this part of town, so I decided to just come over, rather than go home first."

"Your filly looks great tonight, even on the raise."

"Fingers crossed." I pay for my beer and retreat to a table. The televisions are showing the races from Parx Racing and Laurel; they are finishing up their day cards. I sip on my beer and pretend to watch. My mind is focused on what might happen tomorrow. James will disappear. Maybe he would get his sub vet to come in in his place. Surely Timmins will want to have things continue as normal as possible at the track after they go after James. Clare, his sub vet, is pretty good. She generally only comes around the track on the occasional Sunday when James takes the day off. I've always had decent interactions with her. I continue to contemplate.

Amanda calls, I answer. "Hey, you."

"Pete, how was Harrisburg?"

"It was very good." I lower my voice, although there are only a couple of other people at Pokers. It's still early. "They're going to go after James tomorrow, so we'll know more after that. How was your day?"

"Ugh. Hectic, and crazy. The bank wants me to have final plans in place by the end of this week. I'm still working with all the branch managers to finalize everything. It's a nightmare. But what the heck, we'll get through it. What time will you be home?"

"The filly's in the third, hoping a little after eight o'clock."

"Don't eat, I'll prepare us a nice dinner."

"That'll be great."

"Good luck tonight."

"Thanks, we'll need it. See you later."

"I'll be naked." And just like that, Amanda hangs up.

A few more people had come into Pokers. The horses for the first race are walking over from the backside, heading to the paddock. I go outside to take in the scene. The first race is a maiden claiming event for two-year-olds. I hadn't bothered reading the form. The old me would have known as much as I could about every horse in the race. The new me doesn't really care anymore. I'm excited to run my filly, but the other races have become meaningless.

Less than an hour later I'm in the paddock. My nerves are up. Alfie is leading Pink Slippers around the paddock. She looks terrific. The valets file out of the jocks' room, I nod to Alfie to bring her in to be saddled. She continues to be a very professional filly in the paddock; a couple of the other horses are creating a lot of problems for their connections. Once saddled, Alfie leads her back out to walk a few more turns. Emma Sparks files out with the other jockeys.

"What do you think, Emma? Can we keep the winning streak going?"

"I hope so. The race looks good for her. Lots of speed to aim at."

"Yes, it looks like that. Keep her covered up, and see what you've got." Alfie brings the filly back in. The paddock judge makes his call, "Riders up!" and I swing Emma aboard. My nervous anxiety increases. Alfie passes Emma and the filly off to Jake. They head down to the starting gate. I return to Pokers.

"Thanks, Mary." She has my Budweiser ready. It has been a long day, a good day, which promises more later, but the next few minutes will determine the day. I take a few swigs of my beer as I study the TV screen by the bar. She's now the 5-2 favorite, in a competitive field of seven. I'm surprised she's the favorite.

"It's post time." They start loading in the gate. Pink Slippers walks in like she's done it a hundred times. "They're in the gate," the track announcer says, "and they're off!"

She tucks in behind the front-runners nicely. Emma is motionless above the filly. The first quarter is fast, we are three lengths off the lead in fourth place. As they head into the turn, Emma lets out a couple of notches of rein and Pink Slippers starts to move closer to the leaders. Coming off the turn Emma takes her three-wide, and she is able to get her to the front just inside the eighth pole. Then she draws away by a couple of lengths. It is a very nice victory. I'm completely buzzed, that euphoric feeling pumping through my veins.

An hour later, I arrive at home to Amanda waiting for me, sitting at the dining room table, naked.

CHAPTER 43

PETE, WEDNESDAY

MY ALARM BLARES, WAKING ME FROM A BLISSFUL SLUMBER. I need a few seconds to orientate myself. Amanda doesn't seem to have been disturbed by the noise. She continues her rhythmic breathing. Last night we enjoyed a lovely dinner at Zucchini's, followed by a nightcap at Jessup's.

We haven't heard anything from Timmins yet. We don't know how things went with James yesterday. I guess we'll learn, one way or another, soon enough.

Seeing James yesterday was strange. He has a confident, easy-going way about him. We chatted, briefly, as he was passing through. He asked me how my filly was doing after her latest win and even split a doughnut. He seemed genuinely happy for me. You'd never know there is another side to him, a much darker side. I wonder what pushed him in that direction.

I arrive at the barn right at six. The horses are ready for their feed. The filly's appetite seems to have increased lately, which is a very good thing. I've upped her feed, and she's holding very good weight. Oftentimes if you run a filly too many times too quickly, she will lose her condition.

I only have my two geldings to train today, since the filly will be walking the shedrow. It is going to be an easy morning. I go to the tack room to get the tack for Thunder Clouds. Hairy follows me and then drops himself in his corner to go to sleep for the rest of the morning.

My training career is now nearly over. Of the two horses I'm training today, one I don't know what I'm going to do with next, the other I will never run again. I don't know what I will do when I've finished training at Missionville, but I do have a plan for who I want to do things with. I've even contemplated marriage, something that would have been entirely alien to me six months ago. It's funny how life moves in twists and turns.

I'm about to put Thunder Clouds's saddle on when Alfie arrives, right at seven o'clock.

"Filly first?"

"Please, Alfie." He will take the filly out, hose off her front legs, dry them with a towel, and then walk her for thirty minutes. They'll be finished around the same time I return from the track on Thunder Clouds.

The old guy trains well, shuffling around the racetrack. It feels uncomfortable when you're on him, but he has his ears pricked the whole time, which is generally a sign that he's OK. Another month or so, and he should be retired. My other gelding also went well on the track. An easy morning, we are all done at the break.

As I finish things up Clare, James's sub vet, stops by. Maybe the plan yesterday did happen after all.

"Hey, Clare, it's not Sunday is it?" I say, deliberately claiming ignorance.

"Pete, no. James called me. He's pretty sick."

"Wow! That sucks. What's wrong with him?"

"Some kind of summer flu. He said he'll be out for at least a week, maybe more."

"Well, it's good that you can back him up."

"It'll be a struggle with my regular practice, but I'll manage."

"It's good to see you regardless. I'm OK today."

"Great, I'll stop by tomorrow." She heads down Mike's shedrow.

So James is out of commission for at least a week. Something *has* happened. I suppose I'll just wait until I hear more.

I fetch Hairy from my tack room and we head over to the kitchen for some breakfast.

"Usual, Pete?"

"Thanks, Alice." She places two sausages on the grill and starts preparing my sandwich. This I will miss when I leave. The ordinary interactions I have with people I've come to care for, and who care for me, and Hairy.

I receive a text from Sarah, "Call me when you can. Just spoke to Timmins."

I put my phone back in my pocket. Alice gives me my sandwich and two sausages, I head for a table that is furthest from those that are occupied. Hairy chomps down on his two sausages. I call Sarah.

"Pete."

"What do you know?"

"Timmins got to James yesterday. He told him some of the evidence he has on him. Told him to come to his office in Harrisburg next Thursday, 2 p.m., for a more detailed conversation. He also instructed him not to share this with anyone. If he does, he'll bring the full weight of the law on him, or something like that."

"So basically he's told him not to alert Franks or Harry?"

"That sounds about right. Timmins wants you to attend the meeting, if you can."

"Did he say why?"

"Something to do with the syringe we gave him. You can corroborate where it came from."

"OK, I'll be there." I will have to confront James directly. I wasn't prepared for that, but I suppose it makes sense. "His sub vet, Clare, was on the grounds today. She said James was sick, and would be out for at least a week."

"I guess that's his story for now. Hopefully it doesn't raise any suspicions." We chat for a little longer. I finish my sandwich, and head out for a long walk with Hairy.

CHAPTER 44

PETE, THURSDAY, JULY 7

(A WEEK LATER)

ARRIVING AT TIMMINS'S OFFICE, I REALIZE JUST HOW ANXIOUS I am about this meeting. I don't know how James will react when he understands that I've been involved in his downfall. I'm also curious to see the real James. Is he the same person I've come to know over the years at the barn, or is there more to him that I don't know? Obviously he has another side, but what's really driving his desire to go down the wrong path? Maybe I'll find out.

This last week, Amanda and I have been discussing it over and over. What makes someone do something they absolutely know is wrong? I know I've been a little guilty of this, before I started dating Amanda, but nothing to the same extent that James has.

James is in the waiting area as I walk in. Another guy is here too. I glance over to James as I sit down. He doesn't acknowledge my entrance. Timmins comes out and invites us all into his office. We take our seats.

"This is nothing but a meeting. Nothing legal, just a conversation," Timmins begins. "James Norwood, you know Pete Wright, and this is Bruce Smith, a local FBI agent." This time James looks at me and almost smiles. We all make non-verbal acknowledgements.

"We're here to discuss positive drug tests for the drug Dermorphin," Timmins continues, "and to make the connection to James, and then possibly to the connections of the horses involved. We currently have two positives."

"James, do you have anything to say, for now? Remember, everything is off the record." Timmins is seeking a quick explanation. James has had a week to think about his situation. He declines to respond. The James I know from the barn would welcome the opportunity to express his version of events.

"Well the two positives. The first is for Spicy Lemon, after his last win, back in April. This was the first time he raced for Mike Franks and Harry Mitchell. The second is for Rueben Steel, who won a little over three weeks ago for the same people. Are these two horses that you treated, James?"

"I am the private vet for Mike Franks and Harry Mitchell, so yes, I treated those horses."

"Good. Can you explain how they both tested positive for Dermorphin?"

"I can't, but I'm guessing you can," James replies combatively.

"We found a syringe which has your fingerprints on it, and the drug Dermorphin." I assume James already knows this fact, from his meeting with Timmins last week.

"That may be true. I treat all kinds of animals, for all kinds of reasons. I don't see how that ties me to this case." I guess Timmins had told James only so much last week.

"The syringe was discovered in Spicy Lemon's stall, the day of his race," Timmins recounts methodically.

"Can you prove that?" James inquires, trying to avoid the inevitable, but he is starting to look uneasy.

"Remember James, this is just a conversation, nothing legal here. Bear that in mind. Pete brought us the syringe." James looks towards me; he didn't seem to know I was involved. He does now. He looks agitated, like he is losing control of the conversation.

"Where did Pete get the syringe?"

"Jorge gave it to me." I didn't know if Timmins wanted me to answer, but I want it out there. "I believe his print was also discovered on the syringe."

"That still doesn't prove anything. There's a syringe, I used it. It had Dermorphin in it. That's really all you've got?"

"That, and Spicy Lemon, the horse that Jorge takes care of, that raced that night, tested positive for the same drug. That's pretty damning, James," Timmins pushes.

"I could still argue there is coincidence there."

"You could, James, and I repeat, this is not a legal hearing at present. We may move on to that soon, as you're aware. You know that Spicy Lemon is

not the only positive. I think you'll have a tough case to argue, the consequences could be dire." James is listening, and he's a smart guy.

Timmins continues, "We're not interested in you so much, although you
will lose your practicing license in the state of Pennsylvania, no matter what
direction we go in. But we're interested in Harry Mitchell, the owner. Bruce,
why don't you take over for a minute?" James and I look over to Bruce Smith
who's been a silent witness to the conversation up to this point.

"Thanks, Steve, and thanks for inviting me to this. I've been tracking
Mr. Mitchell for a number of years now. He's become somewhat of a local
celebrity as a successful entrepreneur, as I'm sure you're aware. The problem
is, his business practices don't make sense from a legal standpoint. He runs
low turnover pharmacies, yet generates a lot of income, mostly cash. We've
never really figured out what he's doing to create the cash he makes. We're
convinced the racetrack purchase was solely to help him launder some of
that cash. But again, we haven't found the proof that we need."

Smith continues, "James, you could be a real help to us, if you're willing.
If you do help us, Steve will help you through this case."

"OK. I might help. What do you want from me?"

"Who supplies the drug to you? Where do you get it from?"

"Harry."

Bingo! He's rolling. I guess he doesn't have much choice. Harry's ship
might be sinking, but there's no need for James to go down with it.

"He gives it to you directly?" Timmins asks.

"No. I get it from his compound pharmacy. His chemist makes it for me."

"Right Relief Compound, that's the one, right?"

"Yes, just out of town from Missionville."

"And the chemist's name?"

"Ben Blackton."

"Thanks, James. That's all we really need to know for now. You're out sick
from your track work, right?"

"Yes, I have a sub vet doing all my work."

"You need to remain sick for another month. Once we've done our bit,
getting to Harry, we'll resolve the positives, and you'll get as lenient a
punishment as the law allows us to hand down. Make sense?"

James looks resigned to this outcome.

"It makes sense," he acknowledges.

And with that, the meeting is over. Smith and Timmins remain behind,

James and I leave and head to the parking lot. It's pretty awkward.

"I'm sorry James. I liked you. You did good work for me, but I went after you for this." I want to be honest. I want him to know that I care about these horses, and what he did was really wrong. "I noticed you doing something with Harry's horses on race day, it just wasn't right." He remains silent as we continue walking to our cars. "I hope you can understand why I did what I did, and I hope you realize that what you did is awful. Jesus, James, say something!" I raise my voice at the end. I want a response, not just some resigned bull-shit.

"Pete, you did what you had to do. I'd have done the same. Tell Jorge, thanks." It seems like a genuine sentiment, like he's relieved in some way. He goes to his car, our conversation is over.

On my drive back to Missionville, I receive a text message from James, "I was being blackmailed. No excuse. Get him."

CHAPTER 45

PETE, SATURDAY JULY 16

(A WEEK LATER)

I WAKE UP BEFORE MY ALARM. I HAVE THINGS ON MY MIND.
Jake has asked me to do another run up to Canada for Tom. I thought of plenty of reasons to give him why I didn't want to do it, but none of them were good enough. I need to keep doing this until we finally expose the system. Waiting for the documents from the USDA is becoming painful. Sarah reckons it should be very soon. Margaret already has the story prepared.

As I'm getting dressed, Amanda stirs, sits up and stretches, naked.

"Morning, Pete."

"Hey. No need for you to be up yet."

"I like to watch you get ready, when I can." She has that way of getting me aroused with a few simple words. I abandon dressing, and lean over to kiss her deeply. I don't leave the bed for another fifty minutes. Amanda is fast asleep by then.

I arrive at the barn at six forty, my horses are pretty anxious. A few of Mike's help have already arrived, which adds to my horses' agitation. I feed them quickly.

I'm now back up to four horses because Ray had me claim another filly last week for $10,000. Her name is Flower Garden. She'd raced in New York in her early days. Her wins there included an allowance race at Aqueduct. She's been racing at Missionville for about a year now, and was steadily dropping in class. Ray thinks there are a couple more wins left in her. Before, I would have been excited by the prospect, now I just want to take good care of her, and hope I can do right by her.

Pink Slippers is doing well, again, after her last victory. Ray will want her back in the races soon to see if we can keep her winning streak going. I'm relieved that she's done so well, it takes the pressure off me running the two geldings. Although I'm not sure how much longer that can really last.

I strip off all the bandages, my horses' legs look decent. Thunder Clouds's ankle is still big, but there's no heat. Pink Slippers's legs are still ice cold, which is pretty incredible given the work load she's been putting in. The new filly's legs are OK, she has an old tendon on the left front leg I've been working on. If I can shrink it a little more, she might come sounder. When we claimed Flower Garden, she finished third. She looked like the winner at the eighth pole, but weakened quickly. It looks to me like the sore leg might have affected her finishing kick.

"Morning, boss. Gelding first?" I hear Alfie over my shoulder. It's odd, we just call Fred Flintstone 'the gelding.' But he does have a name. We breezed him a little yesterday, so he's just walking today, after Alfie hoses off his poultice.

"Yes, thanks, Alfie. Can you cover for me again tomorrow? I'll ask Jorge too."

"No problem, boss."

I head to the tack room to get the tack for the new filly, she'll be first to train this morning. Hairy follows me, and drops himself in his corner. He'll be fast asleep in minutes.

Fifteen minutes later I'm on the track with Flower Garden. We're both still getting used to each other.

"Hey, Pete. How do you like your new horse?"

"I like her, Jess." Even if I don't, I'd say I do. That's what we do.

"She looks good, you'll treat her well."

"I'll try my best."

"Big horses are working today." Jess and I have discussed Northern Peaks and Dancer's Foil, from time to time, over the last couple of weeks.

"Yes, two more works to their next races. Things could get interesting."

"I can't see anyone really beating the champ though." Jess is a big fan of

Northern Peaks, and who can blame her, he's the Triple Crown winner. But Dancer's Foil did look good in the Wood Memorial before he hurt himself.

"You might be right, Jess. I'll catch up with you on Monday after the works." I walk off, and then move into a jog. Flower Garden is going to be doing my usual routine of galloping a mile and a half from the wire.

She trains quite well. She's a little aggressive in the early part of her gallop. I've been trying to ease her down and get her to relax more. It's starting to work.

Once back in the barn I hand her off to Alfie, and get my other filly ready. I only have time to train two before the break today, so the morning will be a little rushed to get everything done, and be at Tom's by eleven.

Amanda is on the rail, by the time I'm on the track with Pink Slippers. She looks lovely, as usual, chatting away with a couple of horsemen. As I stand my filly in, my thoughts jump to the idea of marriage again. Why not? We love each other, we really like each other, we're best friends. I cannot imagine not being with her. I'm sure she thinks the same about me. Why not? I walk the filly away, and smile at Amanda.

"Can you stop by at break time?" I ask her. She usually stops by my barn last on her barn tour, but I need to chat before I leave for Tom's.

"Sure, Pete."

I trot off. The filly trains beautifully again, floating across the track surface. I think there's another win in her, even on the raise again. We might need to look at one of the little allowance races they run here.

When I get back to the barn, Clare is in my shedrow.

"Hey, Pete. All good today?"

"I think we're fine. I may need you to look at my new filly early next week. I want to see what we can do with her tendon."

"Sounds good." Clare's been subbing for James for nearly three weeks now. She's become one of the fixtures on the backside pretty quickly. From time to time, I ask her how James is doing, and she just says he's still pretty sick. I don't know if she really believes it.

Since James sent me that text, on my way back from the meeting, we haven't communicated directly. But it all makes sense now. Harry has something on James, so James went to the other side for Harry. I just don't know what Harry has on him.

I gave James's contact information to Margaret. She wants to follow up on some of the horses we had identified for the article she's writing about the slaughter issue. James would have documented his treatment of a few of the horses. It would be more damning evidence of the fraud in the slaughter pipeline.

Amanda stops by the barn, during the break.

"Hi, Pete. Nice morning?" She smiles coyly.

"Hey, you." I smile before asking for a favor, "Any chance you can take Hairy when you leave, and then take him for a walk later? I'm short on time."

"Of course."

"Great. I'll just leave him in the tack room. You can pick him up when you're ready."

"Sounds good. You'll call me from Canada when you're in the motel?"

"Of course."

"And we'll have a special meal when you get back on Sunday."

"I can't wait." I really can't. I hope this will be my last trip for Tom.

"I need to see a few people, get a couple more horses photographed and videoed for my site." Amanda kisses me and leaves. I get Thunder Clouds ready. Twenty minutes later we are shuffling around the racetrack. The difference between his stride and Pink Slippers's is stark. Riding him after the filly makes his stride seem worse. Hopefully he'll soon be retired.

After finishing up in my barn, I go to see Jorge, who is in Spicy Lemon's stall.

"Hey, Jorge. How's the old guy?"

"He's OK, runs next week." I make a mental note to tell Sarah.

"Will he win?"

"I don't think so. No James." Jorge knows what's going on, and I haven't really said anything to him.

"Yes, right. Any chance you can help me out tomorrow?"

"Si, 7:30 again?"

"That'll be great. None training, just get their stalls."

"No problem."

"Gracias." I wander back to my shedrow. All sorted. Now a quick sandwich, and then off to Tom's place.

I get to Tom's right at eleven o'clock. He is waiting for me as I drive in. Another thirty horses are in the big barn, ready to be loaded and sent on their way, their USDA tags identifying them as meat animals. I take a look around before we move them into the trailer; there are at least four or five

Thoroughbreds in the group. There are also a number of Standardbreds. Maybe one of the local trotting tracks has closed down for the season. I really don't know how their racing works, or what happens to their horses after they are finished racing, but Standardbreds are ever present in these loads.

"Ready to load them, Pete? Let's get you on your way."

"Sure, Tom." I don't have a lot to say. We move in amongst the horses, bull whips in hand. Ten minutes later the last horse steps into the trailer and we shut the ramp.

"See you tomorrow. Documents are all ready for you in the truck."

"Thanks, see you tomorrow." And that is it, I'm on my way to Canada again. The load doesn't feel as heavy as the last one I shipped. The weather conditions are good and there isn't too much traffic on the road. It all makes for a reasonably easy ride up north. I pull into a gas station, just before the border, like I did last time, and fill back up. I photograph all the documents. I notice Jake Jenkins's signature on six of the EID forms. I see three other familiar names from prior trips.

The border crossing is reasonably uneventful, once I get to the booth. There's a slight delay because I followed two other trucks. The CFIA guy is starting to become a familiar face. He checks around my trailer, performing his usual routine to make it look like he's counting the number of horses I have on board. He seals the truck, stamps and signs some forms which he hands back to me, and I'm on my way. I hate that I'm getting used to this routine.

Two and a half hours later I arrive in Massueville in Quebec, the small village that plays host to the slaughterhouse. Once at the plant, I head to the office.

"Good to see you again, Pete. Another load from Tom, eh." I'm getting familiar with too many people.

"Yes, good to see you." The guy looks at his computer. "Corral six, just pull up there and we'll let 'em off."

I do as instructed. He is waiting for me by the entrance to the corral, and cuts the seal on the truck. The horses move out into their new surroundings, some of their snorting and squealing sets off a little hollering from a couple of the other adjacent corrals. A mass of horses ready to be processed into meat.

"That's it. See you next time." God, I hope there's no next time.

"Thanks, see you." I jump back in my cab and head out of the hell hole as quickly as I can.

I check into the same motel and take a hot shower to clean myself up. I feel a little better. I also bought a six-pack of Budweiser, two empty bottles are already in the trash can.

I pull up Amanda's number on my phone.

"Hey, honey."

"Hey, you. Just get in?"

"Had a quick shower. I needed to get clean after being up there."

"I wish I was there with you. I'd help you get clean."

"I wish you were here too. All good there?"

"Yep. Hairy and I had a great long walk around the lake just out of town. I did some work on my computer this afternoon, and now I'm just a little lonely."

"Me too, to that last point. I'll get up extra early tomorrow and get back by mid-afternoon."

"I'll head out in the morning with Hairy, and then be waiting for you. What do you want to do tomorrow night aside from dinner?"

"Nothing but hang out with you." Our conversation continues for a few more minutes, with plenty of sexual innuendo going back and forth. Finally, we hang up.

I pull up the internet. I'm interested in how the two big horses worked today, and if there is any confirmation regarding their next races. I go to the *Daily Racing Form* site and see, "Northern Peaks bullet work, will headline the Haskell at Monmouth." And "Dancer's Foil continues to do well, getting close to a return."

I read the first story. Northern Peaks worked in 58 and change, just after the break at Belmont Park. It was the fastest work of twenty breezes today at that distance. His trainer was very happy with the performance. The horse had galloped out an extra quarter of a mile in 24 seconds. He'll ship to Monmouth Park late next week, and work one more time over the New Jersey oval, for a start in the Haskell Invitational, the following Sunday. All seems like standard stuff for a leading three-year-old. I exit the story.

I pull up the second article. Dancer's Foil also worked at Belmont Park, going the same distance in 59 and change, a second slower than Northern Peaks; it was still one of the fastest works of the day. He galloped out an extra eighth of a mile in 12 seconds. His trainer was also pleased with the move – you never see trainers quoted as not pleased with their horse's work ahead of a big race – and Dancer's Foil will ship up to Saratoga next week. He will have one more workout at the upstate New York track. If all goes well, he'll race in the Jim Dandy Stakes.

Both the Haskell and Jim Dandy are preps for the Travers Stakes at the end of August. A showdown is looming.

CHAPTER 46

PETE, FRIDAY JULY 22

AS I'M FINISHING UP AT THE BARN, SARAH TEXTS ME, "Call me when you can."

I go to my tack room to make the call.

"Sarah?"

"The USDA documents have arrived."

"And?"

"All's in order. Basically, we have proof those horses were slaughtered."

"What's the next step?"

"I'll get the documents to Margaret. She can finish up her story, and we'll just wait to see it run."

"Do you know if Margaret got a hold of James?"

"I don't know, but I assume so. She's not said otherwise. She told me she has everything else she needs. I think she went back to Owenscreek last week with Amanda too. She's on it."

"Very good. Your horse is in tonight."

"Ugh, I know. I'm freaking out about it. The sooner we blow up the slaughter story, the better."

"I'll go over to the races and watch him run. He's in the second, so it'll be easy enough."

"Thanks, and thanks for keeping an eye on him."

"No worries. I get it. We'll get him back, one way or another. Talk later."

So we've got the story ready, and it should run in the *New York Times* soon.

This is huge. The fallout could be damaging. I'm not sure if it's enough to bring Harry down, but it might get close enough to him that he straightens up his act. I can't imagine Jake can survive the story, nor Tom, or the slaughter pipeline as it currently exists. Fingers crossed. I'm frankly ashamed I've been relatively oblivious to the issue for many years, until Amanda and I got together.

We've started talking about a real commitment. I had been hesitant to bring it up, worried that the thought of the long term might upset what we have 'in the here and now.' But Amanda is all over the idea. We've decided to wait until the dust settles after the Harry cases, and then we'll slide off somewhere and tie the knot. I couldn't happier. We're planning to head to Zucchini's tonight to celebrate.

I text Amanda, "In case you haven't spoken to Sarah, USDA came through, we're a go with the story X"

She calls me right back.

"I just got off the phone with Sarah. Great news!"

"Yes. I can't wait to see the story run. Things will happen."

"For sure. You've done something amazing for the horses here." Amanda is referring to my trips for Tom. I don't feel good about it at all, but I'm glad I won't have to do another one.

"It's a team effort, once the story gets out there." And it really is. Amanda inspired me. Sarah mentored Amanda, and Margaret stepped in with her journalistic experience. We just need to wait a couple more days, to see it all explode.

"I've got to get back to work. I'm pitching my proposal this afternoon to the board. Wish me luck." I'd almost forgotten, Amanda's been crushed with work lately getting this plan together.

"You'll kill 'em. I'll be home by seven thirty tonight, then we'll head to Zucchini's for a big celebration."

It's the last race night of the week. In the summer months we sometimes get a bit of a crowd on Fridays. It might be an office party, or a few students coming together for a different experience. But Fridays in the summer can be a little less bleak at the track. When I arrive at the races just before the first, there are already a couple of groups huddled together with beers and wines in hand, hanging out by the paddock. I head into Pokers.

"Budweiser, Pete?"

"Thanks, Mary." Mary opens a bottle for me.

"Don't see you so much anymore when you're not racing. Shopping again?"

"Not tonight, just killing an hour." I go to a table to just chill out for a little while. Spicy Lemon is in the second race. There isn't much need for me to go out to the paddock to see the maidens in the first.

Pokers is starting to fill up, most of the usual horsemen gather around the tables they occupy each night of racing. We are a very predictable group. As much as I'll miss the track kitchen and Alice, I won't miss this place.

Adam walks in. I didn't realize he had a runner tonight. He gets himself a beer, and heads in my direction.

"Hey, Pete. Good to see you here."

"Adam, you racing tonight?"

"Yes, I've got one in the last. It's 20-1. It'll be a long night for me."

"Good luck, though I won't be sticking around to see how you do."

"Don't blame you. It's hard, not sure I'm cut out for this training game. Galloping horses is much less complicated."

"And easier on your bank account, unless you get winners." A free-lance exercise rider can make plenty of money if he wants to hustle, and Adam is a hustler, in a good sense. He's a hard worker. But training is difficult, unless you have a generous owner. Adam is basically his own owner at this point.

"For sure. I'm nearly broke. This horse running tonight's already cost me $200 to pre-race, and I've little shot at recouping anything."

"You going to stick with it, or go back to galloping?"

"I don't know. I'll give it a little more time. That's all I can afford."

"Best of luck. Unfortunately good horsemanship is less important these days." I've seen some great horsemen struggle at the training game. I've seen some who aren't horsemen at all be very successful. Mike Franks is a good example of the latter. I can't imagine he's ever ridden a horse. He's willing to cheat, and he's got an owner willing to do the same.

Adam and I watch the first race, and then I leave to head to the paddock for the second race.

Jorge leads Spicy Lemon into the paddock. The horse still looks well, his red coat shines brightly. Jorge takes great care of his horses. When he walks by me, he nods in my direction. Mike Franks is standing by saddling stall three, waiting for the valet to come out with his tack. The crowd has filled out a bit more around the paddock area. It's turning into a nice summer's evening. The second race is a $10,000 claiming event. It's the same claiming price they paid for Spicy Lemon. He's the fifth choice in a field of seven runners. If you throw out the race he won for Franks, he'd probably be the longest shot on the board. I don't hold out much hope that he'll run well at all.

Jorge takes his horse over to be saddled. The seven older horses stand almost motionless as their connections put the tack on and get their horses ready. Once done, each is brought back out and led round the oval area. Longman comes out with the other jockeys. He probably knows he's on a loser, and likely doesn't care – just going through the motions. He and Franks talk briefly, as Jorge brings Spicy back in.

"Riders up!" comes the call from the paddock judge. Spicy is third in line to be led out of the paddock. Jorge hands him off to Jake. I go over to see Jorge. It seems like a good time to chat, outside of the barn.

"Hey, Jorge. Horse looks great, as usual."

"Si, thanks. Tough race for him."

"Hard to pick him, with what we know."

"Si."

OK, I need to tell him. "You know why James is no longer around Jorge?"

"They say he's sick, but I don't know."

"Because of that syringe. It tied everything up nicely. James was caught."

Jorge thinks for a moment, and says, "Bueno, gracias."

"You've done a very good thing. James is just the beginning."

"I help. It was no good."

"Hopefully more will happen soon. I'll let you know."

The horses are loading into the starting gate.

"Gracias. I help."

We turn our attention to the race. They're all in the gate.

"They're in the gate," the track announcer begins, "and they're off!"

Spicy Lemon breaks well enough, and settles into third place heading down the backside. Longman is sitting very still on him. As they head into the turn, a horse from behind moves upsides him, and then passes him easily. Spicy is in fourth place, and it doesn't look like he is going to make a move of his own. As they straighten up at the head of the stretch Spicy drops back to sixth place. By the time they cross the wire he's last, about five lengths behind the next to last horse.

"No bueno."

"Sorry, Jorge. He had no kick at all." It was a poor performance. I imagine Sarah will start thinking the worst now – time for them to get rid of the horse.

Jorge goes to get his horse, I text Sarah the bad news. "Spicy finished last, no kick. Will keep my eyes open the next few days."

CHAPTER 47

PETE, MONDAY

STARTING WITH AN INCREDIBLY DEEP RED SUNRISE, this morning is gorgeous. Soon enough, it will be very hot, so I am ready first thing to head out to the track on Pink Slippers. I want to get three horses trained before the break, then Thunder Clouds after the break.

"More good workouts from the top horses, Jess," I say as I stand in at the gap.

"Yes, Northern Peaks's easy half-mile at Monmouth is all he needs. He should be ready."

"The Haskell field doesn't look too strong, just the horse that was third in the Derby."

"Should be a nice gallop around for a million dollars," Jess notes with a little sarcasm. There is a lot of money at the very top of the sport, and not too many good horses competing. I agree with Jess, this should be an easy win for the Triple Crown champion.

"Dancer's Foil's five-eighths at Saratoga was very good too."

"I guess they used it to tighten him up just a little more. Not sure if he's ready for this level of competition after his time off, but maybe," Jess comments, less certain that Dancer's Foil is the real deal.

"We'll see. I think he'll be ready for them." I walk off, and then jog to the wire.

The filly is still training very well, and today is no exception. After standing at the wire for a few minutes, watching horses gallop by, we move off into a perfect gallop. She just eats up the ground with her floating action. We gallop in close behind a set of Jim Johnson two-year-olds. I had to move her to the inside and overtake them; she'd started to get very strong.

Once we are back in the barn, Alfie takes her and I start on the next one, the gelding.

An hour later I ride Flower Garden into the starting gate. Whenever I claim a new horse, I like to do a little gate schooling with it. Too many times you will see a horse lose a race because of antics it performs at the gate. What you want is for a horse to be very quiet and stand square on all four of its legs as the gates open. Getting them used to the gate without racing, helps with that.

Our gate crew at Missionville is decent; they let me take my time with my horses. Flower Garden walks right in, and we stand there with the gates closed for a couple of minutes while two of the gate crew climb up around her. They then back us out. She's perfect. I'll probably do it one more time, close to when I race her for the first time.

At break time, Clare stops by. Alfie is still walking the new filly, so I have him stop her in the shedrow so Clare can take a close look at her tendon on her left front. She picks up the leg, and gives the tendon a couple of good squeezes. The filly doesn't react. She then asks Alfie to jog her back and forth. He does. The horse isn't visibly lame at the jog.

"I think it's old, Pete. We could do an ultrasound to be sure. But I think you should just keep doing what you're doing, it might strengthen it." I've been working one of my liniments into the tendon. There's not much more I can do.

"Thanks, Clare. She's coming around in her training, so fingers crossed." Clare walks down to Mike's shedrow.

I get Thunder Clouds ready. Fifteen minutes later the old guy is shuffling round the racetrack in his training, no better or worse than he's been going lately. I've become very fond of the horse, but he's not good for my back.

I notice Jake's trailer outside our barn when I bring Thunder Clouds back from the track. Jake's in Mike's shedrow as I take the horse one turn around before putting him in his stall. When he sees me he nods a hello. I have a bad feeling.

Twenty minutes later, while I am cleaning my tack, I hear a horse being loaded on the trailer. I step outside to take a look. Another one is ready to be loaded. Jorge is there waiting with Spicy Lemon. Harry is cutting his losses on the horse and getting rid of him.

I immediately go back into my tack room and call Sarah.

"Sorry, Sarah. Jake's taking Spicy Lemon. They're loading him now."

"Thanks, Pete." She hangs up. I guess she doesn't have anything to say. What can you say?

CHAPTER 48

AMANDA, TUESDAY

SARAH CALLED ME IN A PANIC YESTERDAY. Her worst nightmare is unfolding; Spicy Lemon has been shipped out of Harry's barn. I was already planning to go to Owenscreek today for the auction, Sarah wants me to see if Spicy Lemon is there, in Tom's kill pen.

Pete is getting ready for the barn.

"See you over at Sarah's later, right?"

"Yes, look forward to it."

"I think Margaret's coming too. Maybe you guys can ride over together in her car. No need for both of us to drive back."

"Makes sense, I'll call her this morning."

"Perfect."

Margaret is meeting us all today to show us the final version of the story she sent to the *New York Times*. She thinks they'll run it tomorrow, barring any headline news bumping the story. I'm very excited to see it out there, unfortunately the news of Spicy Lemon disappearing has dampened my enthusiasm a little. I know how hard this is on Sarah. She loves that guy, and feels that she let him down.

I'm in the office by seven thirty. Work has been very busy over the last few weeks, but my reorganization proposal has finally been approved. I now need to hire some vendors to help execute the plan. In six months, our branches will be completely overhauled; my major task now is to make sure that everything happens as I detailed in the approved plan. It is the type of work challenge that I thrive on. Even the managers at each of the branches have embraced it, realizing this may well be the future.

My morning at the bank moves along quickly. Soon enough I change into my auction outfit – a T shirt and pair of jeans – and head to Owenscreek. I'm not sure what I'll do if I see a horse in Tom's kill pen, other than photograph it and send the pictures to Sarah to confirm whether it's Spicy. Tom won't resell him to me. Jake won't let any of Harry's horses go for resell. I guess I'll just be confirming Sarah's worst nightmare, giving her some kind of horrific closure. I had hoped the *New York Times* story would run before this happened. It might have given us an easy way to convince Harry to let the horse go.

I arrive at the auction just as the tack sale gets underway. It gives me plenty of time to head out back and check on the horses.

There are two Thoroughbreds in Tom's kill pen. My stomach drops. I don't remember what Spicy looks like, but I assume he is one of the two. I don't usually do anything about the horses already in the kill pens, but I need to get a couple of pictures, very discreetly. From about three corrals away I take some video, then snap five photos. I head to the kitchen area to send them to Sarah; five minutes later she texts back, "He's not one of them."

I guess that's good. Jake's picked up Spicy, but hasn't sent him to Tom, not yet anyway. Maybe Tom can only take a certain number of horses each week from Jake and Harry. Who knows why there might be a delay, but there seems to be one. Jake has a small holding, the horse must still be there.

I head out of the kitchen and survey the other horses, trying to identify the other Thoroughbreds. It looks like there are five of them. I go through my usual routine of documenting who they are. I then go to the gallery and wait for the horse auction to begin.

The auction is busy today, with ninety-three horses selling. Tom buys twenty-one and Fred snags seventeen of them. All the Thoroughbreds go to the two kill buyers. Prices for meat horses remain quite high. There are a few private buyers taking a chance on some of the horses, the rest go to a mix of rescues and dealers. The dealers will try to spin them through another auction, or just bring them back another time.

Jake is sitting in his usual spot in the gallery. As the auction ends I walk over to see him.

"Hey, Jake."

"Amanda, looking lovely as usual."

"Do you have Harry's horse, Spicy Lemon?" I get straight to the point.

"If he's one of the ones I picked up on Monday, then yes, he's at my farm. I didn't have room to bring him today," Jake says honestly.

"What are you going to do with him?"

"He's Harry's horse. He'll come here next week, and go to Tom. You know how it is." I do, I obviously don't like it.

"OK, thanks." There's no point in arguing with Jake, nor asking if I could buy the horse from him. Harry makes it clear to Jake, and I know it. His horses go to kill.

I head to my car, while texting Sarah, "Spicy's at Jake's place. He'll be there until the next auction."

Pete had texted me a little earlier. He and Margaret will get to Sarah's after five. I get there an hour before to find Sarah in her kitchen, I smell the coffee brewing.

"Hey, Sarah."

"Amanda, good to see you. I'm a wreck over Spicy. I can't concentrate on anything else."

"I'm sure you are. Don't give up. We have a week to get him out of Jake's place, one way or another."

"I know. And I know this story is going to swing things, but not sure which way."

"Let's wait and see what Margaret has to say. She says her story is locked-in, should be out tomorrow." No more edits, it's final. It just needs to get out there. Margaret is thrilled to get the *New York Times* byline, but also anxious to share her story with us before it runs.

Sarah and I chat over coffee before we head out to the barn. Always one of my favorite times of the week. But I can tell that Sarah is distracted. She's just going through the motions, without really engaging with what she's doing. No doubt I'd feel the same way. How people can be so nonchalant about sending a horse to slaughter seems strange to me.

When we return to the kitchen, Sarah pulls out the first bottle of wine.

"We might as well start now. I plan on having a few tonight, dull the pain a little."

"I'll join you." We pour the first two glasses of wine. Sarah continues to unload on me about what she thinks of Harry, and how she feels that she's really let down Spicy. There's no consoling her, so I just listen; maybe that's all she wants me to do. That's what friends do for each other, I guess.

Pete and Margaret arrive just on five thirty. Margaret has a briefcase with her, she'd driven Pete over here.

"Welcome, guys. Wine?" Sarah wastes no time making sure everyone is going to have a few drinks and stay over for the night.

"I'll stick to Budweiser." Pete rarely drinks wine and Sarah has plenty of Budweiser in the fridge too. She's also put a chicken dish in the oven.

"OK guys, the editor I'm working with at the *New York Times* says the story will run tomorrow. It will be on the front page, and then continue on the sports pages. That's huge!"

"Wow Margaret, that's fantastic!" I respond. "What's the headline?"

"I'm not sure, the editor writes it. Maybe something like, 'Horse slaughter system full of fraud, racehorses among those illegally slaughtered.'"

Margaret continues, "The story covers each of the horses we identified, establishing that they were in fact slaughtered. I was able to get vet records on the horses James was looking after. Pete, that's a big deal!" Margaret nods towards Pete.

"Good, I'm glad James cooperated."

"He didn't give me any info on the illegal drugs, he said his lawyer told him not to. But the legal drugs he'd given the horses is bad enough, and disqualified each one from being slaughtered and entering the food chain."

"Good, good for James." Pete seems very pleased that James has come through.

"The story details each of the connections of the horses, obviously including Harry Mitchell and Mike Franks. I discuss how the claiming system and slaughter system co-exist, some of this I highlight through the Rupert Bear case. I clarify that these connections did nothing wrong legally, they didn't sign anything; rather their actions have ethical concerns that I make obvious. I mention all the connections of each of the horses. Pete, that includes you." Margaret looks over at Pete, to see his reaction.

"No worries. If it helps the story, I'm good. Might provide me cover at the track if I'm included." I think Pete is taking one for the team here.

"The story goes into the background regarding how the slaughter system works. The kill buyers, the auctions, the slaughterhouses, and so forth. Amanda was very helpful in making sure I got all that right." Margaret glances in my direction and I nod.

"I identify some of the people on the slaughter side in the story, the kill buyers like Tom Baker, and his horse traders, the guys who signed off, fraudulently, on the EID forms. Jake Jenkins, and the three other guys, David Spires, Simon Peterson, and Tony Gardin."

Sarah looks across to Margaret, and asks, "So Jake Jenkins is featured in the story?"

"Yes, he signed off on the racehorse EIDs, his fraud is very black and white." Sarah looks upset. "Why, is that a problem?"

"He has my horse. I'm not sure how he'll react to all this." Sarah has been key in making sure this story happens, now she's worried it might jeopardize her own horse.

"Sarah, we needed to identify the fraud in the system, and those directly involved. That's what makes the piece so compelling. The editor at the *Times* couldn't believe what we have. She thinks there's enough here to end the whole slaughter practice, and end it very soon. She'll send the story, as well as my source materials, to the USDA, CFIA and their contacts at the EU." Margaret defends the piece, as she should. She's worked hard to get it to where it is.

"I know you're right. It's just hard for me to focus right now." Sarah gets up and grabs a new bottle of wine and fills up our three glasses. She hands Pete another Budweiser.

The evening proceeds with lots of alcohol, some useful discussion about next steps, once the *New York Times* article runs, and a gorgeous chicken dish that Sarah prepared.

When I get up the next morning I find five empty bottles of wine on the kitchen table.

CHAPTER 49

PETE, WEDNESDAY

AS AMANDA AND I LEAVE SARAH'S BEFORE FIVE IN THE MORNING, groggy, I pull up the *New York Times* story on my phone. There it is, our story, front and center on the main page: "At Missionville, horses race to death, then pollute the food chain." It's a provocative headline. I read the story out loud for Amanda as she drives. Its detail is as described by Margaret last night. I squirm a little when I read my name. This morning at the track will be interesting.

I arrive at the track a little after six o'clock, after getting my car and Hairy. He stays with a neighbor when I go away for the night; luckily that neighbor also works at the racetrack and gets up early. It's an arrangement we've had for years.

I feed my four horses, and go through the usual routine of checking their legs and enjoying the quietness of the time.

I'm curious how quickly the news of the story will spread around the backside, and then of course, how people will respond. It obviously doesn't paint us in a good light.

Alfie arrives right at seven o'clock.

"Morning, boss."

"Hey, Alfie. Can you start with Slippers, please?" The filly worked yesterday, so she's just walking today.

"OK, boss." Alfie doesn't know anything, yet. He'd have mentioned it.

I go to my tack room and get the tack for my other filly. Hairy follows me and drops down in his spot for the morning. A few minutes later I'm up on the track, standing at the gap.

"Have you heard, Pete?"

"What, Jess?" I play dumb.

"The story in the *Times*, it's awful."

"What story?"

"They ran a story about this track, and sending horses to slaughter. I just read it on my phone, after hearing a couple of trainers talking about it when they got up here." The news will spread fast, thanks to mobile phones and internet access.

"Christ! I'll look for it when I get back to the barn."

"Just go to *Paulick Report*. It's their new headliner."

"Thanks, I will."

"You're in it, Pete. I'm sorry." OK, that's good. Hopefully no one else will suspect I had anything to do with the story. I move my filly off into a walk, and then jog back to the wire.

When I get back to the barn I load up the *Paulick Report*, and sure enough, the *Times* story is already linked. I read the story again, and then start to look at some of the comments. There are eight already. Five are very damning of Missionville and all us horsemen. Harry especially gets some very colorful criticism. A couple of commenters ask questions about what should happen to racehorses when they stop running; one suggests some kind of euthanasia program. I hand my phone to Alfie, and ask him if he's seen the story yet. He stops and reads it.

"Very sad, boss," Alfie responds. "I heard a couple of Mike's grooms talking about it." Of course, Mike and Harry are a key focus of this side of the story. Things are probably very weird over there right now. Harry loves press, but not this kind of press. I imagine he's freaking out somewhere.

Out at the track, all the gossip has turned to the *Times* story. I must have been asked a dozen times over the rest of the morning, "Did you read the story?" and "What do you think of the story?" I try to remain reasonably neutral in my responses. I focus on my own involvement in the story, mentioning the two-year-old I had, and how upset I am that it ended up being slaughtered.

The one person I'm keen to see this morning is Jake. The story will definitely make his life uncomfortable. He was exposed as the connection between Missionville and the slaughter pipeline, and he committed serious fraud, which is a felony. By the break time I still hadn't seen Jake.

Clare stops by the barn.

"Hey, Pete. How are the horses?"

"Good today. Did you read the story yet?" I want to get an outsider's perspective, and Clare is still somewhat of an outsider to this community.

"I glanced at it. Didn't know anything about it until I got here."

"It's pretty deplorable, right? But is it shocking?"

"How do you mean?"

"Does it shock you that horses from here go to slaughter, some of them anyway?"

"Not really. I can't say I like it. But I'm not naïve."

"Right. It's something we do. We know it goes on. We couldn't really survive as a track without the slaughter pipeline outlet, I guess. It'll be interesting to see what happens next."

"If the story's half what I think it is, based on my quick glimpse, plenty will happen next."

"I think you might be right."

"See you tomorrow." Clare walks down into Mike's shedrow.

I get my last horse ready, and head to the track. There is more chatter and questions about the story. I still haven't seen Jake, which is very unusual by this time of the morning. Andy, one of Mike Franks's exercise riders, is standing in at the gap.

"Not seen Jake today, is he around?"

"I don't think so Pete. That story's screwed him." Andy is pretty friendly with Jake, as you would be with someone you've worked with for four or five years.

"Yes, I guess it has." So Jake hadn't come in at all this morning. Someone must have tipped him off about the story before he even got here. I walk off from the gap and head to the wire.

An hour later I'm in my tack room when my phone rings.

"Pete, it's John." Wow, my Penn State lawyer friend in Washington, DC.

"Hey, it's been a long time." We rarely speak on the phone anymore. We trade the occasional Facebook message to keep in touch.

"You OK?" Of course, John must have read the story, and seen my name.

"Yes, all's well. I assume you read the *Times* story."

"I have it in front of me right now. As soon as I saw the headline I figured something was up." John knows very little about racing and my career in racing, but he does know I train at Missionville.

"Then you saw my name in the story."

"Yes, if you need help with all this, I can help you."

"That's very good of you. But it's OK, I helped write the story." I lower my voice, but I'm already in my tack room where no one should overhear.

"I don't understand?"

"It's all good. I'll call you over the weekend for a proper catch-up?"

"OK, Pete. If you ever need anything, just holler."

"I will, thanks." I hadn't expected the story to reach my non-racing friends, and so soon, but I guess that's what a front-page story in the *New York Times* will do.

I look at the *Paulick Report* on my phone again. The story has been on the site now for four hours and there are nearly fifty comments. This will be the story of the day for the industry. I browse through the comments. Harry has become a pretty big target for the commenters, which I like. Some have made the connection that Harry owns Dancer's Foil, who is running on Saturday in the Jim Dandy.

After I finish up, I go to the kitchen with Hairy.

"Usual, Pete?"

"Thanks, Alice." She places two sausages on the grill, and starts preparing my sandwich.

"Shocking story."

"Yes. Real, I guess, but shocking," I respond.

"It surprised me, Margaret Collins writing it. I knew her a long time ago. She covered racing here for a few years, up until Harry bought the place. I always thought it was a shame the *Missionville Times* stopped covering racing."

"I didn't know that." I hate lying, but I need to keep my cover.

"I always liked her. She wrote some decent stories, got the community excited about this place. This story's obviously different."

"Yes, I can't imagine anyone coming racing for the first time after reading this piece."

"It's a shame what this track has come to. Nothing good ever really came out of Harry's purchase." Alice hands me my sandwich and Hairy's sausages.

"Thanks, Alice."

I wander over to a vacant table.

My phone vibrates, it's Jake, "Pete. How are things at the track?"

"Jake, I was looking for you. Things are a bit crazy."

"I figured. Someone messaged me this morning about the story. When I saw it, I decided I shouldn't be around. I'm screwed."

"It looks tough, no matter how you look at it. The comments on the *Paulick Report* are a bit crazy too. Have you seen them?" Jake doesn't seem to suspect my involvement with the story. I know Tom Baker will figure it out in no time. When he talks to Jake, Jake will know.

"I've been reading them. Over a hundred when I last checked. Harry is furious." So Jake has talked to Harry? "Mike called me. Harry wants to kill me." So Mike called Jake, and Harry is furious.

"Harry's probably embarrassed he's been caught. Especially now that he has a top horse."

"It's more than that. He'd assumed I'd make his horses unidentifiable. He'd instructed me to obliterate their lip tattoos." Oh, that would have eliminated any chance he'd be caught. "He even gave me a chemistry lesson on how to do it. It's gruesome. I didn't think it would be necessary. The horses were going to a hell hole anyway. No chance of rescue, straight to Tom."

"Well screw Harry. You need to protect yourself somehow."

"We'll see. I'm in big trouble. The law will get me first, but Harry might come back after me later. I have a couple of horses at my farm. I need to get rid of them, but I don't want to send them to the auction right now for obvious reasons." One of those horses is Spicy Lemon. "Can you get your friend Amanda to call me?" So he knows Amanda and I hang out. I wonder why that didn't spook him, and he kept me working for Tom.

"I will. I'm sure she'll help you as much as she can." She can get both horses to Sarah's. They can then decide what to do with the second horse.

"Good, the sooner I get rid of the horses, the better. I'll catch you later." He hangs up. I need to get Amanda to get those horses out of Jake's property before he realizes I was in on everything and he has a change of heart.

I call Amanda.

"Hey, honey."

"How's the track?"

"As you would expect. Pretty crazy. Anyway, I have something else for you. Can you call Jake, and arrange to pick up horses from him to go to Sarah's right away. He just called me. He's freaking out, and needs to get rid of his horses quickly."

"I will. Text me his number. I'll call Sarah once it's all arranged. She'll be ecstatic!"

"You need to get it done ASAP, before Jake realizes I was in on the story, and he will. I kind of feel bad for Jake, he got himself in this mess, but maybe he's not such a bad guy. Harry's going crazy for him because he didn't remove the lip tattoos of the horses."

"Harry's worse than pond scum. That asshole will get away with all this. He didn't commit fraud, he had Jake do that for him."

"Sure, but maybe we'll get him for the drugs later."

"I really hope so. We haven't heard from Timmins in a little while, but I assume they're doing their thing."

"I'm sure they are. OK, got to go, see you tonight."

"Love you, Pete."

"You too, Amanda."

CHAPTER 50

PETE, SATURDAY

MARGARET JOINED AMANDA AND ME LAST NIGHT AT ZUCCHINI'S. Since the story ran, she's been contacted by both the USDA and the CFIA. She spent two hours on the phone with both of them. She thinks that some major things are going to happen in the next week or two. We drank plenty of champagne to celebrate.

This morning, with a mild headache, I start to get ready for the barn. Amanda wakes up, "Hey, honey."

"Hey, Amanda, no need for you to get up yet."

"I was thinking, now that Jake's disappeared, should I just come in with you? And you should come back to bed first." She comes over to me, and literally drags me back into the bed. I'd only managed to put my jeans on. She removes them, slowly.

Later, the three of us – Hairy in the back – head to the racetrack. I'm late.

Three days after the *New York Times* bombshell the track is still humming with the news, as well as rumors and gossip related to the story.

Jake hasn't been at the track since Tuesday. Some speculate that he's been locked up. I suppose that's plausible, but I haven't heard anything definitive. On Thursday, Sarah went over to Jake's and picked up the two horses he had at his farm. Jake had told her he wouldn't be there, but to grab a couple of halters and haul them out. Sarah is thrilled to get Spicy Lemon back. The other horse was another one of Harry's.

Paulick Report's story now has four hundred comments. Some of those comments speculate that Missionville will be closed down after all this, either that or Harry will need to find a buyer. There is an increasing call to close down the racetrack-to-slaughter trade. Thankfully no one seems to have figured out that I had anything to do with the story.

I have all four of my horses to train this morning; given my late start, it's likely I'll only get two ridden before the track break and two after the break. After we arrive, Amanda heads to the track kitchen for her first coffee of the day. I take Thunder Clouds out first this morning, and have him on the track, at the gap, a little before seven thirty.

"Hi, Pete. What about Dancer's Foil today? Are you watching?" Jess and I have been discussing the *Times* story for the last three days. It's nice to get a chance to talk about something else.

"I might head over to Jessup's to watch, or watch online. I think he should win. You?"

"I'll watch at home. I think it'll be tough for him. I'm more interested in seeing Harry." So we aren't completely off the topic of the *Times* story.

"Yes, it'll be interesting to see if he shows up. Some of the comments on *Paulick Report* would scare me if I were Harry."

"He's an ass. I bet he doesn't show. If he does, I wonder if they'll try to interview him."

"Because he's an arrogant ass, I think he'll show. Let's hope his horse wins, we're more likely to hear from him then!" I walk away and move Thunder Clouds into his shuffle jog. Soon enough I will get this horse retired.

By the time I get to the track on my second horse, Slippers, Amanda is on the rail. She's having a conversation with two trainers who are watching their horses. As I ride by, we exchange glances. I wondered how the horsemen would react to her this morning, given Jake's absence. She is now the only known outlet for horses that are finished with their racing careers.

My filly trains beautifully, as she's been doing for the last month and more. When I get back to my barn, Clare is waiting for me in the shedrow.

"Need anything today?" she asks.

"I'm good. May need a pre-race next week if I get the gelding in. I'll let you know."

"Great. Want to let you know, James isn't coming back. You're now officially my client."

"Sounds good to me. Any reason?"

"He told me he needs to move on, look for off-track vet work. He says it burnt him out, working here." Sounds like a credible explanation. And getting burnt out here when you're on Harry's payroll makes sense. I wonder how Harry'll take the news.

"I guess it can get to all of us at some point. Good luck with your new business!"

"Thanks. Some clients I really like, like you. Some, maybe I'll try to lose." I assume Mike Franks might be one of those clients. Clare walks over to his shedrow.

I have two more horses to train, I get the tack for my new filly. Hairy is snoring away in his corner of the tack room.

We walk up to the track with Adam, who's just come out of his barn. I haven't seen him to talk to since the *Times* story broke.

"Hey, Pete."

"Adam, how's training treating you?"

"This horse is my last hope. She's running next week. If I don't win with her, I'm selling up."

"Back to galloping? It's a tough business."

"No, I'm out of here. It's too hard, and that story really woke me up."

"How do you mean?"

"There's more to life than just trying to exploit these animals. This filly, I treat her well. If that doesn't get me her win, I just don't want to keep doing it all."

"I get what you're saying. You're competing in a tough place. I've struggled with it. I hope you win next week." I really do get what he's saying. And I want to tell him just to quit now, and get the hell out of here before it sucks him in. But I don't want to blow my cover just yet. We enter the track.

"I'll catch you later." Adam moves off. I wait longer. Adam reminds me a lot of myself when I was starting out. He's a good, decent guy.

My new filly trains nicely. She's starting to settle in her gallops much better. That's good progress. My last horse also goes well. The track is much quieter by that point, I was probably one of the last out there to train today.

I haven't chatted with Jorge since the story broke. I want to see how he is doing. I imagine that whole outfit is kind of freaking out, given the scrutiny on Harry and Mike. After I finish galloping, I head over to Jorge's part of the shedrow, where he's grooming one of his horses.

"Hey, Jorge. Everything OK?"

"Si, Pete, bueno." Jorge seems relaxed and positive.

"You see the story?"

"Everyone sees the story, bueno."

"It's all good?" I'm a little puzzled by his response.

"Si, gracias."

"We've got your horse. Spicy." I want to make sure Jorge knows the horse is safe.

"Bueno. Gracias."

"More soon, I hope."

"Gracias." Jorge might know more than he's letting on.

When I get back to my shedrow Amanda is waiting for me. She's a little later than usual.

"Hey, you," she greets me.

"How was your morning?"

"Very busy, which is interesting. I have four horses to add to my site."

"Wow, that's more than I think I've seen you add on one Saturday?"

"Yes. A couple of the horses are for trainers I've not dealt with before."

"That's good!"

"It is. I need to make sure the site gets the traffic it needs to move more horses if this is how it's going to be." We discuss this a little longer, then wander over to the track kitchen.

We decide to head out to Jessup's to watch the Jim Dandy Stakes at Saratoga. The race is one of two key preps for the Travers Stakes. Northern Peaks is in the Haskell, the other prep race, which is slated for tomorrow. Our focus in the Jim Dandy is obviously Harry's horse, Dancer's Foil, who is the third choice at 5-1. He hasn't raced since his second place finish in the Wood Memorial. He is facing eight other runners, three of which ran in the Kentucky Derby, finishing second, fourth and tenth. Two other starters won their last races in convincing style in New York allowance races. I think that Dancer's Foil has more quality than these runners, we'll see very soon. We arrive at Jessup's an hour before the race is due to go off.

"Usual, guys?"

"Thanks, Charlie."

"Crazy piece in the *New York Times*." Of course, Charlie would have heard all about it, as well as the reactions from the horsemen at Missionville.

"Yes, pretty sad really," I respond.

"Do you think they'll shut the track down?" It would be tough on Charlie's business if that happens. He took a big hit when the mine closed down all those years ago.

"Let's hope not."

"I really hope not. You guys are my business these days. You like Harry's horse?"

"More than Harry," Amanda replies.

"I don't blame you for that. Honestly, I don't think I've ever seen him in here, and he's from this town." Charlie hands us our drinks and we head to one of the few empty tables.

There is a good crowd in Jessup's, more than half of which are from the backside of the racetrack. A lot of the buzz of conversation still seems to be focused on the *New York Times* story. There's still no inclination that I'd helped with the piece, I do wonder where Jake is though. He's bound to have talked to Tom. Tom will have figured it out as soon as he saw which horses were identified in the story.

Amanda and I keep to ourselves, pretty much, in the lead up to the race, although one or two horsemen come over and ask Amanda more about her placement service. More evidence that she's currently the only option for the horses at Missionville.

By the time the horses are in the paddock for the Jim Dandy, we're all now focused on the race, and Harry's horse. It's hard to root for a horse if you don't like its connections, but we're all closer to Harry than to anyone else in the race.

Dancer's Foil looks very good in the paddock, as he is led around. He's a big, rangy, bay horse with a long striding walk. Like Northern Peaks, he's a great grandson of Northern Dancer.

Harry is in the paddock surrounded by three or four people, one of whom is Todd Brown, his trainer. Dancer's Foil remains at 5-1 on the board. The horse that was second in the Kentucky Derby, Fletcher's Crime, is the 2-1 favorite. He'd been beaten by six lengths in the Derby. The second favorite is Gustav's Legacy, who recently won a New York allowance race by ten lengths. He seems to have a lot of potential, but this is a big move up in class for him.

By the time the horses are being led out onto the track, Jessup's is full and focused on the race. A few call-outs from the crowd come through, responding to the commentator's analysis. Dancer's Foil's odds fall to 4-1. Maybe Harry's stopped betting in Vegas, and he's now betting at the track.

The nine horses look terrific as they parade in front of the stands. Saratoga is absolutely packed. It's one of the few race meets that draws large crowds each day of its six-week season.

Five minutes later, they are in the gate, just below the clubhouse grandstand. Dancer's Foil, in the fourth post, loads professionally. The starter lets them go and Harry's horse goes straight to the lead. He is two lengths in front as they head into the clubhouse turn. He is just galloping along, and the others are letting him get easy fractions on the lead, unable to put any real pressure on him.

As they move onto the backside, Dancer's Foil is three lengths clear. Fletcher's Crime is in second, two lengths ahead of the rest of the field, which are all bunched together. Down the backside Dancer's Foil extends his lead, the fractions have quickened, he's running a terrific race. The rest of the field is beginning to struggle. Harry's colt moves around the final turn on his own in the lead, and is ten lengths clear inside the eighth pole. His jockey then wraps up on him. He wins by twelve lengths without being pressured.

The camera turns to Harry as the horse gallops out. He's high-fiving those around him, making the same ass of himself as he's done before when the horse has won. I wonder whether the last few days have affected him at all.

It was an impressive performance, and the time of the race was very good too. He will be a formidable foe for the Triple Crown winner, I'm sure of it now. The crowd at Jessup's seems to agree. Horsemen know when they see a good horse put in a strong performance.

Dancer's Foil heads into the winner's circle. I hope that after the picture is taken, Harry will be interviewed, which is usual after a big race. Harry is in the winner's circle. He has a big smile across his face. He's standing furthest away from his horse. The colt doesn't look like he's been in a hard race at all. He just pricks his ears. The picture is taken and the group begins to disperse. The camera switches to a close up with the trainer, Todd Brown. It's interview time.

"Todd, that was very impressive," says the reporter.

"Thanks Jeannine. Yes, I was hoping for a good performance. He's been training very well. I didn't quite expect that."

"He was only just shy of the track record, and was hardly ridden in the end. Very impressive. Travers next?"

"That's our target. I'll see how he is in a few days."

"Well done." The camera moves over to Harry. "Harry, congratulations, you must be thrilled."

"Thanks, I am." He has a huge grin on his face. All of Jessup's is now back focused on the TV screens.

"Your biggest win to date?"

"It is yes. This is the best horse I've had, so far." Harry has only been playing on the elite circuits for a few short years. He is very lucky to have this caliber of horse already.

"You think you can compete with the Triple Crown winner, Harry?"

"Of course. We should have beaten him before the Derby." True to character, Harry gives an arrogant answer.

"Harry, the *Times* story, do you have any comment?" Wow, I wasn't expecting that. Go Jeannine! She obviously isn't worried that Harry might not interview with her if the horse goes on to win the Travers.

"Just enjoying the win today, thanks." Harry remains composed.

"Congratulations, Harry. Back to you, Steve." Jeannine tried, which I think is impressive. And it shows that the *New York Times* story is the major industry news right now.

"Thanks Jeannine. No comment there from Harry Mitchell, Dancer's Foil's owner, on the *New York Times* story that's sending shockwaves through the racing industry. We'll have more on that story during tomorrow's coverage from Monmouth Park.

"Dancer's Foil made a remarkable return to the races. We'll see how the Triple Crown champion, Northern Peaks, does in tomorrow's Haskell Invitational. These two horses could be on a collision course at the end of the month in the Travers, right here at Saratoga. Good night!"

CHAPTER 51

PETE, SUNDAY

WE RETURN TO JESSUP'S TO WATCH THE HASKELL BROADCAST. While I want to see Northern Peaks's return to the races, we are more interested in the coverage the *New York Times* story gets. I am pleasantly surprised that it is getting any kind of TV time at all.

The telecast from Monmouth is scheduled to begin at five, we get to Jessup's a little beforehand.

"Two days in a row, you're becoming regulars again. Usual?"

"Thanks, Charlie."

"Dancer's Foil was very impressive yesterday. Harry's got a hot horse."

"He does. Let's hope Northern Peaks wins today. A showdown between the two would be great for the sport."

"And keep the spotlight on Harry." Charlie winks, as he hands us our drinks and then moves on to another customer.

The Haskell broadcast begins. It's another good gathering of horsemen from the track. One of the advantages of no racing on the weekends is that we can all hang out and watch the big races together.

The beginning of the broadcast shows Dancer's Foil's stretch run from yesterday's Jim Dandy. The racing analysts then discuss the performance, praising Harry's horse, and discussing that there might be a real challenger to the Triple Crown champion. They then remind the audience of the Triple Crown series, replaying each one of Northern Peaks's wins. Finally, they replay the stretch duel between Northern Peaks and Dancer's Foil, in the

Wood Memorial. They make their best attempt to build up the drama of a show-down between the two horses.

Returning from a commercial break, they introduce Ian Cresswell, from NTRA's Safety and Integrity Alliance, to discuss the *Times* story.

"Ian, for our audience, can you explain the role of NTRA's Safety and Integrity Alliance?"

"Yes, and thanks for having me on your program. We look at the different racetracks around the country, and design a set of standards that are important for the welfare of the racehorse."

"Is Monmouth Park, where we are today, a member of the alliance?"

"Absolutely. All the top tracks in this country and in Canada are part of this alliance. It's important for the trust of the racing fan."

"Is Missionville a part of the alliance, a racetrack owned by Harry Mitchell."

"Unfortunately not." Strike one against Harry.

"Is this because it doesn't comply with your standards, or for other reasons?"

"Actually, they've never asked for a review. Sadly, there are a number of racetracks around the country that aren't in the alliance."

"The *New York Times* story. How did you first hear about it?"

"As soon as it was on the *Paulick Report*, I was alerted."

"And generally, what are your thoughts on the matters the story uncovers?"

"It's a huge black-eye for the industry. How they were able to get the information for the story is incredible. They must have had an insider at the kill lot. Regardless, the story highlights a huge problem the industry needs to tackle if we want to remain relevant to the public."

"Will the story impact your alliance program?"

"It will. We're going to look more closely at the options each racetrack provides for horses that can no longer race and are not going to the breeding shed."

"Do you know if they do a good job of that here at Monmouth Park?"

"Monmouth has a couple of retirement programs, one of which is directly affiliated with the racetrack. Relative to other racetracks, they do a very good job. That said, we are going to examine if more needs to be done."

"Obviously Harry Mitchell was singled out in the story. Any thoughts on that?"

"I'm not sure I can answer specifically on Mitchell's situation and his involvement in what happens at Missionville. It looks to me like he didn't do anything illegal, as the law stands. I don't think that's the case for the person who signed his papers. I understand he's disappeared."

"Thanks. That's Ian Cresswell, from the NTRA's Safety and Integrity Alliance, as we struggle to come to terms with the shocking *New York Times* story of last week. Now over to the paddock."

Not bad coverage, at least the story is being discussed, and the guy from the Alliance has suggested they plan to make some changes. Good can come of all this.

The Haskell ends up being a pretty boring race. Northern Peaks is the 1-3 favorite, he only has four other runners to beat. No one really wants to face the Triple Crown champion, not even for the million dollars the track put up for the race. His biggest challenger is a local horse who won the local prep race for the Haskell. The other three runners are all eligible to run in allowance races, and that's where they belong. Northern Peaks won the race by four lengths, without being asked to run at all.

CHAPTER 52

AMANDA, TUESDAY

THE *TIMES* STORY REALLY SEEMS TO HAVE SHAKEN THINGS UP. I've added five more horses to my website over the weekend, and I'm trying harder to promote the new horses through online forums and other means. I've even started a Google AdWords campaign. I need to do my bit to make sure the horsemen around here can't complain too much about losing an easy disposal option. It's quite possible someone will take over Jake's place, and things return to business as usual, but obviously our goal is to make sure that doesn't happen.

Fortunately I've been able to coast at the bank for the last few days, otherwise I might have gone mad. I'd signed on some vendors to help with the branch restructuring project, before the story was published. Work on the branches will start in a couple of weeks. In the meantime, I can relax a bit at work.

Pete and I are also doing great together. It's hard now for me to imagine that it's only been five months since we started dating, and in that time we've even managed a brief separation. It seems we've belonged together forever. Pete is easy to be with. We connect, respect each other, and the sex is great. I haven't had a chance to get bored, which is usually the first fatal blow to any of my prior relationships. Once the Harry situation is resolved, finally, one way or another, we're going to tie the knot. We've discussed it, we'll get married either in Vegas, or Elkton, Maryland.

My morning at the bank is very straightforward, giving me more time to think. We haven't heard anything more from Timmins yet. I imagine he's heard about the *Times* article; I hope it might give him some fresh angles to pursue as he examines everything about Harry. I must admit, it's nice to imagine that Harry is starting to realize that his kingdom is crumbling, just at a time when he's hitting the national stage with his horse, Dancer's Foil.

At eleven o'clock, I head to the auction. An hour later I arrive, just as the tack sale begins. The horse sale won't get started for about another hour, giving me plenty of time to go to the back and check for Thoroughbreds.

There aren't any.

It's the first time I've been at the auction and not seen any Thoroughbreds. I guess it's either the impact of Jake disappearing, or people getting spooked by the *Times* story, or both. I go over to the kitchen. I figure I might as well have a coffee and hang out for a while. I have plenty of time before the sale starts.

The kitchen is busy, so I sit down at a shared table. I know one of the guys on the table, Mark, who drives horses for Fred, the kill buyer. He's a reasonable guy to talk to, the odd occasion we've chatted. I figure he might give me some sense as to how the *Times* story has impacted his world. I glance up at him.

"Good to see you here as usual, Amanda." I try to make it easy for Mark to make the opening comment. I don't want him to think I'm fishing for gossip.

"You too, Mark. How are things?"

"Well you know, that story's created a lot of a mess around here."

"How so? There seems to be plenty of horses here, although no Thoroughbreds."

"Yep. I think you'll find your Thoroughbred business will slow down. Jake's missing."

"Yes, I've heard that."

"Tom's not here either. His contract is suspended for the time being."

"Wow! I didn't know that. Will that slaughterhouse he buys for find someone else for this area?"

"Maybe, maybe things'll die down and Tom will be back in business."

"What about Fred's business. Any impact, Mark?"

"For now, we'll be OK. We're not taking Thoroughbreds though, that's a no-no. They're too easy to identify."

"Some of those horses were sold through this auction. Is that a problem for them here?"

"I don't know, might be. CFIA up in Canada might also close down the border, temporarily anyway. If they do that, our business is screwed too. Lots of crazy things happening, it's not good for business."

"Do they know how the *Times* got the story?"

"No, not yet. People think it must have been a driver for Tom. Tom's not said anything yet." They'll figure it all out soon enough, but it's good no one has spoken yet. "Of course, Tom's going nuts. This deal is costing him a fortune, probably four or five thousand dollars each week he's not shipping. He also thinks he'll get a hefty fine."

"Can't say I'm too upset." He knows I'm on the rescue side, there's no point in hiding it.

"I'm sure. But what happens to all these horses, if we can't ship 'em?" It's the age-old argument used to support horse slaughter, if you can't ship them, they'll be starved and abused.

"Something will happen. Things have a tendency to sort themselves out." That's always my answer. If we eliminate slaughter, we'll then find a solution for unwanted horses. We have no incentive to find that solution while slaughter remains an option.

We continue chatting and then I go out back to take one more look around before waiting for the start of the auction.

It's strange to see Tom's place empty in the gallery. He always stands in the same place, leaning on the rail in front of him. He always has three or four people huddled around him during the sale. That space is now entirely empty. Fred's position is on the other side of the gallery, but still at the front. He has his people around him, one of whom is Mark.

Eighty-five horses go through the sale today. Fred buys thirty of them, which is more than usual for him. He can afford to do it, the prices dropped by at least a hundred dollars per horse. It's simple economics: you remove a kill buyer, you lower the demand by about a quarter, prices do the same. Fred can afford to keep some of these horses at his place for a week or two because they were very cheap to buy.

Fred seems to enjoy his celebrity, being the only major buyer of the day. He usually operates in Tom's shadow.

When I arrive at Sarah's, she is in the kitchen, coffee is brewing.

"Hey, Sarah."

"Amanda, great to see you. What a week we've had!"

"Yes, how's your new horse?" I ask about Spicy Lemon.

"I can't believe it. It was destroying me, knowing what I'd done to him. To have him back, it's crazy but I can't stop crying." And right on cue, a tear appears below her right eye. She wipes it away. "I'm just so relieved."

"I'm very happy for you. I know it's been hard." Sarah passes me a cup of coffee.

"Yes, but it's just so good to have him back. He seems OK, too. I turned him out for the first time yesterday. He raced around for a while, enjoying the sun on his back, and then he stopped, dropped his head, and grazed for a solid three hours. He loved it. It was good of Jake to let me have him."

"Pete says no one knows where Jake is. I chatted with that guy Mark, at the auction. He also said Jake's missing."

"Fred's driver? What else did he have to say?"

"Tom's contract is temporarily suspended, the CFIA might shut down the border, and basically no one is taking Thoroughbreds for now. There were no Thoroughbreds at the sale."

"This is real progress. I called Timmins to make sure he's seen the story, in case it helps with his case on Harry."

"Any update there?"

"He said there is, too early to say anything, but the *Times* story is definitely on their radar too."

We chat for a few more minutes as we finish our coffees, then head to the barn. Spicy has his stall back. The two-year-old who's been in his stall is now in the annex part of the barn. Sarah is really enjoying herself as she tends to her horses. Spicy gets an extra carrot or two in his dinner.

Pete pulls up the driveway after we're back in the kitchen. The three of us plan to hang out for the night, and enjoy what has happened over the last week or so.

"Hey, Sarah, glad your horse is back?" Pete asks, as soon as he walks through the door.

"Yes, thanks. I was pretty shocked how all that worked out. For all Jake's faults, this is a huge deal for me."

"I'm glad. I'm a little worried about Jake, but there's not much to do about it."

"It's weird that no one seems to know where he is. I assume we'd know if he was locked up somewhere?" I ask.

"I think so. Maybe he's holed up at Tom's farm? He and Tom are pretty tight. If he is, he knows I was the whistleblower."

"It's possible. Maybe he does know. He's not tried to contact you again, has he?" Sarah asks.

"No, not yet, and I've not heard from Tom either, thankfully. I'm sure he's pissed."

"Mark, Fred's driver, reckons this is costing four or five thousand each week he's not shipping. They suspended his contract, Pete."

"They should! Hopefully there's more fall out."

"Mark thinks the CFIA may close the border. Tom might be in for a hefty fine too on this side."

"Well, we have a lot to celebrate, I bought some champagne." Sarah goes over to the fridge and gets out a bottle of Veuve Clicquot. "We've got one bottle of the good stuff, and a few cheaper bottles." She smiles. She also puts a large dish in the oven. We spend a wonderful night at Sarah's; three good friends enjoying a moment of victory.

CHAPTER 53

PETE, FRIDAY

RAY HAD BEEN SPOOKED A LITTLE BY THE *TIMES* ARTICLE. He asked me earlier this week if we should just retire Thunder Clouds. Amanda is thrilled. The old guy went over to Sarah's farm yesterday. I must admit, it choked me up a little seeing him loaded up and off to a farm. I imagine he's lived in a racetrack stall pretty much every day for the five years he's been racing. Sarah will have him turned out in a paddock soon enough.

Ray hasn't talked about another claim, and I don't push it. Before, I would have been spotting horses and discussing them with him. Now I'm happy to let our operation wind down. The gelding we have is likely going to need to find a home soon, if I can convince Ray. Slippers will be racing for someone else. She definitely has a decent future ahead of her. And then she'll go to the breeding shed. She's already proven her worth. I'm not a 100 percent sure my new filly was a good claim, but we'll see.

After feeding, I remove my horses' wraps, all seems well.

Alfie arrives right at seven o'clock. I have Slippers ready to go, he gives me a leg up. I meet Adam on the horse path, on the way up to the track. We turn our horses in together.

"Hey, Pete."

"I see you're still here, Adam."

"Yeah, but only until I can sell these horses. I need to go and do something else."

"Sorry to hear that, but it's good to get out now, not leave it too long. What'll you do?" We start to head back to the wire.

"I have a cousin in Ohio who has a construction business. He says I can start at the bottom, but maybe things can work out over there for me."

"It's something, I guess."

"I'll miss the horses, but I won't miss this place too much."

"Good luck, if you need help moving your horses, let me know."

"Thanks, Pete, good luck to you." Adam pulls his horse to a stop, and I keep going back to the wire.

Slippers trains very well, as usual. She'll be running again soon, and I have to think she can win another race, too. I'd only ever had one horse win four races in a row for me before, at the very beginning of my training career. Fingers crossed she can do it for me again, before I quit.

My other two horses train OK. The new filly is getting more relaxed, but there's something about her airways that bothers me. When I work her next week, I'm planning on getting her scoped to make sure there's nothing there.

By break time I had all three trained. Jake calls me, as I'm putting my tack away.

"Hi, Jake."

"Pete, Tom knows it was you." I'm shaking. I figured he would, but why is Jake calling to tell me?

"I'm sorry, it is what it is. When I took the first trip…"

"Don't worry. I don't care. Just steer clear of Tom. He's completely insane. He can be a little psycho anyway."

"Where are you?"

"I'm at Tom's. He bailed me out. I'll stay here for a little while, 'til things quiet down."

"I'm really sorry. Once I got driving, it was something I had to do."

"I really don't care. I'm done with all this. When I started a few years ago, I thought I'd just do it for a little while, earn some extra cash. It got out of control. Then Harry wanted me to remove the tattoos, I couldn't do it. I've made money. I'll have a big fine to pay. I'll move on. Go to another racetrack and stick to ponying."

"Sarah was very grateful to get her horse back." I want him to know the importance of that gesture. He could have just as easily gotten rid of him in some other way.

"Good. Timing worked for that guy. You know how it was with Harry's horses. Pete, you remember Hank's suicide?"

Of course I do, it's still fresh in my mind. "Sure, why?"

"He'd just given me a horse. I figured that had something to do with it, just too much for him. It unnerved me big time. Hank was a big trainer around here years ago when I first arrived."

"I know."

"Do me a favor."

"What's that?"

"Don't let Harry get away with this. It looks like Tom and I are hanging for what owners like Harry do, just dumping their horses. Harry knew what I was doing, he wanted me to make them unrecognizable and get rid of them. Harry should pay for this."

"I get what you're saying. Harry will pay, one way or another."

"Good luck. You probably won't hear much from me again." Jake hangs up.

I'm relieved to have heard from Jake. It was bugging me that he'd disappeared. I suppose it makes sense he's with Tom for now. Harry wasn't going to bail him out. And Jake seems to have shown compassion, despite his role in all this. It takes me back to one of our early conversations about the slaughter trade. If I didn't drive, someone else would. I guess if Jake wasn't the horse trader at Missionville, someone else would have done it. Maybe that someone else would have followed Harry's instructions and obliterated the tattoos too; maybe Harry wouldn't have been exposed.

I want to catch up with Jorge, I haven't seen him, to talk to, over the last week. I walk over to his part of the barn, where he was putting leg wraps on one of his horses.

"Hey, Jorge. Are things good for you?"

"Si, Pete. Soon I go back to Mexico. This place no good, but we help."

"You've done an amazing thing. We should know more soon."

"Si. I go, a week or two maybe."

"OK, we should have a few Coronas before you leave."

"Bueno, Pete."

I return to my part of the barn to get Hairy. We head over to the track kitchen.

"Usual, Pete?"

"Thanks, Alice." She puts a couple of sausages on the grill, and starts preparing my sandwich.

She leans over, lowering her voice a little, "Did you hear the rumor?"

"What?" There is no one else in line, so it's OK to talk.

"There's a big drug case, a few trainers have been talking about it." If there's gossip going around the track, it will be discussed in the kitchen. Alice hears most things.

"Is there a hearing scheduled? Do we know who it is?"

"A couple of people have noticed their purses haven't been released."

"Any ideas who's been caught?" It has to be Harry's horses.

"No one seems to be sure. But it's more than one horse, more than one race." So Timmins's team has been busy. I presume they're now going after Harry directly.

Alice hands me my sandwich and sausages. I wander over to an empty table. Hairy chomps down his treat.

CHAPTER 54

AMANDA, TUESDAY

I ARRIVE AT THE AUCTION A LITTLE BEFORE TWELVE. I'm not here for very long before I realize how different today will be. Usually when I'm out back looking at horses, I will see the key buyers and sellers milling around, catching up after their week's work. Last week Tom wasn't here. This week neither Tom nor Fred are here. Something has spooked Fred. There are still plenty of horses, but like last week, there are no Thoroughbreds.

I go to the kitchen to see if I can catch up with what's going on. I order a coffee, and see Mark sitting at a table on his own. I wander over.

"Hey, Mark. Is it OK to sit here?"

"Of course. Wasn't sure if you'd bother coming today. It's going to be quiet."

"What's happening? Your boss not here too?"

"Rumor has it, CFIA is closing the border to slaughter horses before the end of this week."

"Wow! How do you know?"

"Fred heard from the slaughterhouse in Canada where he ships. They've suspended his contract for now." Change is really happening. This is what we want, but I can't believe it is happening so quickly.

Mark continues, "Apparently the EU's scrutinizing everything. If the CFIA doesn't get things sorted, they might suspend imports of horse meat, like they did with Mexico a couple of years ago."

"It's going to have a big impact on this auction, right?"

"It'll be interesting to see the prices today, and how many horses actually sell. There will likely be lots of buy-backs. The dealers will be freaking out, trying to unload horses."

"And you? What are you going to do?"

"I'll find other driving jobs. It'll just take me a little while, but I'll be fine. Fred's job was OK money-wise, but there are other long-haul options around here."

"Jake's at Tom's, I hear." I thought I should share something I've learned since Mark's been very forthcoming with me.

"Yes, Tom bailed him out of jail. I guess he felt bad he'd made Jake, and his other traders, sign those forms. He's taking care of all of them."

"I guess the whole thing is a complete mess for Tom and Fred. Not that I'm sorry about that."

"Yes, that about sums it up. And for Abel. His auction is going to suffer big time with half his buyers gone."

"Of course. Well I'm not too sorry about that either." I smile a little. In another world, I think I would like Mark. We chat for another ten minutes as I slowly finish my coffee. I then go up to the gallery to wait for the sale to begin.

Eighty-two horses go through the ring, at least twenty of which didn't sell because they didn't reach the prices the buyers were seeking. The average prices were down again on last week, especially for the cheaper horses. A horse that would have gone for four hundred a couple of weeks ago is now going for two hundred, or not selling at all. There is a new buyer, however, a guy I don't recognize, using a bid number that is new to me. He bought twenty-three horses, all very cheap.

I leave the auction around two thirty and head to Sarah's.

I walk into Sarah's kitchen, the coffee is brewing.

"Hey, Sarah."

"Amanda, how was Owenscreek?"

"Fred wasn't there today, apparently the CFIA is ready to close the border for kill horses."

"Great news! Any Thoroughbreds?"

"No, and prices have dropped more, plenty of horses didn't sell. But there was a new buyer I wasn't familiar with."

Sarah hands me a coffee. "Oh?"

"He bought twenty-three horses. All the same types of horses Tom and Fred would buy."

"Interesting. Can't be someone with a contract in Canada, not if the border is about to be closed?"

"No. I didn't have time to make any inquiries. Maybe next week I can find out more."

"Check the trucks and trailers out back. See if you notice any unusual ones, ones with non-Pennsylvania plates. I hope he's not buying for Mexico."

"You think he could be? I know the EU has stopped importing horse meat from Mexico."

"It's possible. They eat horse down there, they have other markets too. If the prices here get so low, it might make sense." Wow, marketplaces adjust quickly.

"Christ, I hope not. The slaughter pipeline is never-ending."

"We can only do what we do. You going to that auction each week is amazing." We head outside to get the horses in and feed them. I'm excited to see Thunder Clouds. We walk out to a paddock together to get him.

"How's the old guy doing?"

"Great, considering he's only been here a short time. I turned him out yesterday for the first time. He just stood still, looked around, and then dropped his head to eat the little grass we've still got. It's almost like he's been turned out all his life. I turned him out again first thing this morning. He's loving it." He looks great, just standing and grazing in the corner of the paddock. Sarah calls him, he wanders up to us, ready to come in. He's an easy pleaser.

"What do you think of his ankle? Is he rideable? I know Pete's been worried about it."

"It's not pretty, and more racing might have really hurt him. I think in a few months we can get a saddle on him, and see what we can do. He might not make a four-star eventer, but there are plenty of other options." We are now back in the barn. All the horses are ready for their feed.

"What are you planning to do with Spicy?"

"I'm not sure yet. I'm still just relieved to have him back. Whatever I do with him, it won't be for a few months. He's having some time off for now." Sarah has run a few horses over the summer at Missionville. She's had a couple of second place finishes, but no wins. She isn't in a hurry with anything at the moment. I'm curious how she makes the farm work financially, but it isn't any of my business really.

Pete's car is pulling up the driveway as we leave the barn to head back into the house.

We have another very pleasant evening at Sarah's. We chat about the slaughter situation, and the progress since the *New York Times* story. *Paulick Report* now has more than five hundred comments on the story, and the interest isn't dying down. Pete also shares with Sarah the rumors on the backside about the drug positives. We are convinced they're for Harry's horses, and consider it a good sign that Timmins's investigation is going forward.

Sarah cooks a delicious meal. We drink lots of wine, and Pete and I make love.

CHAPTER 55

PETE, FRIDAY

SLIPPERS IS RACING IN THE FOURTH TONIGHT, so I only have two to gallop.

The horses enjoy their breakfast as I take off their leg wraps and check them over thoroughly. I'm still surprised how cold and tight Slippers's legs continue to be. Hopefully they'll be the same tomorrow, after her race.

When Alfie arrives at seven o'clock, I already have two stalls mucked out.

"Slippers first, boss?"

"Thanks, Alfie." He'll walk her for thirty minutes. I get the tack for my other filly.

Fifteen minutes later I'm on the track.

"Morning, Pete. Gorgeous morning," Jess remarks.

"It is." We'd just seen a beautiful sunrise. There is no wind and it's still a pretty cool seventy degrees.

"Good luck tonight with your filly. Keep the winning streak going."

"I hope so. Each race is a little tougher, but she's improving."

"You've got her going great. She looks good in that race." I know there are one or two tough horses to beat tonight, but Jess is more often right than wrong.

"Thanks. Big works tomorrow?"

"Yes. Be good to see how Harry's horse and Northern Peaks do with their first works back."

"Should be easy works, but maybe then we'll get confirmation they'll face each other in the Travers."

"I'm sure we'll see them both in the Travers. Too much is at stake for one of them to duck out." Jess has become a bit more of a believer in Harry's horse since his win in the Jim Dandy. The Travers does promise to be a very interesting contest. End of year honors might be at stake.

I walk off, then move into a jog, heading to the wire. I stand my filly in for a few minutes. I have plenty of time this morning. We watch a couple of workers heading down the lane, the outside horse moves ahead of the inside horse close to the wire. The rider on the inside horse is trying to urge his horse forward, but honestly, he's not the best breeze rider – he's hopping up and down rather than being in the rhythm of his horse.

After a few more horses gallop by I move my filly forward and to the right, and begin our gallop. She's now relaxing more and more in the early parts of her gallop. Her breathing has also improved in the last couple of days. She switches her leads at the right places, going into and coming out of the turns. She was less inclined to do that when I first claimed her.

As she switches back onto her outside lead, coming out of the turn, I hear the track siren. It's very loud. There is either a loose horse on the track or a breakdown. I ease my filly back to a jog and then a walk as I survey the track to see what is going on.

I spot Darren, one of the two outriders, starting to gallop fast, the wrong way, around the far turn. I look in front of him, and sure enough, I see a riderless horse. It is galloping the wrong way on the inside fence moving down the backside. It's only two furlongs away from me, heading toward us. I move my filly to the outside fence. We are now standing still as I watch Darren start to bear down on the loose horse. They are going at a flat out gallop. Darren leans closer and closer to the runaway, and then snags it by its bridle. As soon as he does this, he starts to ease his pony back. In less than a minute he has the loose horse walking alongside the pony, they look very relaxed. It's a remarkable piece of horsemanship to witness.

The second outrider is at the quarter pole, standing over a prone rider, who had obviously come off the loose horse. I wait with my filly for what seems like ages – but it's probably no more than a couple of minutes – before the rider gets up and walks slowly to the outside fence. The loose horse has been taken to the gap. The track is now clear again for training, and I move my filly back into an easy gallop.

There's an old saying: if you haven't fallen off, you haven't ridden enough. It's obviously very true. While I haven't fallen off for a good while now, you never know when it's going to happen next, you do know it will happen.

My filly completes her mile-and-a-half gallop steadily. We head back to the gap, and I turn her in.

"A bit of excitement, Jess. You see who it was?"

"It was a new rider for John Swank. She might not be coming back tomorrow."

"Let's hope she isn't hurt too bad. I thought it was Swank's saddle cloth." That's pretty much how you identify whose horses are whose out on the track.

"The horse was fine coming off the track. Must have gotten spooked or something," Jess adds.

I exit the gap and take my filly back to the barn. Ten minutes later, I manage to get my gelding back up to the track before the break; thankfully his training session is much quieter. Adam is out there on one of his horses, so I wait for him and we walk back to the gap together. I feel a responsibility to keep an eye on him in case he needs anything as he unwinds his racing stable.

"Adam, how's things?"

"Fine, Pete. Still trying to get homes for a couple, but making progress. You hear the rumors?"

"Which ones? This is a racetrack, there are always rumors."

"The drug positives. I'm hearing there's a big case coming up soon, multiple horses involved."

"I'd heard something, didn't pay too much attention though." I'm curious if Adam knows any more, and how he'd heard.

"I know three trainers have been whispering, some of their purse money hasn't been distributed. Apparently that's what happens when they're looking into the outcome of races. You'd know better than me?" We are at the gap now, standing in.

"Sure, happened to me once. It turned out the winner was taken down, and I got the first place purse. But they didn't pay out for a while." We start walking off the track.

"So if it's multiple trainers, would be multiple positives?"

"Possible."

"I hear a Franks horse won at least one of the races." So now the rumors are focusing in on who the trainer might be.

"Interesting. I guess we'll know soon enough." We should. First there's a hearing, and then once that's complete, we'll get the ruling. It couldn't come soon enough for me.

I enter my barn, Adam heads on his way to his barn. Larry, the state vet, is waiting for me.

"Alfie just showed me your horse. All good for tonight."

"Thanks, Larry. Alfie'll be here all afternoon for Lasix."

"Usual?"

"Yes, thanks."

It's a short exchange. Larry is on his way to approve all the runners for tonight's program. The field sizes are getting smaller and smaller, he has to approve the runners.

Alfie takes my horse, and I start grooming Slippers. This whole drug positive offense would be another nail in Harry's coffin, if indeed it is Harry's horses, which I assume it is. But it wouldn't be enough to bring him down. I hope Timmins has more to throw at him, but he is keeping his cards close to his chest. Sarah hasn't heard anything from him for a week or two. I half expect to see him at the track, snooping around, but that hasn't happened. Not yet anyway.

My phone vibrates, it's Sarah.

"Hey, Pete. The border is closed."

"Wow! How did you hear?"

"A friend who works on the rescue side, she heard. She called me about it, asking what I know."

"Thanks for letting me know."

"You did a good thing there, Pete. I know it was hard."

"Thanks, but very worthwhile right?"

"Yes, of course." Sarah hangs up. She wasn't my biggest fan when Amanda and I started hanging out. She's now become a good friend. I really look forward to our Tuesday evenings at her farm.

I text Amanda, "In case you didn't hear, CFIA has shut down the border. X"

An hour later I'm finished at the barn. I collect Hairy and we go to the kitchen for his treat and my sandwich. Alice doesn't disappoint. She also updates me a little more on what she's been hearing about the positive tests. She also mentions a Franks horse.

Hairy and I leave the track and go on a nice long walk. I have plenty of time to chill out and relax before I need to get back for the races.

I arrive at Pokers just as the first race goes off. It's another maiden race; I won't be around long enough to see these horses develop, so there wasn't much point in getting here sooner.

"Budweiser, Pete?"

"Thanks."

"Good luck tonight, filly's on a win streak for you."

"Yes, we've been lucky." Mary hands me my beer.

"I hear there's a drug problem on the backside." So the positives have been discussed at the races too.

"Sounds like something's up. I guess we'll get confirmation soon."

"The cheats ruin the sport for everyone." She's right of course. But sometimes it's human nature to take an edge. Obviously Harry has taken this to the extreme, assuming it is Harry.

As I sit down with my Budweiser and *Daily Racing Form*, I hear a message from the track announcer, "Would the following trainers contact the racing secretary's office for a change of rider: Franks races two and five, Martin race three, Johnson race seven."

Mike Franks and Jim Johnson get up from their respective tables and head out of Pokers. Neither acknowledges the other.

I look at my *Form*, Marcus Longman has been taken off all his mounts for the night, or he is a no-show. That's unusual. Of course, everyone in Pokers notices the same thing. Whispers start flying, lots of people speculating.

A couple of jockeys do this from time to time, but it's usually because they fail a sobriety test, or they hear that one is being used for that night. Longman hasn't done this before, not to my knowledge anyway. Of course, in the back of my mind, I hope there is a very different reason.

I go out to the paddock to watch the horses for the second race. It is a $15,000 claiming race for horses that haven't won two races. There are only six horses in the field. These horses are still a little green, having only raced about a half a dozen times each. Franks's horse is the favorite for the race, a big red filly. Jennifer is leading her around.

The track announcer notes, "Rider change for number four, Manoy replaces Longman." Jennifer's horse has a new rider; Rafael Manoy has only been at Missionville for a month. He came up from the southwest circuit, looking to restart his riding career. After he lost his bug at Louisiana Downs a year ago, he'd struggled to establish himself on the Louisiana circuit. He stopped by my shedrow a couple of times to introduce himself. I got a bad vibe from him.

Franks's horse is the 2-1 favorite in the race. I decide to place a ten dollar bet on a different horse. I won fifty dollars. Franks's horse came fourth, she was well beaten. Franks's stable has been on a losing slide over the last month or so. They usually win at about a twenty five percent rate, which is impressive, if done fairly. For their last twenty runners, they've only won one race, and it wasn't even one of Harry's horses.

The third race is for the old-timers. A $10,000 claimer for horses that haven't won two races in the last year. It's another six-horse field. The racing secretary is having a harder time filling races. Two runners in the race have made over $300,000 each. One had started his career in New York, the other in Maryland, at Laurel. Both have now raced at Missionville for more than a year at the $10,000 level, both had been much better in their youth. The favorite for the race is a horse called Stephen's Folly. He's raced his whole career at Missionville, and has won ten races. He's a popular horse, currently in Jim Johnson's barn. He won his last start, which was his first race back for four months. The track announcer states that Manoy has the ride on the three horse, a horse from a ship-in trainer.

Stephen's Folly wins the race quite easily. The two horses that had made over $300,000 trail the field. Their best racing days are long gone, they'll be in at the $5,000 level soon. Manoy's new mount, which was the second choice, finishes a weak fourth.

Now it's my turn. My nerves are getting to me, as they always do before a race. I enter the paddock and stand by saddling stall number one and wait for the runners to be led over. This is a seven-horse field. There are a couple of good 'come-from-behind' fillies in the race, which makes our task a little more complicated. I feel good about how Pink Slippers is training, and she is a soft favorite for the race, but this is not an easy task for her. She's against a better group of fillies than she has faced so far in her career.

Alfie brings her into the paddock and they begin circling as I wait for Emma's valet, who soon files out with the other valets.

"What happened to Longman?" I ask Greg, the valet, as we put on the saddle.

"Don't know. There's rumors, but no one really knows. He didn't show."

"Sounds very unusual. No sobriety testing?"

"Not tonight." So that rules out that reason, not that Longman is stupid enough to lose mounts for a few drinks at lunchtime.

"Weird."

"Good luck." Greg returns to the jocks' room. Alfie takes Slippers back out to the paddock while I wait for Emma. My nerves are increasing. Soon it will be time for my quick Budweiser and see how the filly runs. Emma files out of the jocks' room with the other jockeys and comes over.

"Tough spot, Emma. I know we're favorite, but this is not like the last couple of races."

"Yes, but you've got her in great shape."

"What'll you do?"

"I guess I'll sit and wait, but try to get first run on the other closing fillies?"

"Sounds good." Alfie brings Slippers back in. The call comes, "Riders Up!" and they head out of the paddock. I have a new pony rider, Kelly, to take them down to the starting gate. I head back into Pokers.

"Here you go, Pete." Mary already has my Budweiser ready.

"Thanks, Mary." I study the TV screen next to the bar. The horses are nearing the starting gate. My filly is now at 5-2 joint favorite with one other. The next horse in the betting is 3-1. It looks like a three horse race.

They are loading in the gate. Slippers goes in nice and easy. The other fillies also load well.

"They're in the gate," the track announcer says, "and they're off!"

Slippers breaks well, and is just in behind the leader as they head out of the shoot. Emma soon has her relaxed in second place, two lengths off what is a fast pace. The other runners are a little strung out behind her. As they head into the far turn, Emma nudges Slippers a little closer to the leader. The filly looks great, and is in a good position. As they come off the turn Emma takes her a little wide, and she passes the leader with ease. Emma is now in a full drive. Coming from behind are the two key closers, and they start their charge as the horses hit the eighth pole.

Slippers still had a half-length advantage inside the sixteenth pole. I will her on, almost shouting. But the inevitable happens. She is just headed on the wire by the filly on the far outside. It is a good second place finish, just not quite good enough for the win. I head outside.

Emma brings Slippers back and Alfie takes hold of her. The filly is breathing very heavily, she'd really put in a strong effort. Emma looks similarly exhausted after putting the filly into overdrive coming down the lane.

"Sorry, Pete. She ran terrific. Maybe I went too soon."

"No worries, as long as she runs her race, I'm happy." Emma is off the horse by now. We start walking back towards the jocks' room as Alfie takes Slippers back to the barn.

"I really wanted to keep her streak alive for you."

"It was a tough race. I'm happy. I think you rode her perfect."

"Thanks." Emma disappears into the jocks' room.

I text Ray, "Second, just beaten, ran huge. Should be tough back in that spot next time. Will call tomorrow." I hope Ray will wait for the call tomorrow. I don't need to hear from him tonight.

I send Amanda a text, "Filly ran huge, second, just beaten. Will be home in twenty minutes. Let's head out to Jessup's. Longman's gone missing. X" Amanda has grown to be OK with Jessup's. I know it's not her favorite place, but she likes Charlie. He always makes her feel welcome.

Amanda replies almost immediately, "Nice, glad she ran well. See you soon X"

We arrive to a crowded Jessup's at a little before nine. The all-you-can-eat buffet attracts its usual Friday night crowd. I'm curious if Longman shows. On a normal Friday he would be the life and soul of the place, staying long into the night.

"Usual, guys?"

"Thanks, Charlie. Already getting busy."

"It's another Friday night."

"Did you hear Longman was taken off his mounts?" I'm interested in what Charlie knows. He's usually up to date with the goings on, like Alice I guess.

"Yes, lots of rumors. Don't expect I'll see him here tonight. You hear anything?"

"Only that it wasn't a sobriety test."

"I heard security checked his car, found something. From someone who knows his valet." Excellent, so Timmins is making progress.

"I guess we'll know soon enough." Charlie moves on to his next customer. Amanda and I find one of the only remaining empty tables.

"Phew, long day, not a bad day though." I sigh.

"I'm surprised Timmins is going after Longman. I thought he'd only focus on Harry."

"I guess it's all related. If they can get Longman to talk, maybe he'll have something to say to help their case."

"Maybe. When do you think we'll know about the positives?"

"Based on the volume of noise on the backside I can't imagine it'll be more than a few more days. Once that's out in the open, things will really start to happen."

"I should tip off Margaret. Maybe she'll want to write something, keep it all in the news."

"Smart." I hadn't thought much more of Margaret's involvement, but surely she deserves any scoop on Harry. Longman would help make the story a little more spicy.

We enjoy the all-you-can-eat buffet, and hang around the place for a couple of hours. I want to make sure Longman doesn't make a late appearance. His valet does, but he doesn't. We chat with his valet for a little while, but he wasn't too forthcoming with what he knows. He does mention that he doesn't think Longman will be around for a while. It's going to hit his pay check hard. I buy him a beer, but I don't feel too sorry for him.

We arrive home at a little after eleven thirty. Amanda suggests a night cap. It sounds like a fantastic idea to me. She goes to the kitchen to get the drinks as I retire to the living room. When she comes over with the drinks, she'd removed her blouse and shoes.

CHAPTER 56

PETE, SATURDAY

MY ALARM WAKES ME UP AT FIVE. I'M EXHAUSTED, but it's a good exhaustion. I creep out of bed, not wanting to disturb Amanda, who is sound asleep. I gather my clothes and go to the bathroom. Last night was simply amazing. Amanda has no limits to her imagination. She's also very in tune with my desires. It's just all crazy good.

Once washed and clothed, I tiptoe downstairs and let Hairy out before he gets too boisterous. His energy this morning is in sharp contrast to my own.

I have an easy day ahead of me at the track. Amanda and I have decided to take a little road trip later and spend the night in a log cabin up in the mountains. It's something I used to do as a kid. It seems like a good idea right around now. I'm really looking forward to it.

My three horses nicker to me when I enter the barn. I feed them quickly, and then just watch them eat. They each dive into their feed tubs. Slippers is first to finish, you wouldn't think she just ran a race. I remove all their bandages, as usual. Slippers's legs need to be washed off before I can figure out how they look after her race. Alfie will take care of that. I start mucking the stalls, as Franks's help begin to arrive. David Arts, his assistant, comes over to my shedrow once things quiet down a little for him, after his crew has settled into its routine.

"Pete, you hear all the rumors?"

"About the drug positives, or Longman?"

"The positives."

"Sure, I heard some of the chatter. Is it you guys?"

"It is. Mike told me yesterday. He has a hearing on Monday. He's expecting a big problem. He wants me to take my trainer's test."

"He thinks he'll get stood down?" I fake stuff well, there's no doubt he should get a hefty penalty if his runners have tested positive for frog juice.

"Yes, it's apparently very bad. Harry's going crazy. He can't understand what's happening. It was all his horses." What he can't understand is how he got caught, not how it happened.

"Was Harry in on it?" I want to see how David responds. I know the answer.

"I really don't know. Mike's job is good for me, but I don't fully understand everything that goes on. Apparently, Harry likes you, says you might be able to help me, during any transition." I wasn't expecting that. Harry always did have a soft spot for me, ever since I had that bad spill from one of his horses. Now I'm wondering if he felt guilty because the horse was drugged.

"I wish I could. To be honest, I'm winding down my operation. I'm going to be looking for a new line of work."

"Oh, sorry to hear that. You've always been a good barn mate to us." I was, for a very long time, but not for the last couple of months. I'm sure they'll figure that out soon enough. But David, who is the hard-working manager of the operation, has always seemed pretty decent. He spends all day in the barn, making sure things run as well as they can. He's much more of a trainer than Mike Franks. The horses will be in good hands, but perhaps not in as corruptible hands.

"Thanks. I wish you the best if you do have to take over the operation."

"Appreciate it, Pete. Can you keep this conversation to yourself, at least until the hearing?"

"Sure." So there it is. Franks will soon be suspended, and it'll all be out in the open.

Alfie arrives right at seven o'clock.

"Filly first, boss?"

"Sure, Alfie, can you cover for me tomorrow?"

"Sure, boss."

"Thanks, I'll see if Jorge or Jennifer can help you out, we've nothing to train." I head to my tack room to get my other filly ready. Hairy drops down in his spot, ready for his morning nap.

A short while later I'm standing in at the gap.

"Tough loss last night, Pete," Jess offers.

"Thanks. She ran her race."

"She ran great. Emma did her best for her, just didn't quite set up." Jess would never criticize Emma, but I do agree, this race was just a tough loss, no jockey error. Jess continues, "See Northern Peaks worked this morning at Saratoga already. Easy half-mile in 50."

"Sounds about right. One more work next week should get him ready again. When's Dancer's Foil supposed to work?"

"After the break up there, another half-mile work." Jess is always on Twitter keeping up to date with what's going on.

"Let's hope it's more of the same." I walk off, then move into a jog back to the wire. I haven't heard any whispers about what happened to Longman yesterday. I was sure the news would be all over the track this morning.

The filly trains nicely, and we enjoy a quiet track. I did pass a set from John Swank's barn. I didn't see a new rider. I'm assuming the girl who fell off yesterday hasn't returned today.

I'm back on the track in thirty minutes aboard my gelding. Amanda is on the rail in conversation with a trainer. Since Jake's disappearance, she's experienced a real uptick in interest for her site. Four new trainers have asked her to add horses, trainers who wouldn't have given her the time of day before.

As I walk past her, I smile. She smiles back, then returns to her conversation without missing a beat. My gelding does his thing, getting me around the track. I think he's run his last race for me. Ray will have to make a decision about him soon. I'll be talking to him later today anyway, so maybe I'll bring up retirement for this guy too. Thunder Clouds is definitely enjoying his new life.

At break time the p.a. system across the backside announces that Longman is off all his mounts for Monday and Tuesday, the two days that entries had already been taken for next week. All involved horsemen are asked to go to the racing secretary's office to make alternate arrangements. It doesn't involve me, but Longman's absence is becoming more noteworthy. He's definitely staying away.

I text Amanda, "Will be done within the hour, stop by? X" I go about my tasks of grooming and doing up my horses' legs. Slippers has another day of poultice, her legs seem to be fine after her race last night. The other two horses are just getting done up in alcohol for now. I mix it up from day to day, but their legs seem to react best to a straight alcohol rub. Tomorrow they'll all be left open.

Once I finish, I head over to see Jorge who is also attending to one of his horse's legs.

"Jorge, can you cover for me tomorrow?"

"Si, Pete, no problem."

"Gracias."

"Next week is my last week."

"Where are you going?"

"Mexico. I am ready for home."

"Will you come for dinner before you leave? I'll drive you."

"Si, would be nice."

"When's good for you? Any day works for us." I really want to hang out with Jorge. I feel bad he figured he needs to leave.

"Monday, is OK?"

"Monday works, Jorge. Pick you up at the kitchen. Six?"

"Si, gracias." I head back to my shedrow. Amanda is waiting for me. We head into the tack room.

"Longman's gone, Timmins raided his car." Amanda's first words.

"How did you hear?"

"Three or four guys on the rail. One trainer said he saw his car pulled over with Longman standing outside it. If it's not true, it's the rumor that most believe."

"Makes sense. It would be good if Sarah spoke to Timmins and gave us an update."

"Yes, I'll ask her. Good morning?"

"Not bad, I'm done early. How much longer do you need to be here?"

"I told Shawn I'd stop by. He has some feedback on the banking program he wants to talk about. I need to visit two more barns, get pictures and video. I should be done in an hour or so."

"Great, see you at home when you're done. We can get an early start up the mountain." Amanda kisses me and departs.

CHAPTER 57

PETE, MONDAY

I COME BACK TO FEED THIS AFTERNOON, SOMETHING ALFIE usually does for me. I need to be at the track to pick up Jorge and bring him over for dinner. Amanda is preparing a fun Mexican evening at the house; she is happy to have an excuse to leave work early, since it's starting to get hectic again at the bank.

Mike Franks was absent at the track this morning. I'm guessing he's attending his hearing for the drug positives. If that's the case, we'll know for sure tomorrow when the ruling is announced. Other than that, it was a pretty uneventful morning at the track. There was a little buzz about the two Travers horses' works over the weekend. The works were nothing special – easy half-miles – but the announcements that they're both now confirmed to race in the Travers, barring any unfortunate injuries, has captured the imagination of the racing public, and the backside at Missionville.

Feed time in the afternoons is usually a quiet time in the barns. Franks has two runners tonight; he has two grooms waiting by their stalls. David is in his feed room getting everything ready for the other horses. The two runners will be fed after they race. Half his other grooms are here, picking out stalls.

For me, it's just a case of picking out my stalls, topping up the water buckets, throwing in some hay, and preparing the horses' feeds. It takes me less than fifteen minutes.

I head over to the kitchen. I have an hour to kill to wait for Jorge.

"Unusual to see you here in the afternoons, Pete," observes Alice.

"I know. Something different." I smile. "May I get a cup of coffee?"

"Sure. So who do you like of the top two?" There are only two other people in the kitchen. Alice is a little bored I think.

"Dancer's Foil. I like how easily he won the Jim Dandy, and he's a fresher horse."

"Be crazy to have a Triple Crown winner and he not be the best three-year-old?"

"It would, but Dancer's Foil might have stopped that Triple Crown streak if he hadn't been injured."

"Sure, but staying sound's important." This conversation with Alice is similar to three or four other conversations I've had in the last twenty-four hours. As much as it irks me, I think Harry's horse is the better horse, and Northern Peaks might be on the downswing. The rigors of the Triple Crown series can ruin a good horse.

I go over to one of the many empty tables, sit down and chill out. Right at six o'clock, Jorge appears.

I drive Jorge back to the house. Amanda has a plate of cheesy nachos prepared and some margaritas already poured.

"It's nice to see you again, Jorge. Welcome to our home." I like the way Amanda said that. It is our home. She's now ended the lease on her house.

"Gracias, Amanda. It's nice to be here."

"Margarita or Corona?"

"Si, a margarita is nice." We move into the living room and sit down. For whatever reason, I haven't socialized too much with the sizable Mexican community we have in Missionville. They usually stick together, and the rest of us don't make much of an effort to do anything about it. On the odd occasion, like the Kentucky Derby, you'll see a few Mexicans visit Jessup's. But mostly they'll stay on the backside and keep to themselves. It all means we don't know much about each other.

"Jorge, you heard the rumors of the drug positives?"

"Si, everyone knows."

"You know who it is?"

"Maybe my boss?" Jorge guesses, or maybe he is hoping.

"Yes, I think there was a hearing today. It'll be confirmed tomorrow."

"Si. It's bueno."

"It's all because of the syringe you gave us. You made this happen. It tested positive for Dermorphin, a class-one drug. They created a test, and then snagged another horse of Franks." I can tell Jorge doesn't understand everything I'm saying, but understands its meaning.

"It's bueno. I'm happy."

"How long did you work for Franks?" Amanda asks.

"Over two years now."

"Did you like the job?"

"It was OK at the beginning. I get paid cash, money's good. I need money for my family in Mexico. Then I notice things I no like. I keep quiet. Then Pete asked me about a horse went to slaughter. I no like. I want to do something and I'm ready to go home."

"Where's home?" Amanda asks.

"Just outside Mexico City. I have wife, two young children. We build house." Jorge pulls his wallet from his pocket and takes out a couple of pictures of his family.

"Your wife is very cute Jorge, your kids are gorgeous!"

"Gracias, Amanda. I miss them very much."

"And you're heading home this week?"

"Si, payday is Friday. I leave after that."

"If you didn't like Franks's job for a while, why did you stay?" It's my turn to ask. I hope Jorge doesn't think we brought him here for an inquisition.

"I have to. I'm no legal, like most that work for Franks. We get paid cash. I get the money home quickly. If I try to leave, it may be no bueno to return." Paying cash to undocumented workers is an aspect of Harry's money-laundering operation no doubt.

"So you couldn't work for anyone else?" Amanda jumps in.

"Is possible, yes. But Franks help me get my track license. New job means I need to change license. May be problem." So Franks and Harry work with security to get the help Harry needs. It all makes sense. Jorge continues, "Franks's job popular in Mexican community. I hear it at Beulah when track closed. I decided to move here, no problemo."

Amanda serves a chicken enchilada dish that Jorge seems enthusiastic about. Our conversations continue late into the night. It's a pleasant evening, not that I should have been surprised.

Jorge tells us about how he met his wife, who was his childhood sweetheart. He talks about his journey over the border for the first time, in order to come to the United States to try to make more money for his family. He recollects how hard it was for him to leave his wife for the first time, and every time since.

He talks about his visits home, each time running the risk of getting caught by immigration. He tells us about the birth of his first born, his daughter. How hard it was for him when he was so far away in Ohio. It was no easier for him when his son was born. With the growth of his family, it has become increasingly difficult for him to leave them to try to do what he thought was right – providing for their future. His mother has recently become quite ill, making his decision to finally return home for good much easier.

Jorge now has nearly enough money saved for a house he's building; his family currently lives with his wife's parents. He plans to set up a farm in Mexico. His more than ten years here were simply to set himself up so he could pursue his dreams with his family.

I've always liked Jorge, but I now feel I know him a little better. I have a new-found respect for him, and what he's given up to help set himself and his family up for the future. I imagine his story is not too dissimilar to those of other Mexicans who toil away on the backside at Missionville, and racetracks around the country.

CHAPTER 58

PETE, TUESDAY

THE WORST KEPT SECRET ON THE BACKSIDE IS POSTED in the racing secretary's office, in the "Notice of Rulings": Mike Franks has four positives for Dermorphin.

Dermorphin is a class-one drug, and the penalty for this series of infractions is a ban for one year and a thousand dollar fine. Franks is prohibited from any racing properties in the state of Pennsylvania. Other state racing jurisdictions will uphold a similar ban if Franks tries to license in another state.

Each of the horses involved are owned by Harry Mitchell. That is obviously not a surprise to me, but it catches a few off guard at the track. What I didn't realize was that there are four positives. I had presumed they only had two. Maybe a couple more came in before James stopped working for Franks.

What is becoming pretty clear, Harry's rule of his own track is now very fragile. His horses have been caught up in a doping scandal, and his jockey has been caught up in a new battery scandal.

I text Amanda, "It's official, Franks is banned. Have Margaret call me if you want? x" It might be good for this story to get some press, keep the pressure on Harry. Margaret could write it for her paper, it's probably not big enough for the *New York Times*. But even a story in the local paper would be great, the *Paulick Report* should pick it up.

Half an hour later, just as I am finishing up my morning work at the barn, Margaret calls.

"Pete, Amanda just let me know the ruling is official."

"Yes, four horses. Is it enough for a story?"

"Of course, I can tie it to the Longman situation too. Should make for a very entertaining piece."

"Great, when will it run?"

"Friday's paper, online on Thursday I should think."

"You need anything from me for the story, just let me know."

"Will do. I think I have things straight, thanks for pushing me to do this."

"I'm hoping this keeps the pressure on Harry. I imagine Timmins is still working on other aspects of Harry's business. Let's hope so anyway."

"Yes, I spoke to Sarah last week. She said Timmins wasn't revealing much about what he's learning, but we assume the Longman shakedown means Timmins is making progress." Margaret is right. I wasn't expecting Timmins to go after Longman. He must be using Longman, much like James, to build a stronger case against Harry.

"Can you email me when the story goes online? I'll forward it to the *Paulick Report*, see if they'll run it. I imagine they will, with all the buzz around Harry's horse, Dancer's Foil."

"Will do." Margaret hangs up.

I get Hairy and head over to the kitchen.

"Usual, Pete?"

"Thanks, Alice." She places two sausages on the grill, and starts preparing my sandwich.

"Mike Franks is banned then, all Harry's horses, what do you make of it?" Alice asks.

"I think it's odd that the four horses are all Harry's, Franks trains for quite a few others."

"Yes, you might be right. I suppose this has something to do with that vet quitting." Of course, people will now start putting two and two together. James quits, and horses that he treated turn up with positives.

"I guess. I was told it was stress related. Though I suppose cheating creates stress." I didn't think I should mention the blackmailing situation James had found himself in. I still have no idea what Harry has on James.

"These are interesting times at Missionville." Alice hands me my sandwich, and two extra sausages. I go over to an empty table and sit down to eat. Hairy chomps down his treat in two gulps.

CHAPTER 59

PETE, SATURDAY

I ARRIVE AT THE BARN RIGHT AT SIX O'CLOCK. My three horses are waiting and ready for their morning feed. I plan to work my new filly today, her last work before a race next week. Fortunately, Emma is one of the jockeys at Missionville who doesn't go to Jessup's on a Friday night; she is happy to come in and work the filly. They will be my first set.

The track has been buzzing all week with the Franks situation; with both Franks and Longman gone, some are starting to wonder what's next. Margaret's new piece did make it to the *Paulick Report*; she tied both incidents nicely back to Harry. No doubt Paulick ran the piece because of Harry's horse, Dancer's Foil, which is getting a lot of press up at Saratoga. The new story has already accumulated more than a hundred comments on Paulick's site, and people are connecting the story with the *New York Times* slaughter story.

David Arts is now the official trainer of all Franks's horses, and it's become pretty clear to me that he wasn't involved in any of Harry's dodgy dealings. It will be interesting to see what happens over the next months, if Harry starts to return to his instincts. David has asked for my opinion on a few training matters. I hope he's able to do well, but I think he's in a bad situation. A couple of owners have already moved their horses to Jim Johnson's barn.

Jorge's last day was yesterday. I bid him farewell. He gave me his mother-in-law's address in Mexico. Maybe we'll visit one day.

I start to get the filly ready as I wait for Emma and Alfie to arrive. It's a glorious early morning at the track.

Emma shows up a little before seven.

"Hey, Pete."

"Emma, thanks for coming in on a Saturday."

"No worries. I'm excited to ride the filly next week."

"Cool. Easy pre-race work. Let her find her own rhythm, and just ask for a little more down the lane."

"Sounds perfect." I pull the filly out of her stall. I give Emma a leg up, and we head out to the track.

"Flower Garden, to go a half-mile, Jess."

"Sorry, Pete. No official works today."

"What do you mean?" I ask Jess, as Emma and the filly wait at the gap.

"None of the clockers showed this morning. Very strange, but no official times." That is strange. But maybe not so strange given other circumstances.

"OK, no worries, she's got official times so she can race anyway. Emma, whenever you're ready." Emma moves the filly off to head back to the wire.

"Northern Peaks already worked this morning, Pete. Five-eighths in 59 flat. Last eighth was in eleven." A decent work from the Triple Crown winner. "Dancer's Foil is due to go after the break. Let's hope it's a good work, and we're set for next Saturday!"

"Fingers crossed." I head over to the backside, so I can clock my filly. The clockers going missing must have something to do with Longman and Harry. I can't remember a time when no clockers showed up for work.

I text Amanda, who should be getting here just about now. "Clockers are a no-show today. More evidence Timmins is doing something? X"

Emma has my filly at the wire. The track is pretty quiet, as it can be on a Saturday morning. It's a great sight to see a filly so relaxed, and a rider who's willing to just take her time. After a couple more minutes, they move off, and break into an easy canter. I decided not to use a pony to help Emma ease her into her breeze. The filly has been so much more relaxed over the last few days I figured Emma would be fine, and she is. As they swing into the backside, Emma starts to move the filly close to the rail and lets out a notch of rein. The filly needs no urging, she visibly lengthens her stride and moves into her breeze.

Emma sits motionless aboard the filly for the first three-eighths, and clocks a nice 37 seconds. Then she starts to urge the filly inside the eighth pole, with her hands and heels. The filly quickens to finish the work in 48 seconds. They then gallop out an extra eighth of a mile in twelve seconds.

It is a perfect pre-race workout. When Emma brings the filly back to me at the gap, she is hardly blowing.

"Pete, you have her in great shape."

"She looked good, perfect job. Any noise?" I inquire if there's anything wrong with her breathing.

"No noise, all's good."

"Great. Thanks." We walk back to the barn.

I'm not in a hurry this morning, so I figure I'd get one more before the break, the gelding, and then train the other filly after the break. I want to hear what Jess thinks of Dancer's Foil's work, she'll be following the updates closely on Twitter.

The gelding trains fine. Amanda is out there on the rail, chatting away with a few horsemen, making progress with her racehorse website.

I'm still struggling to figure out what to do with the gelding in terms of racing or retiring. Fortunately Ray hasn't seemed to be too bothered about racing him lately, so I don't bring it up with him. I see Adam as I'm on my way back from the track. It sounds like he'll be gone in another month or so. He's down to one horse and looking forward to getting to Ohio.

Clare is in my shedrow when I return.

"All good, Pete?"

"I think so, Clare. I was going to get the filly scoped who just worked, but I think she's fine. I'll enter her next week, so may need a pre-race."

"Sounds good, I'll see you on Monday." Clare wanders into Franks's shedrow, I mean David's shedrow. She's managed to keep hold of most of James's clients since she took over from him. I thought she might have tried to lose Franks's business, but hasn't. She's never really discussed James over the last few weeks. I'm tempted to ask her if she knows any more, or even what James is up to. But I haven't yet. She's very reliable, I like that. She knows her vet work. And I haven't seen her duck into the stalls of horses that are racing on the same night.

I get Slippers ready for the track. I want to take her out a little after the break to ensure that the track is quiet. It's starting to get hot, so that's not ideal, but it is late August in Pennsylvania. She's come out of her last race nicely, but she's run a few races in a row now. I want to take it easy with her for a couple of weeks, before gearing her up again.

Fifteen minutes later we are standing in at the gap.

"Your other filly worked nicely for Emma, Pete."

"She did. I was very happy with it. How did Dancer's Foil work up in Saratoga?"

"A bullet. Fifty-eight and change. They say he looked like he made no effort, very easy for him. He had a stablemate ahead of him for the first three-eighths, then went by him and drew away by ten lengths."

"Wow! That sounds impressive."

"I'm now a believer. This horse is something else. I wouldn't be surprised if they make him the morning line favorite. Pretty crazy really."

"Well, let's hope we see a great horse race next weekend." I just wish Harry wasn't involved, but you can't blame the horse for that. I move my filly off to a walk, then jog her back to the wire. She trains beautifully. When we get back to the barn, Amanda is waiting for me.

"You all done?"

"Not yet, Pete. I just wanted to say hello." I give my filly to Alfie. We head into the tack room for a little privacy.

"So, you think the clockers not showing is related?"

"It has to be. In all the years I've trained at Missionville, this hasn't happened. Remember when I worked Thunder Clouds that first time with Longman, they reported a time bang on what I'd asked Longman to work the horse, but the horse had worked much faster. There's a connection between Longman and the clockers, and I'm sure with Harry too."

"Crazy stuff."

"Yes, but I think it shows Timmins is getting closer to Harry. I'm sure Harry must be going ape shit by now. Clockers, Longman, James, he must know they're really digging. And this has nothing to do with Jake, and his slaughter trade. Reading some of the comments on *Paulick Report*, they've already tried and convicted Harry."

"Good. I just hope Harry gets what he deserves."

"Yeah. In the meantime, he may well have the best horse in the country. Dancer's Foil just posted a bullet work up in Saratoga. He really does look like the real deal."

"I guess next weekend will be very interesting. I'm heading off, I need to chat with Shawn again. He wants to run another program. I've also a couple more barns to visit. See you at home later?"

"Can't wait."

CHAPTER 60

PETE, SATURDAY

TODAY IS TRAVERS DAY, THE MARQUEE RACE OF THE SARATOGA meet. It's the midsummer classic, pitting the best three-year-olds against each other before they start racing against older horses. It is always the longer-term target of the leading three-year-olds after they've battled through the Triple Crown series. Oftentimes, they'll meet fresher horses that avoided those three races in the spring.

This year we have a classic confrontation between the Triple Crown winner, Northern Peaks, and the upstart, Dancer's Foil. The racetrack community at Missionville is equally divided in their opinion regarding who will win. Northern Peaks was so impressive in his Derby win that some argue that he is the best we've seen since the late '70's. Others believe that Dancer's Foil is a far superior animal, and his last workout at Saratoga was otherworldly. The *Paulick Report* has a poll for the race; it's almost evenly split with more than ten thousand votes. The NBC evening news last night mentioned the upcoming race. Horse racing is benefitting from this potential rivalry.

Only two other horses are set to race against these stars, making this the smallest Travers field in living memory. Dancer's Foil shares morning line favoritism with Northern Peaks at 4-5. The other two runners are at 20-1. They may as well have been 100-1 for all anyone cares.

I only have two horses to train this morning. My filly ran a nice second-place finish last night. She made the lead coming off the final turn, and was just beaten by a filly that was closing on the wide outside. We were the third favorite in the race so it wasn't a bad performance. Even Ray seemed reasonably happy. He still hasn't bothered me about claiming another horse. I have a feeling all the recent news at the track has rattled him a little. Maybe he's winding down his interests, which would suit me just fine.

All morning at the track people share their opinion on the big race. It's a welcome distraction from the gossip about Harry and his enablers – rumors that have been central to the Missionville community over the last few weeks. Alfie is firmly in the camp of the Triple Crown winner. Jess was too, until the workouts last week; now she's swapped to Dancer's Foil. Alice has remained with Northern Peaks. Adam favors Dancer's Foil, while Shawn is praying for a safe race for all. Jessup's will be the place we'll all go to see the outcome of the duel.

The missing clocker saga of last Saturday remains a mystery to the backside. Three clockers have basically vanished. Three days ago they were replaced by three new clockers. I'm certain this is all related to the Harry investigation. I just wish Timmins would move directly onto Harry. It does bother me that he will be at Saratoga today with one of the best horses we've seen in a very long time, enjoying the attention he craves.

By ten o'clock I'm finished at the barn. I head out of the track and take Hairy for a long walk. Amanda is still busy on her barn tours. She'd added four new horses to her site last week. She told me she needed to photograph and video three more horses this morning. She is stressed because she now has to get a few more horses actually moved from the site to new homes. She used to normally have about fifteen horses listed at any given time, she currently has thirty-five.

Her visits to the auction over the last couple of weeks have also indicated some uncertainty in the slaughter market. The border to Canada has remained closed for slaughter horses; no one seems to know for how long. There's definitely a buyer at Owenscreek picking up horses to ship down to Mexico, but nobody seems to know which kill buyer he's working for. With the low prices, he's now buying upward of forty horses a week, which is nearly as many as Tom and Fred bought between the two of them when the Canadian border was open. The whole thing seems like a nightmare to me, but Amanda appears to be thriving on the situation.

When Hairy and I get home, Amanda is waiting for me. She has a bottle of wine open on the kitchen table, along with a few nibbles for lunch. She's just gotten out of the shower, and only has a towel loosely wrapped around her. This is how she is sometimes, and it's irresistible. Within ten minutes, we move up to the bedroom with the bottle of wine. The towel remains in the kitchen. We don't reappear for three hours.

We get to Jessup's at nearly five o'clock. There is a huge crowd of mostly the backside at the track. We push our way through to order our drinks.

"Like Derby day, but more, Charlie!" I had to practically shout.

"Yes, crazy. Those two horses have really brought everyone out. Usual?"

"Please." Charlie gets my Budweiser and Amanda's glass of wine. We retreat to a small space in one of the corners of the bar.

"Crowded!" I had to shout so Amanda could hear me.

"Yes, never seen it so busy."

"Me neither. You know anyone?"

"I see a couple of trainers I've talked to, that's about it."

"Yes, pretty much all backside people."

Two talking heads, on TV, are doing a point versus counter point discussion, one favoring Dancer's Foil, the other favoring the Triple Crown winner. Neither really raises any new thoughts that haven't been discussed on the backside over the last few days. Then one of the broadcasters mentions Harry Mitchell, and some of the troubles he seems to have faced recently. This is better, this is more of what I want to hear. If he's going to be on the national stage, at least make sure he has to suffer some criticism.

The criticism only lasts for a couple of minutes.

The horses are being led over to the paddock from the backside. It's odd to see only four horses, but it does mean that a lot of attention can be focused on the two leading contenders. They both look magnificent as they enter the paddock. With only a four-horse field, the paddock looks a little sparse. Usually for the big races, the inside of the paddock is packed with owners, trainers and other hangers on. Today there are four groups of people spread quite far apart, and a few media. Harry's group is the largest, which seems like an accurate reflection of his ego.

The horses continue to walk around the paddock as the four valets file out of the jocks' room with their saddles and number cloths. The horses are led into their saddling stalls, Dancer's Foil in number one, Northern Peaks in number three.

Then something weird happens. Four uniformed officers enter the paddock and go straight toward Harry's group. The camera moves away from them and focuses on the horses. Something is up. The commentators don't mention anything, they simply go from horse to horse, reminding us again of their accomplishments, or their lack of accomplishments as the case is for two of the contestants. When the horses are saddled, they are led around the paddock again. I keep my eye on the inside of the paddock, to see if I can see Harry's group, but they aren't there.

"What do you make of that?" I ask Amanda.

"I don't know, they're not saying anything, but something happened." It didn't go unnoticed in Jessup's either. There are plenty of whispers wondering where Harry went, and who had come into the paddock heading in his direction.

The horses are being lead out of the paddock and onto the racetrack for the post parade. There is still no word from the commentators as to what has happened. They're either ignoring the situation, or have been told to do so. The TV switches to a commercial break. The whispers at Jessup's grow louder. A few wonder if Harry has finally been caught. Others presume it's nothing.

Amanda receives a text message from Sarah and shows it to me, "Just heard from Timmins. He says enjoy the show."

He's got Harry!

The four horses enter the starting gate. One of the two outsiders is reluctant to load. He probably understands what a task he has in front of him; he's only won two races in twelve starts. Once they are all loaded, the starter lets them go quickly. They break right in front of the stands.

Immediately the top two horses charge to the lead. The other two settle in three lengths behind. It looks like it's going to turn out to be no more than a match race. By the time they come out of the clubhouse turn, the top two are six lengths in front of the third horse, which is already pulling away from the reluctant loader.

Dancer's Foil is on the inside and moving along easily with Northern Peaks on his outside. The fractions for the race are solid, and the two horses look comfortable heading down the backside and into the far turn. Then the jockey on Dancer's Foil asks him to lengthen his stride a little, and he does. Northern Peaks responds, and they both go the next quarter in a quick twenty-three seconds. All the time, Dancer's Foil is just cruising.

Coming out of the far turn, Northern Peaks starts to come under pressure from his rider. Seeing this, Figuaro, the jockey on Dancer's Foil, smacks his horse down the shoulder one time, and he accelerates again. He moves away so quickly that he is three lengths in front at the eighth pole, and by the time he crosses the wire he is five lengths clear. It's a very impressive performance. Dancer's Foil has also broken the track record. He is the fastest winner of the Travers Stakes in its long and storied history. His jockey is having a hard time pulling him up, he was running so easily and fast at the end.

The crowd at Jessup's starts to applaud, it's a magnificent performance. We know we've witnessed something very rare – greatness.

Five minutes later, the outrider has returned the winner to the winner's circle for the customary post-race ceremony. There's some confusion. No one seems to know what's going on, and where Dancer's Foil's connections are. His groom leads him into the circle. Todd Brown follows, and the photographer keeps waiting. Then someone yells to hurry things up. She takes what has to be the oddest win photo of a grade one race that many will have witnessed.

Now it's interview time. The usual procedure would be to interview the jockey, owner, and trainer. Sometimes just the trainer and the owner, but usually the owner gets some air-time. This should be Harry's moment, but obviously it isn't going to be. It is just the jockey and the trainer, and both appear a little at a loss to explain what has happened to Harry. Of course both are enthusiastic about the horse, which has just proven his worth at the top of the three-year-old division.

Amanda receives another text message from Sarah. She shows it to me, "Just heard from Timmins again. He wants to thank us all personally for what we did."

PETE, FOUR MONTHS LATER

AMANDA AND I ARE NOW MARRIED. We celebrated Harry's arrest with a trip to Elkton, Maryland. It's easy to tie the knot there. My parents came down from Philadelphia for the occasion. During our three-day stay, Amanda and I visited the Fair Hill Training Center, which is a beautiful place to train a horse. Sometimes horses from Fair Hill ship in to race at Missionville.

Dancer's Foil raced again, winning the Breeders' Cup Classic. It was his first try against older horses. He won easily. People are now debating whether he will race as a four-year-old or retire to stud. There is little question as to whether he deserves Horse of the Year honors. He will be the first horse to defeat a Triple Crown winner in the end-of-year awards. Northern Peaks didn't race again after his Travers defeat. He'll always be remembered as a Triple Crown winner, he just wasn't the best three-year-old of his generation.

The horse slaughter situation in America is still in flux. The European Union still imports horse meat from Canada, as long as the border from the United States remains closed. Kill buyer Tom has refocused all his business on other livestock slaughter. Fred appears to have retired. The mystery buyer for Mexico is still the main buyer at Owenscreek.

The horse community is divided on the horse slaughter issue. I know which side I'm on, and am proud of the role we played in closing the Canadian border. Amanda's site is starting to move more Thoroughbreds. She still visits the racetrack every Saturday morning and Owenscreek every Tuesday. We regularly stay at Sarah's on Tuesday nights.

I'm no longer training racehorses. Ray let me retire his gelding. He moved his two fillies to another trainer. This all happened the week after the Travers. I started taking some college courses in the fall, pretty much as soon as I quit training. I'm not sure what I'm going to do, but I'm happy trying to figure it out while undertaking a couple of side projects.

Missionville Racetrack is up for sale again. Because it has a casino, there are interested parties willing to make the purchase. The consensus view of the horsemen at the track is one of relief that Harry no longer influences their livelihoods. The racetrack also has a new set of stewards.

The track has been working with the NTRA to join its Safety and Integrity Alliance. The NTRA has asked me if I was interested in doing some work for them during this process, and I agreed. I am also helping them determine better solutions for retiring racehorses from all its member tracks. That's a problem that has been avoided for far too long, and it's a pretty big task.

Amanda's doing well at the bank. The new branches she helped design have now been rolled out. It's too early to tell how successful they're going to be, but customer reaction has been positive so far. There are a few things she plans to tweak, but it looks like she might have helped save her community banking system. She is the best thing that's happened to me, by far.

Sarah continues to train her horses at her farm. After giving Spicy Lemon a month off, she decided to bring him back to the races. He's run twice so far, with a third place finish his best effort. I am guessing he'll soon be retired. She's retrained Thunder Clouds to be her pony horse. She uses him to help her educate some of her younger horses. Sometimes I go over to her farm and help her out with them.

Amanda and I wrote a long letter to Jorge, once the Harry situation was resolved. In his reply, he let us know that the construction of his new home is well underway, and his family is pleased to finally have him back home. We are planning a visit next year. I've never been to Mexico.

Alfie is now hotwalking horses for David Arts. The hardest part of giving up training for me was letting Alfie go. He's worked for me since I started. David was happy to take him on. David has twenty horses in training, in the same barn. He obviously doesn't have any horses for Harry.

James got back in touch with me shortly after the Travers. It turns out that he was being blackmailed because of his sexual orientation. He's gay, but he wasn't out. Harry knew, God knows how. I guess in some parts of the country and in some work environments it's tough for those who do not fit the norm. We hang out a little. James is now in a steady relationship. He had no problem telling Timmins whatever he wanted to know about Harry.

Jake's up in the Cleveland area, ponying horses at the track up there. He texted me about a month ago, out of the blue. He sold his small holding just outside of Missionville, and is looking for a similar set up where he is. He plans to focus on rehabbing horses from the track.

Marcus Longman won't ride races anymore under Jockey Club rules. He avoided doing jail time by providing additional information about Harry. No doubt Longman will reappear on the bush track and match racing circuits somewhere. Like Harry, he's broken. He has no empathy for the horse.

Harry will spend a long time in jail. It turns out all the cash he was making was from a large and sophisticated drug making and dealing network. He supplied significant parts of East and Central Pennsylvania, prescription drugs and crystal meth. I don't understand all the details, but his compound pharmacy was central to his operation. James helped identify everything along with Harry's chemist, Ben Blackton.

Harry used the track to launder his cash. At first he just operated the track in a legitimate way, but it didn't take long for him to realize how he could increase his odds of winning, and therefore gain more legitimate money, by cheating. Longman was a part of that, so were the clockers, as was his hold over James. He would bet big in Vegas on horses he knew had an edge. He wouldn't bet every horse, he didn't always expect to win. But when he bet, he expected to win. When he was done with his horses, he gave them to Jake. He didn't want them identified, which is why they went straight to Tom's kill pen.

Basically I think Harry is a psychopath who wanted to be accepted by the elite. His foray into high-brow racing, which started only three years ago, was a part of the latter. I guess he will wonder if it was all worth it. He has a lot of time to think about it. He had to sell Dancer's Foil before the horse won the Breeders' Cup Classic.

The headline stories the day after Dancer's Foil's Travers win were rather amusing. The *New York Times* went with "Dancer's Foil defeats Triple Crown winner, owner locked up." The *Washington Post* led with "Drug kingpin defeats racing's elite, on his way to jail." The *Daily Racing Form* used a nice play on words, "Travers winner foiled." Each of the stories detailed

Harry's downfall, and mentioned that there was a small committed group of horsemen from Missionville who were instrumental in his undoing. I saved a copy of each of the stories to give to Jorge.

RESOURCES

If you are unfamiliar with racing in America, the following will help you understand *Missionville* better.

Missionville's backside is a barn area with accommodations for backstretch workers. Because there's also a kitchen, rec room, and other services, some workers, like Alfie, never leave the racetrack. The majority of races at Missionville are claiming races, so trainers and owners have few other options to race their horses. This is why Sarah runs Spicy Lemon in a claiming race, for example.

To race a horse, an owner and trainer must both be licensed by the track. The owner will have an account with the racetrack bookkeeper. That account is where money needs to be available if an owner wants to make a claim; it is also where purse money – the money an owner wins from their horse's placement in a race – is distributed after a race. A trainer, like Pete, may act on his owner's behalf. An owner can also be a trainer, like Sarah.

As an owner, Ray pays a training fee to Pete, his trainer, for each horse he has in training. Ray is also responsible for the veterinary expenses for each of his horses. Like most trainers, Pete makes his living off of training fees paid by his owners, and any bonuses received from winning races and selling horses.

The racing secretary at Missionville writes the condition book, which lists the upcoming proposed races for each race night. There are usually twelve races proposed for each night, eight of which will be used. The condition book is distributed to trainers and owners, who then enter their horses in races at the time of entries, which is a pre-set date, either three or four days before the scheduled race night. The racing secretary then selects which eight races to use based on the races which have the most horses entered at the time of entries.

To claim a horse, a claim slip must be filled out by the potential new owner or trainer, before the race. The claim is made official after the race regardless of how the horse runs, and even if it does not finish the race. The claiming owner now owns the horse. Any purse money won by the horse from the race goes to the original owner, as does the claiming price paid by the new owner.

The racetrack provides stalls for free to the trainers. Trainers are allotted a number of stalls based on their level of activity at the races. The racetrack doesn't like horses that don't race to be on the backside. Trainers run the risk of losing stalls if they don't keep racing their horses.

Horses train in the early mornings on the racetrack. There is one twenty minute break during training, which allows the maintenance crew to refresh the surface. Missionville races are at night, four days a week, year-round.

Like all racetracks, Missionville has a team of clockers who time workouts and make them official. Each horse that races needs to have at least one official workout published in the thirty days prior to a race, unless it raced in those thirty days. This workout time is published with the racehorse's past performances in the *Daily Racing Form*, as well as in the racetrack program.

Horse race gambling happens either at the racetrack, online through Advanced Deposit Wagering, in an off-track betting facility, or in places like Las Vegas. Bets made through bookies in Las Vegas do not impact the odds of a race, which are calculated by the amount of money that is bet on each horse by all the other means of gambling. This is why Harry and Ray prefer to make their big bets on races at Missionville in Las Vegas, through a bookie. This type of betting is actually illegal for anyone who is not a resident of Nevada.

A racetrack is a private enterprise. The fictional Missionville is owned by Harry Mitchell, a local entrepreneur. All the racetracks in Pennsylvania run under the jurisdiction of the Pennsylvania Racing Commission.

A horse can live well into its twenties, sometimes longer. A racehorse generally races only for a few years, and its racing career is often cut short due to increasing injuries. There is a persistent need to address what we do with horses after their careers are over. Some great organizations focus on this issue; while Amanda's work at Missionville and Owenscreek is fictional, it's typical of what this effort entails.

Horses are not currently slaughtered in the United States. They are shipped to either Canada or Mexico for slaughter.

RACING TERMINOLOGY

Shedrow is the walkway inside a racing barn outside the horses' stalls. It also refers to an area of a barn belonging to a specific trainer. For example, Pete's shedrow is Pete's area of the barn he shares with Mike Franks, another trainer.

A **hotwalker** walks horses either after their exercise to cool them down, or instead of their exercise. That's what Alfie does for Pete.

Frontside and **backside** are areas of a racetrack. The frontside refers to the part of the racetrack that is accessible to the public, the backside refers to the area that only the licensed horsemen have access to, and where the horses are stabled. Backside also refers to the part of the racetrack that is opposite the grandstand.

On the racetrack an **ankle** is an ankle. Some equestrians may wonder why it's not called a fetlock.

On the racetrack a **pony** is actually a horse, but not a racehorse. Ponies are used to help keep racehorses calm, either in training or before races.

We measure horses in **hands**, not feet. Each hand is the equivalent of four inches.

Pre-race refers to the administration of drugs before a race. This occurs one or two days before a race, depending on which drugs are being administered: Bute is one day, and Banamine is two days, in Pennsylvania. Administering drugs in this way is designed to ensure that there is an acceptable level of drugs in a horse's system during post-race testing. This is legal.

A horse's standard training routine is to **gallop**. This is really a steady canter. When a horse **works**, also known as **breezing**, it is going at racing pace. This might happen once a week in training, or about a week before a race.

ACKNOWLEDGMENTS

This book is the result of a lot of help from folks who know some of the details of the story better than I do. They include Caroline Betts, Liz Collard, David Iwersen, Kim Moscato, David Rollinson, Terry Torreance, and Tim Woolley. While this is a fictional story, it was crucial to me to make sure the story is based on reality.

I am very grateful to Lynden Godsoe for her cover artwork.

I am also indebted to those who gave me feedback on the story throughout the entire writing process, including Clare Davison, Nadezda Dohnalova, Kristen Halverson, Ellen Harvey, Paula Hogan, Jayne Lornie, Fernando Molina, Louise Mur, Bob Murphy, John Myers, MaryAnn Myers, Jessica Rich, Dan Ross, and Jaimee Williams. The writing is much better for all the feedback I received.

Finally, I'm indebted to all those horsemen who gave me jobs on the backside of racetracks and Fair Hill. Without those jobs, I couldn't write this story.

ABOUT THE AUTHOR

Alex Brown is the author of *Greatness and Goodness, Barbaro and His Legacy*. He also covered horse racing for the *Cecil Whig* and has covered the Triple Crown series for the *New York Times*.

Alex has been a horseman all his life. He galloped horses for many years at the Fair Hill Training Center in Maryland. He's also worked at a number of racetracks throughout North America. Alex has also visited the main kill auctions on the east coast. He is a vocal proponent of ending horse slaughter. Alex now lives in Cornwall, U.K. He can be reached at alexbr4cornwall@gmail.com

CPSIA information can be obtained
at www.ICGtesting.com
Printed in the USA
LVOW12s1842150218

566740LV00004B/887/P